S0-BCK-645

A Lifetime of Investing

Benjamin Calvin Korschot

Printed in the United States of America
Richardson Printing, Inc., Kansas City, Missouri

ISBN 0-9656197-0-2

PREFACE

◆

───────────────────────────────────────

This book had its beginning in the late 1970s. Two, perhaps three times in some years, Mary and I drove to Minneapolis to visit our daughter Barbara Carver, her husband, Craig, and our granddaughter, Mischelle. It was about a nine-hour trip when the speed limit was 55 miles per hour. I was president of Waddell & Reed at the time, and many events we were experiencing were traumatic and stressful for both of us. It was Mary's suggestion that we should begin to keep a record of what was happening to us, so that our children and grandchildren would have some insight into our lives that they might find interesting. I had a micro-cassette tape recorder that I used at times in investment seminars, and Mary drove about half the time on trips of this type. So on one of the trips, I dictated while she listened and reminded me of facts and events. To our surprise, time passed much more quickly, making the trip quite pleasant. It worked out so well that we began to look forward to the time in the car to do our recording. The result was that, by 1983 or 1984, we had recorded a great amount of miscellaneous recollections and information about both the family and business aspects of our lives.

A few weeks after Mary died on May 9, 1988, it became obvious to me that working on this book would provide an avenue of activity that would help me adjust to life without her. The process of having a professional independent secretary transcribe my disjointed dictation was time consuming, with the end product being something quite different than I had hoped to read. On these trips I had never had available the background data that I soon realized was an essential ingredient in melding our memories into some cohesive form. Fortunately, I had maintained detailed information about all my business and investment activities, and, from a variety of sources, including photograph albums, I organized in sequential form our memories of the personal side of our lives.

I am not at all sure that my dictating in the way I did was as efficient as a book written from scratch. I am convinced, however, that the book would never have been written if the tapes had not been available as a visible reminder of Mary's strong conviction that it should be done. Both of us had come from family backgrounds where there was very little in writing to help us understand what had influenced and guided the lives of our forebears. We did not want our descendants to be without the information in this book.

ACKNOWLEDGMENTS

◆

Life has been good to me. Only one event prevents me from using a word like "great" or even "fantastic." It is my loss of Mary when she was only 67 years of age. This is a selfish feeling to which I plead guilty because our life together was so precious. Having a positive mental attitude had been a guiding influence all my life. When Mary was dying and when she was gone, it was extremely difficult for me to retain this attitude. But gradually, although not completely, I regained my optimistic attitude toward the future and once again started to think of adversity as a source of inspiration and strength. Perhaps my three children, Barbara, Lynne and John, who know my life so well, would say that life has truly been "great" not just "good" to me.

So it must be obvious this book is dedicated to Mary and the three kids whom she really raised with a little help from me. I believe I was always there when they needed me, but anyone who reads this book will know that I was very self-centered in the pursuit of my career and objectives. My motivations came out of the experiences of the Great Depression and the love and guidance of my parents. I did not know what was influencing me at the time, but I can look back and, without reservation, say I wanted to be admired and respected by all those I associated with as I passed through the stages of my life: a student; an athlete; a husband; a father; one who fought for our country; a businessman; and an investment specialist in managing other people's money. Respect and admiration to me did not mean being number one, the best at everything or earning the most money available to me. Instead it meant words like dependable, hard-working, thoughtful, honest, intelligent and knowledgeable. Also within me was a deep-seated need for a feeling of security. Even today I believe I would panic at the thought that I did not know where my next meal was coming from. When Mary and I were buying a house, I would never assume a mortgage that could become a problem. This need for security is also an explanation of why I only worked in situations (like banking) where I could feel secure. I also believe this facet of my personality was a major factor behind my success in managing other people's money.

It is important for me now to look back and identify certain individuals besides my parents who had a great influence over me. My boyhood friend, Gordon Robbins, came into my life when we moved to West Lafayette. His mother, an artist and high school teacher, and his father, a professor at Purdue, provided almost a second home, where I saw firsthand a side of life that had been hidden from me. My high school basketball coach and history teacher, Lloyd "Bill" Chase, guided me to Purdue and my fascination with history. Marshall Ketchum, a professor at the University of Chicago, created my interest in investments. Art O'Hara and Henry Bodwell, my mentors in the art of managing money, inspired me to emulate them to the best of my ability. Rolly and Virginia Davis, the personal friends who came into our lives in 1952, were always there. My sister Ruth was closer to me than my other sisters when we were growing up. In our adult lives, I was always just her "little brother" she watched and loved. And finally, my sister Mary (seven years older than me), who lost her husband, Neal Grond, about six months after Mary died, became very important to me. When we were young and in our married lives, we seldom did things together. But even though she lived on the West Coast, we became brother and sister in the finest sense of the word.

Eight of the 23 chapters in this book are devoted to my 13 years at Waddell & Reed. They were the most rewarding years of my life. But four of them, from June 1974 until about the middle of 1978, were, by far, the most stressful I ever experienced. This was the time when I was president, and our parent company, Continental Investment Corporation (CIC) was in financial difficulty and ultimately bankruptcy. Waddell & Reed, as a financial service organization, could not escape the consequences. It was a tremendous challenge just to keep the company alive and thriving. It is tempting to mention here the names of those individuals who were involved with me, in one way or another, during some part, if not all, of those stressful years. I hope that, by reading the forthcoming eight chapters, you will come to know how and why so many people worked together to survive those four years and then move forward to make Waddell & Reed a company to be admired.

The words in this book are mine, but a good many people have helped me with either suggestions or comments that I have appreciated. My daughters, Barbara and Lynne, my son, John, and my sister, Mary Grond, are familiar with most, if not all, I have written. Two of my management associates at Waddell & Reed, Rod McWhinney, our general counsel, and Bob Hechler, our chief financial officer, read chapters 11 through 15 at an early stage in my writing and provided suggestions that were helpful. Hank Herrmann and Herb Evert have reviewed the chapter on my retirement. Clarence M. Turley, Jr., chairman of the board of directors of Roosevelt Financial Group, Inc., and Stanley Bradshaw, president, have shared their recollections with me.

I also appreciate the assistance provided me by my granddaughter Schelle (Mischelle) Miller in the typing of the manuscript and, as a graphic artist, in the designing of the book cover. She and her husband, Michael, also guided me in my purchase of the Macintosh computer, which has proven to be an extremely important part of this production. Finally, my secretary for 13 years, Margie Hein, helped immeasurably to make my life in the office a place of enjoyment. I liked what I was doing and wish the words "mandatory retirement" had never become a part of our business culture.

TABLE OF CONTENTS

◆

Preface iii
Acknowledgments. v

CHAPTERS   PAGE NO.

Chapter 1   Bits And Pieces Of My Early Years 1
Chapter 2   The Depression Of The 1930s 7
  My Father 8
  Rebuilding A House And Starting A New Life. 9
  Some "Growing Up" Recollections 13
  My Grandfather. 19
Chapter 3   Special Insights Into My Family 23
  Dad's Death And Some Regrets 24
  A Christian Environment 26
  The Tillotson - Goodman Family 28
Chapter 4   High School, Purdue And Marriage 33
  High School 35
  Purdue 36
  Making The Team 38
  Making It Financially 39
  Life Begins With Mary Schelle. 41
  Automobiles And Accidents. 44
Chapter 5   Involvement In World War II. 47
  Getting Into The Navy 49
  To The U.S.S. Knapp DD653 51
  To The Pacific. 53
  Our Role In The Task Force 54
  We Sank A Ship 56
  Halsey And The Typhoon 56

I Almost Drowned 59

Home On Leave 59

The Kamikazes Missed Us 60

Trying To Get Home 63

My Shipmates 66

Chapter 6   Graduate School, First Job And First Home . . . 69

Mary Goes To Work 70

Some Big Decisions At School 71

Looking For A Job 73

My First Three Years At The Northern 74

Teaching At Night 77

A New Car And The Suburbs 78

The Organized Reserves 79

Chapter 7   Back In The Navy 83

726 Michigan Without Me 84

The Mediterranean, Europe And England 86

A Search For Ancestors 89

Living In Norfolk 90

Chapter 8   The Northern Trust Company 93

Measuring Investment Performance 96

Pioneering In Pension Fund Management 97

The People With Whom I Worked 99

Art O'Hara 101

The Decision To Leave 105

Chapter 9   Glen Ellyn 109

Founding The Glen Ellyn Kiwanis Club 111

Krebiozen 114

The 6259 Investment Club 114

Family Life 115

How I Began To Acquire Some Assets 122

Our Attitude Toward Money 123

Chapter 10   The St. Louis Union Trust Company 125

Family Life 129

Business Life 139

Leaving The St. Louis Union Trust Company 144

Chapter 11   Managing Mutual Fund Money.............. 149

My Money Management System 150

The Central Value Index............................. 151

Selecting Individual Securities........................ 152

Evaluating The Performance Of Investment Analysts 153

Measuring The Performance Of Fund Managers 153

Chapter 12   Taking Over As President Of

Waddell & Reed 155

The Presidency Of The United Group Of Mutual Funds 158

Cutting Costs....................................... 159

Working With The SEC............................... 160

Chapter 13   Managing Waddell & Reed.................. 163

Adverse Publicity.................................... 164

Important Decisions 166

Our Marketing Organization 168

Managing The Investment Operation 173

The Development Of RMA 178

Chapter 14   Communicating During Time

Of Adversity 181

Chapter 15   From Bankruptcy To Torchmark........... 187

Unpleasant Financial Publicity 188

CIC Is Declared Bankrupt 189

Out Of Bankruptcy 190

Torchmark 191

Torchmark And Boston Separate 192

T.M.K. United, Inc. 194

My Presentation To Investors.......................... 195

The Presidency Of Waddell & Reed Investment

Management Company.............................. 196

Chapter 16   The FAF And ICI 197

The Financial Analysts Federation (FAF) 197

Chairmanship Of The FAF 199

Chairmanship Of The Investment Company

Institute (ICI)..................................... 204

Two ICI Committee Assignments 206

The ICI Organization 209
Chapter 17   Speaking — Writing 211
Newspapers, Magazines, Radio And Television. 212
Shareholders And Salespeople 218
Speaking To The Public. 220
Published Articles 222
Chapter 18   Retirement 229
My Resignation From The Board Of
  The United Group Of Mutual Funds. 232
Professional Recognition. 234
Chapter 19   Roosevelt Financial Group, Inc. 235
Higher-Yielding, Low-Quality Bonds 236
Smith Breeden Associates, Inc.. 239
Management Changes. 240
Roosevelt — A Public Corporation 241
April 24, 1992. 242
Chapter 20   Insights Into Our Personal Lives 243
The Move To Lakewood. 244
Our Lake Of The Ozarks Home 246
Our Social Life. 247
Beaver Lake, Arkansas 249
Our Personal Finances 251
Chapter 21   Mary's Illness And AIDS 255
August 31, 1984. 257
The Mayo Clinic. 259
The USC-Kenneth Norris, Jr., Cancer Hospital 259
Living With The AIDS Virus. 262
Mary's Other Health Problems. 263
More Surgery Then Europe 264
Reno, Nevada, And October 31, 1986. 266
I Told Barbara, Lynne And John 269
Physicians And Tests. 270
November 26–Thanksgiving. 271
Chapter 22   Mary's Death 273
The Inevitable Decision. 276

Chapter 23   Living Alone..........................281
   The Family...282
   The Church, Golf, Movies And Basketball..................292
   Still In The Business World 295
   Management Of A Portfolio..........................296
   My Sister Mary Grond's Death.......................298
   About The Epilogue................................299
Epilogue   Managing Money 301
   Investing In Mutual Funds..........................301
     Common Stock Mutual Funds....................302
      Aggressive Growth and Growth Funds...........302
      Small Company Growth Funds..................302
      Growth and Income and Equity Income Funds.......303
      International and Global Funds..................303
      Science and Technology Funds 304
      Balanced Funds............................304
      S&P 500- Stock Index Funds 304
      Convertible Securities Funds 305
      Specialty Domestic Funds....................305
      Specialty International Funds 306
     Fixed-Income Mutual Funds 306
      Money Market Funds.........................307
      Government and/or Government Agency Funds......307
      Taxable Bond Funds 307
      High-Yield Taxable Funds....................308
      Medium Maturity Taxable Funds...............308
      Tax-Exempt Bond Funds.....................308
      High-Yield Tax-Exempt Bond Funds 309
     A Mutual Fund Portfolio 309
     How Mutual Funds Manage Money 310
     Selecting The Fund Manager.....................311
     Transaction Costs 314
     Mutual Fund Boards Are Vital 315
    Unit Investment Trusts and Closed-End Funds...........316
    Buying Your Own Bonds........................318

Managing Your Own Stock Portfolio 319
Picking Stocks 325
    The Business 327
    Earnings 328
    The Balance Sheet 328
    Price Earnings Ratios 329
    The Price Action of a Stock 331
    Building a Portfolio 333
    When to Sell 335
    Capital Gains and Losses 336
A Final Summary 336
Appendix–A Authored Articles 339
Appendix–B Family Trees 340
Index 343

CHAPTER 1

Bits And Pieces
Of My Early Years

Morton Street in Lafayette, Indiana, is a blue-collar, working man's street in the north end of town. My grandparents lived in the middle of the block on the north side of the street, between Nineteenth Street and the railroad. When my father, Benjamin Garrett, married my mother Myrtle Goodman in 1913, he built a new house for them at the end of the street next to the railroad tracks. Four girls preceded me into the family, so when I was born on March 22, 1921, my parents and sisters were delighted. In my "growing up" years, I never lacked feminine attention.

In 1924 we moved one block away to 1924 Greenbush Street, a new house that was built by my father and his brother Henry. On this street in this one particular block, the two brothers worked together to build five houses. My Uncle Henry Korschot's family lived in the house at the corner of Twentieth and Greenbush while my Aunt Mary and her husband, Garrett Dunnewold, lived in the second house from Nineteenth Street. Two families from our church, the Charles

Vanderweilens and the Otto Bols, bought the two houses between us and Uncle Henry. Since all of us belonged to the same church and had a Dutch heritage, it was natural for it to be a cohesive neighborhood. It was truly a great place to live.

We lived there until the summer of 1931, a seven-year period of tranquility when I never lacked opportunities to be happily active in a wholesome environment. Our next door neighbors, the Vanderweilens, were a very important part of my life. The father, Charles, ran a grocery store in downtown Lafayette. The mother's name was Becky, and the children were John, Charles, who was my age, Cecil and Ruth, who was about two years younger. Charles, or Chuck as he was called, and I were virtually inseparable. However, the most vivid recollection I have of growing up together was when, for one reason or another, I chased Chuck up a telephone pole and threw rocks at him. I hit him a few times but did not hurt him too much. Finally, I left him alone, and when he came down I was sitting on the front step of our house. Chuck threw a rock at me and hit me on the crown of my nose. I still have the scar.

We played a great deal of sandlot baseball in an empty lot about half a block from our house. We also had a basketball hoop behind the garage. Charley Korschot, a son of Uncle Henry, was some four years older than I, but that never prevented my joining with him and his friends in the various kinds of games we had in the neighborhood. Baseball and basketball were our favorites, but throwing horseshoes occupied a lot of our time, too. Sometimes we played behind Charley Korschot's house, but frequently we walked down Twentieth Street a few blocks to play horseshoes with four of the sons of my Aunt Frances and Uncle Johannes Bol. One of their sons, Bennie, was just two years older than me, so we spent a great deal of time together. He and his brothers, John and Otto, both Charley Korschot's age, were frequently in our neighborhood to play basketball and baseball.

We also played the usual kinds of kids' games in our neighborhood. One was Andy Over, in which you throw a ball over the house. The person who is "It" catches the ball and tries to hit one of the kids on the other side before they can get around the house.

I do not remember doing things inside the house, but I can still visualize the time when a coffee pot was spilled on the stove and on my sister Ruth. The coffee ran down her leg and into her ankle socks, resulting in severe burns.

I have very few recollections of my older sisters, particularly Alice, Mary and Johanna, while we lived on Greenbush Street. They were respectively 11, 7 and 6 years older than me. Alice's fiancé, Clarence Vanderkleed, liked to tease me, and for that reason I did not care for him. Later Clarence and I became good friends as brothers-in-law. Other than that, I remember very little about Alice in that period. My sister Ruth was four years older than me and a very athletic girl who was always in our ball games. It was not unusual for her to pull bigger boys off me when I was losing a fight. This usually happened when we were on our way home from school. I was always the instigator of a fight, for it was my way of proving I was not a sissy. I was willing and anxious to fight anyone, anytime, anywhere.

One interesting and enjoyable pastime was to play marbles on the way to and from school. It usually took us an hour to an hour and a half to get home from school because we would play marbles in the gutter all the way home. I wish I had kept all of those agates and plixters.

A big event on a summer evening was when my father or mother would decide we could have some ice cream. One or more of us would be sent around the corner up Nineteenth Street about two blocks to a little ice cream store that was next to the St. Lawrence Catholic Church and School. They hand-packed the ice cream, with vanilla being our favorite. Those were also the days when the ice man would deliver ice (usually in 25-pound blocks) because we did not have refrigerators. As soon as he started toward a house, we would climb on the ice wagon for small pieces. Since they were of no value, he never interfered with our enjoyment.

The railroad tracks were only two blocks away, and once in a while, we could scavenge ice from the railroad trains when they were parked along the sidings. We looked for refrigerated cars that we would open to get at the ice that was on top. No damage was ever done to the cars, but it was great fun to get some ice to chew on.

The only opportunities we had for swimming were to walk to Columbian Park, at least two miles away. Swimming was a great way for my mother to get us out of the house. With the Vanderweilens and Bols as well as some of my cousins, there were usually about a dozen of us. We would also play on the different kinds of playground equipment while we were in the park.

As I mentioned, the second house from the corner of Nineteenth Street was where my Uncle Garrett and Aunt Mary Dunnewold lived. I was much younger than their three children, so I never had anything to do with them when I was growing up. We would visit with them once in a while, usually after church on Sunday morning. Uncle Jess and Aunt Maggie lived eight blocks from us at the corner of Fourteenth and Morton Streets, where Uncle Jess also had his sheet metal shop. My folks were quite close to Uncle Jess and his family, one reason being that their four children were close in age to me and my four sisters. When we visited them on Sunday evenings after church, I often went to sleep sitting on the floor in front of my mother with my head against her dress.

The Christian Reformed Church, one of two churches established for the Dutch people who lived in and around Lafayette, was very important in our lives. My grandparents, John and Gertrude Korschot, had 13 children. Eight of them lived to be adults, and seven of them had a total of 24 children. All of my uncles and aunts were active in the church, so the 24 grandchildren in the family grew up in an environment that brought us unusually close to each other.

Church services were held twice on Sunday, just as they are today. We went to both services and also to Sunday school, except during the summer months. We also had catechism classes on Saturday morning. I enjoyed them, as well as the Sunday school classes, which were very well conducted. The teachers were good and effectively used visual materials, such as big maps of Paul's journeys around the Middle East and, of course, the places Jesus went during his brief time on earth.

My father was a Sunday school teacher all of his adult life. He was also superintendent of the Sunday school for several years. He was very well liked by the students and was always called Uncle Ben by those attending Sunday school.

I started in Linwood Grade School half a year earlier than I should have. My birthday was March 22, but I started when the semester began in January 1927. My only important memory of Linwood was the inter-school basketball program which commenced in the fifth grade. I made the first team, and we never lost a game.

After Dad finished building some houses in the middle 1920s, he went back to painting houses, a trade he had learned when he was younger. He organized a crew of men to work with him that included one of my cousins, Lawrence Dunnewold. Another member of the crew was Fred Slopsema, a man I later worked for while I was in college and after my father died. The men would come to the house first to pick up tools, paint and ladders before they went to the various jobs. I enjoyed being with them in the morning and listening to them talk. Once I showed them my expertise with a slingshot by killing a blackbird on a telephone wire near our garage.

Mentioning the garage reminds me of when Chuck Vander-weilen and I were playing with matches and set the garage on fire. We would set the curtain on the door ablaze and then blow the fire out before it burned very much. As you might expect, the fire finally got away from us. My mother reacted very quickly and sent me next door to have Becky Vanderweilen call the fire department. In the meantime, she hooked up the water hose and had the fire out before the fire truck arrived.

Halloween night was a great time for us. We went to enough doors to get a few treats, but most of the time we were trying to figure out what we could do to trick somebody. One time, when I was at the rear of a house, I looked through a cellar window and saw a neighbor, the husband, lying at the foot of the stairs in a pool of blood. All I remember is that for some unknown reason he had fallen down the stairs. Our family had never had any contact with the people in that house.

One neighborhood lady, Mrs. Schreckengass, was a problem for me. She lived across the street and down about three houses. I detested her because she insisted on calling me Calvie. It had a sissy sound to it that I resented. Whenever I walked down the street, I made sure I walked on our side and not hers.

Sledding was an important wintertime activity. When the snow was just right, we would go to the corner of Nineteenth and Greenbush and wait with our sleds for a car to turn the corner. One of us would grab hold of the bumper, and several other kids would hold onto the feet of the person in front of them. We would let a car pull us for several blocks on Nineteenth Street. After we dropped off, we went to the other side of the street, where the cars had to stop at another corner, and got a similar ride back. It was dangerous, but it was a lot of fun. I thought the cars went very fast. Actually, I suppose they went quite slowly.

I remember my father began to talk to me about my temper problem when I was about six or seven years old. His approach was to take me aside after any display and talk about the necessity for me to learn to control my temper. He would always say that, if I did not, someday I would do permanent harm to somebody and would live to regret it the rest of my life. My father did not spank me often, although I vaguely remember one time in the dining room where I was taken over his knee for a couple of swats.

Two other events in that period of my life are worth noting. One was the enjoyment I had in going to silent movies. They were shown in an old run-down theater-type building on North Eighteenth Street near the headquarters of the Monon Railroad, and about three blocks from the home of my Uncle Johannes and Aunt Frances. We went on Saturday mornings, but not many times, perhaps two or three.

A block away on the corner of Nineteenth Street and Schuyler Avenue was a favorite spot for medicine shows. I saw several of them. It was always a man or a couple doing a little entertaining, while someone passed through the crowd with a bottle of something or other that was supposed to cure a great number of things. What a change from today, when the government approves everything of a medicinal nature. I was young, but I knew the product being sold was misleading. I assumed most people knew that whatever it was they were buying would not do all of the things it was supposed to do.

CHAPTER 2

The Depression Of The 1930s

The most important development in my life was the Great Depression of the 1930s, resulting in my father's financial disaster. In the middle of the 1920s, he was a home builder and followed the practice of renting houses instead of selling them. In the late 1920s and early 1930s, my father owned a number of homes that were heavily mortgaged. One by one, families failed to pay their rent. He was reluctant to remove them, but there was no choice. However, the laws then, as now, tend to protect renters, and with the inability to move the people out quickly and rent the houses to someone else, my father was unable to make the mortgage payments and began to lose them.

Finally, the day came when Dad told us there was no way he could keep the house in which we lived. Although the mortgage was held by a friend and an elder in our church, this did not influence or change the situation. Dad was very much aware of the need to have some place for the family, and he fortunately owned (clear of any mortgage) a house on five acres of land just outside the city limits of West

Lafayette, near the Purdue University Football Stadium off Northwestern Avenue. The house was about 100 years old, thoroughly dilapidated, with no furnace, no inside plumbing and no basement. The family living there had not paid their rent, so we had frequent family discussions about how to get them out so we would have a place to live. It was a shocking and traumatic experience to see that house for the first time. But it was a place to live, and it would do no good to complain about our situation. It was just something we were going to have to live with until we could fix it up.

My Father

My father was not a healthy man. His problems started when he was 13 years old and had major surgery. In those days, surgery being what it was, some major mistakes were made. I do not know the exact nature of the mistakes, but the surgery occurred when he was young, and one side of his body grew while the other did not. The side that did grow pushed out toward his back so that he had a hump on one side of his back. This also forced the collapse of one lung and squeezed his heart into the opposite side of his body. This combination of an unusual heart position and only one lung made him a frail person, and as he grew older, his condition became very serious.

His frailties became apparent to me in 1933 (when I was 12 years old). He was out of work, and the only opportunity available to him was to apply for a job with the Public Works Administration (PWA). This federal program was one of those New Deal projects created by President Franklin D. Roosevelt so that people could work and have enough food to eat. Specifically, Dad was given the job of carrying water to other workers because it was the only thing they could find for him to do. It was very hard on him physically, and he had to give it up. He then came up with the idea of getting a truck to haul dirt for the workers. He found an old Model T Ford truck that he managed to buy with the idea of converting its rear end into a more heavy duty one. My Uncle Jess Korschot and his son, John, helped make the conversion. The truck broke down the first day, so that attempt to make a living ended.

8

For a period of time, he tried selling real estate by working with a man named Chris Held, who had a real estate agency in Lafayette. This was not productive either because it was almost impossible to sell real estate during the Depression. I remember Mr. Held as a frugal man who turned off the motor of his car at the top of every hill and coasted to the bottom before starting it again.

During most of the 1930s, what kept us going was that Dad painted and wallpapered houses. He did this successfully enough through the middle and late 1930s to put bread on the table for our family and even to provide work temporarily for some of my cousins. The one cousin who worked full-time for Dad and therefore with me through that period was Ed Bol. Ed was a caring, thoughtful and considerate person who died of leukemia in the early 1940s.

In his effort to earn some money (particularly in the early part of the 1930s), Dad would borrow money to buy an old run-down house (perhaps for five hundred dollars), remodel it and sell it at a slightly higher price. He did this with two or three houses. There were different kinds of things we did to make a house more attractive and increase its value. These included painting and wallpapering, replacing rotten wood, etc. One of the unusual techniques he had (and which I later demonstrated in college) was to take the flooring in an old house, which was usually six-inch-wide white pine, and make it look like regular hardwood flooring. The technique he used was to apply a base coat of paint, draw a line down the middle of the board so that it would look like a normal groove, and then stain and varnish the wood. When he finished a floor, it would look like hardwood flooring. As I look back on it now, I am amused at the decision I made in my sophomore year at Purdue University to present this technique for working with wood to one of my speech classes. I suspect my fellow students did not relate at all to the idea of taking old flooring in a run-down house and trying to make it look like good hardwood flooring.

Rebuilding A House And Starting A New Life

My recollection of the summer of 1931 and the time before school commenced is vague; however, most important to my future was meeting my neighbor Gordon Robbins, who became my best friend through grade school, high school and college. His mother, Belle Bogardus Robbins, was the art teacher at my new school and, in some ways, a second mother. His father was a Professor of Agronomy at Purdue University. They soon perceived our family's financial situation and helped us in various ways. My sister Ruth became a baby-sitter for their youngest son, Bill, and she also cleaned their home on a regular basis. Their house was about a quarter of a mile away on Northwestern Avenue. Quite soon there was a well-worn path across the fields between the houses. Gordon and I became inseparable.

My most vivid memory of my new environment was the first day in school in the fall of 1931, which was about two months after we had moved into the house. Our home was just outside the city limits of West Lafayette, so our new school, Klondike, was a country school with about 80 students in the high school and around 200 in the first eight grades. My mother went with me because I had only completed the first half of the fifth grade. Mrs. Harriman was the fifth grade teacher. Mrs. Frisby was the sixth grade teacher. They and the principal of Klondike met with my mother and me and were of the opinion I should go into the fifth grade and do the first half of the grade over again. My mother was as emphatic and as strong-willed as any person could conceivably be under the circumstances. She would not consider for one moment the idea that I should go back a half year in my education. Since my grades had been very good at Linwood Grade School in Lafayette and she had such a strong conviction, they agreed to my entering the sixth grade. My mother ended the controversy by saying that, if my grades were not satisfactory after six weeks, I should go back to the fifth grade.

I realized there was some challenge for me in this situation, but I was not concerned and do not recall any conversation with my parents about what was expected of me. At the end of the six-week period, I was at the top of the class and no longer was there any question about whether I should continue in the sixth grade. My age difference of at least one year was not important in grade school or in high school, but it was later on when I played basketball at Purdue. It had a direct bearing on my physical strength at a time when more maturity would have been of great value to me. However, I was never unhappy with my mother for insisting on my skipping the second half of the fifth grade.

My first strong recollection of my first year in the new house was the winter of 1931. The house rested on a foundation that was old and had holes where the wind could come through. The floor of the house was made out of soft pine and was in such bad condition you could see through the floor into the area underneath. The basement was dug out to some extent, but it was still unfinished. We had an old, black, wood-burning potbellied stove in the living room. After school one of my jobs was to collect firewood by cutting down trees on our property. Many evenings after supper, we would sit around the stove in the living room, with my Dad peeling apples and cutting pieces for each of us. We sat as close to the stove as we could because the wind would come whistling around and through the house so hard it would raise the rug off the floor. I can remember the center of the rug rising several inches.

Our kitchen stove was also a wood-burning stove, although we managed to get corn cobs at times and use them along with the wood for fire. My mother had to work pretty hard to make that stove function halfway efficiently. One of the nice things about the stove was that, in the winter, when it was so unbelievably cold upstairs in the two bedrooms, my mother would heat bricks on top of the stove, wrap them in towels, and after I had crawled into bed, she would put them under the covers by my feet. How wonderful it was! It was not unusual for me to wake up in the morning with snow having blown in on my bedcovers.

Our drinking water was in a well located in a ravine about 80 feet from the side of the house. The well was only about 10 feet deep, but we never questioned the quality of the water, which had a good taste, even though it had a slight sulfur odor to it. We also had a cistern close to the back door that collected the rain water from our roof. This was the water we used for bathing.

Our outside toilet was at least 50 feet from our kitchen door. It was a cold place in the wintertime and smelly all the time. We were typical for those days and used a Sears Roebuck catalogue because we could not afford regular toilet paper. The girls had named our outside toilet "the hoosey" for reasons no one ever mentioned. In effect, however, it was a way to bring some humor to something no one liked. But none of us ever complained. We just wanted indoor plumbing as soon as we could afford it.

We were not there very long before Dad began to remodel the old house with whatever money he could scrounge together. One of my jobs in the summer of 1932 was to help him mix cement so we could patch the outside of the foundation to keep the wind from coming through and making the house so cold in the wintertime.

It was in the second year after we moved that Dad found an old furnace we could install. Gordon and I dug out part of the basement to provide space for the furnace. We also had to tear down the chimney and rebuild it so it would be close to where we could put the furnace. That meant we had to relocate the stairway to the second floor. There were other projects for the house, and I did some of the heavy work when we put in cement porches at the front and rear of the house.

Not too long after we moved in, a very nice thing happened. A big white Collie dog named Lindy, who lived with the Ayers family on Northwestern Avenue at the end of our lane, mated with an Irish Setter that had stayed close to our house. The result was a litter of pups that we had to raise. We only kept two of them, naming one Spot and the other Buster. My sister Johanna decided Buster was going to be her dog, but unfortunately, Buster was killed when someone backed a car over him. Spot lived for nine years, and whenever I was home, he was my constant companion. He was always with me when I went hunting, and he took on the role of my protector. If anyone looked as if he were going to harm me, Spot was ready to protect me. All his fights were with other dogs, usually if he thought they were getting too close to me. Spot slept in our detached garage, but every morning he was allowed to come in the house, run upstairs and awaken me. He was killed by other dogs while I was away on a basketball trip playing against the University of Wisconsin in my junior year at Purdue. I buried him in our back yard, and I still know the exact location. The loss of Spot was a sad experience.

Since we were so poor, we had to do some extra things to keep the family supplied with food. Behind the house was an area about one acre in size that we converted into a garden. It was my job and Ruth's to take care of the garden. The soil near the house was clay and very difficult to cultivate, but it was well suited to tomato plants. We allowed them to grow wild and had a tremendous number of pear and plum tomatoes, along with regular tomatoes. We planted the rest of the garden in sweet corn, green beans, potatoes, etc. I grew to detest that garden. I did not like that kind of work and did not get any satisfaction out of growing things. And, that garden was a struggle in every way. To cultivate it, we tied a rope around my waist while Ruth would guide the cultivator. I joined the 4-H Club one year and had the embarrassing experience of having the members come around to see how I was doing. All the boys in the 4-H Club were farm kids with good-looking gardens in good soil. Mine was an obvious disaster.

We also had a lot of chickens and a cow. As would be expected, the chickens, eggs and raw milk were a significant part of our diet. We had a shed for the cow behind the garage, and one of my chores was to clean out the stall. My procrastination at getting this job done usually did not end until the exasperation of one or both of my parents would galvanize me into action. I do not look back with great pride on the way I carried my load during that period. I was not as thoughtful as I should have been, particularly as I think of my father's physical strength.

At first, we could not afford to fence in the five acres of land; accordingly, we tied the cow on a chain and moved the chain so the cow could graze in different areas. Moving the cow was one of my less onerous chores. Later, we put a fence around the five acres.

Some "Growing Up" Recollections

One strong recollection I have of those days is the heat in the summertime. Of course there was no air conditioning, so when the hot summer days came, my sisters and I would usually sleep outside on the front lawn. Northwestern Avenue was also Indiana 52, the main road between Indianapolis and Chicago. With lots of truck traffic, the noise caused by the trucks shifting gears as they climbed a hill made it rather difficult to fall asleep. About five or six o'clock in the morning, it would get cool enough to move inside.

Gordon thought it was a great idea to camp outdoors, so once in a while when he was particularly fired up about it, we would pitch a tent back in the woods and sleep out for a night or two. I never enjoyed it.

One of the games we played in those days was one I would consider extremely dangerous now. We would climb the trees where they grew close together and play tag in them. We thought nothing at all of climbing to the top of a big oak tree, climbing out on a limb and, as the limb would sag, catching hold of the limb below it and going all the way to the bottom of the tree, just simply by going on the outside. We did this without any concern or any fear. I wonder how my mother survived that kind of game. She knew we were doing it, but we were away from the house and out of her sight.

Another great source of enjoyment was a swing we made by tying a rope to a large limb of an elm tree that hung over the center of a ditch behind our garage. You could run about 15 feet along the ditch and swing out so you made a big circle that might have been over 40 feet in diameter. One of my cousins, Edna Korschot, broke both arms when she dropped off the rope while still over the ditch.

I grew up liking to hunt because my older cousins, the Bols and Korschots, all did a lot of hunting. Within a year after we moved to West Lafayette, I had my own shotgun and rifle. No one in our family liked the taste of squirrels, so when I went hunting for them, it was just a test of my skills with a rifle. Rabbits tasted good to some of the family, so I went rabbit hunting whenever I could find the time, either after school or on Saturday. I could easily kill a couple of rabbits in less than an hour. My cousins also did a lot of trapping of animals, so I went through a three- or four-year period where I trapped rabbits. I would run the trap line of about 10 traps every morning in the wintertime before school. Most were steel traps, but with others I would put food inside a box and the rabbit would trip the trigger. Whenever I killed a rabbit, I would wring its head off immediately but do the skinning and cleaning outside our garage. My parents and sisters appreciated my having the interest, as well as the ability, to supply food for the family in this way. Every once in a while, my cousins and I would go hunting for rabbits on various farms in the area. When the group was large, perhaps 10 or more of us, we made sure we organized ourselves so no one was in danger of getting shot by someone else.

We also did a lot of fishing for catfish. My favorite place was on my Uncle Charlie and Aunt Hattie Galema's farm. It was named Hadley's Lake and was about four miles from our house. Gordon and I rode our bicycles to get to the lake. My Uncle Charlie and Aunt Hattie were my favorite uncle and aunt, partly because there were so many things to do on their farm. Also, our house on Northwestern Avenue was conveniently located on the way to their farm from our church, so they regularly stopped for coffee and cake on the way home.

One of the exciting things that happened on the farm was the annual get-together of the farmers in their area to harvest their wheat and oats. Being around the threshing machine, helping them load the wheat and oats in the field on their wagons, and eating the lunch prepared by the women made it a very enjoyable as well as an exhausting day. I do not recall exactly how many farmers pooled their efforts, but there is no question that many people were involved, and it was vitally important to them. Another custom, no longer a part of a farmer's life, was the harvesting of corn with a team of horses and a wagon with a high sideboard on one side. I did this with my uncle a few times and marveled at how efficiently he would keep the horses moving with the reins around his shoulders, while at the same time quickly pulling the ears off the corn stalks and removing the shucks to throw the corn in the wagon. It was not unusual for farmers still to be shucking corn in the middle of the winter. Every year late in the fall, our high school sponsored a corn-shucking contest for the farm boys.

One spring, when I was with my Uncle Charlie and he was ploughing his fields, I had the experience of helping him try to kill the bumble bees in a large nest in the ground he was ploughing. We collected some wood for a fire that he started adjacent to the nest. Using a feed sack to wave them toward the fire, he was very successful in killing them without getting stung. He kept asking me to help him, and after observing his success, I joined him. I did not stay with him for much more than a minute or two before I panicked and started running down the field. As I recall, about 10 bees stung me on my face and neck.

Every year for several years, we also held the annual Korschot family reunion in a large wooded area on Uncle Charlie and Aunt Hattie's farm. At that time, we were holding the reunion on the Fourth of July, so playing with firecrackers, playing softball and throwing horseshoes were just a few of many ways we enjoyed ourselves. All of these various things I did at the farm, along with doing a great deal of fishing at Hadley's Lake, left me with many fond memories.

A most exciting and meaningful experience for me occurred when I was about 13, on a trip to Chicago with Gordon Robbins and his father. Without too much preparation or explanation of what it was all about, he took us sightseeing and for a visit to the Chicago Board of Trade. We drove up to Chicago and stayed at a YMCA Hotel on the South Side. Gordon and I shared a room that was only about five or ten feet from the tracks of the elevated railroad. We got up early the first morning and had breakfast at the YMCA. Gordon's father then took us to the Board of Trade building without telling us what was going to happen. We arrived at about five minutes to nine; trading commenced at nine o'clock. Without any warning whatsoever, they rang the bell that signaled the start of trading. I had been casually looking at the mass of people down on the floor and around the various trading pits, and I had just begun to study a booklet explaining what it was all about. Immediately it became a noisy, frenzied place with people waving their arms and shouting at each other. I was completely naive about the business world, so it is easy to understand why it left a tremendous impression on me. All the way through high school and college, whenever I was asked to write on the most unusual experience in my life, I used that event.

During my grade school years at Klondike, I continued to struggle with my tendency to lose my temper and also with my willingness to engage in a fight if there was the slightest provocation. I do not mean to imply that I was in a fight every day. It was nothing like that. But there always seemed to be occasions that arose where this attitude or weakness on my part reared its ugly head. Shortly after I arrived at Klondike, the boys in my class began to test me in various ways. One was to see how good I was at fistfighting. Naturally I did not back away from the opportunity to prove myself. One of the first opportunities came when we were leaving school as I sat on the bus with my arm out the window. Two of the boys in my class grabbed my arm and tried to pull me out the window. When I finally got loose from them, I got off the bus and fought until we were ordered back on the buses. Both of those boys eventually became good friends of mine.

The culmination of my belligerence was in the eighth grade when I challenged a girl in our class by the name of Elizabeth Rubright (a cousin of my future wife) to a fistfight with my right arm tied behind my back. The school had a boxing ring set up in the gymnasium, and the athletic coach for the school arranged for boxing matches of different kinds at lunch time. He consented to my doing this with Elizabeth, and as you might expect, she promptly beat the stuffing out of me. That was the end of my fistfighting.

Summers were different for me compared with most boys my age. The reason was I painted houses with my father every summer from the seventh grade on. I was strong enough and had the ability to produce just about as much as any of the painters working for him. I was never paid and had no time off before school started in the fall. When the weather was bad or there was rain, I would help one or more of the fellows hanging wallpaper. Dad always tried to schedule it so wallpapering could be done in rainy weather. Also, throughout the winter, at Christmas time, and sometimes when we had days off from school, I would be expected to work with one or more of the men either painting or hanging wallpaper. The result was that I was pretty good at doing both kinds of work. Moreover I enjoyed it and never envied kids who did not have to work.

Life wasn't all work, though. I first became interested in movies about a year after we moved to West Lafayette. Every Sunday after church and dinner, the Robbins family would go to a movie at one of the downtown Lafayette motion picture theaters. Gordon always told me afterward what they had seen. I would listen with fascination and envy to the details because movies were a form of entertainment forbidden by our church. The rationale of the church was that it was a sin because you were providing the livelihood of people who were sinful, particularly the actors and actresses. I could not accept this type of reasoning, and, as soon as I could find an extra 10 cents, I found ways to sneak off to the movies. My cousin, Bennie Bol, and my neighbor from the old neighborhood, Chuck Vanderweilen, felt the same way I did. To see a movie on a Sunday afternoon, we walked the Wabash Railroad tracks into town in the belief no one from church was likely to see us. To go to a movie in the evening, I told my parents I would be at Gordon's. When I got there, we would ride our bicycles to downtown Lafayette, a distance of about five miles. My enjoyment of movies was greater than his, so, a few times, I went alone. Frequently I would not get back home until 11:00 or 11:30 at night, and I had to make up some story about what we had been doing. After I had been doing this for a while, my conscience got the better of me, and in a very emotional meeting, I confessed to my mother and promised I would not lie again. She made me realize that lying about it was worse than breaking the taboo on movies, and from then on, they always knew when I was going. Sometimes on a Saturday, I would go to a triple feature in the afternoon and a double feature in the evening.

Mary, Johanna and Ruth were very helpful to the family during the Depression years, particularly in those first three or four years. They were able to get jobs cleaning houses, usually for professors at Purdue University. In those days, professors were the wealthier people in the community because they had steady incomes. Ruth also had a job after school at a golf course located not too far from where we lived. That course is now known as Purdue University's North Golf Course. Ruth worked after school and earned 50 cents a day in the Pro Shop. Although the girls did not earn much money, it was vitally important to our survival. We were a close-knit family; the girls were cooperative in every way; and to my knowledge, no one ever expressed any resentment at having to work and share the expenses.

My three sisters were all married within one year of each other: Johanna to Leonard (Len) Rhoda on December 1, 1936; Ruth to Arthur (Art) Smith on March 10, 1937; and Mary to Cornelius (Neal) Grond on August 26, 1937. Among other things, this meant that our front bedroom upstairs was available to our parents so we had the space to convert their bedroom downstairs, next to our kitchen, to a bathroom. So in the summer of 1938 after I had graduated from high school, we finally had our inside toilet and "the hoosey" was history. I was happy for my sisters and their decisions to be married to three very fine men, but I was truly delighted to have a bathroom inside the house and that I no longer had to take a bath in a small galvanized tin tub. As might be expected, however, I never missed the opportunities to use the shower facilities at Klondike. With gym classes every day and frequent participation in athletic activities, the baths in the little tub were not much of an inconvenience for me except in the summer.

My Grandfather

Dad's mother, Gertrude, died in 1923 when she was 62 years of age. I was about two years old. My grandfather, John Bernard, was 67 at the time of her death. When we moved to West Lafayette in 1931, he was 75 and, at that time, living on a rotating basis with his children. So off and on during the years from 1931 until his death on February 3. 1936, he lived with us for several months at a time. When he was at our house, he slept in my bedroom at the back of the house on the second floor. He always helped me gather the wood and oftentimes would help me cut down a tree. I do not remember too much about him, for we never seemed to have much to say to each other. Perhaps it was my fault. He was reasonably healthy, but he seemed very old for his age. He was a very quiet person in that stage of his life, quite different from when he was a much younger man. Most of the time, he sat in the yard with both dogs, Lindy and Spot. Long after his death, I learned that his children believed the change in him came when my grandmother died.

My great-grandfather, Henry John Kortschot, had come from Holland in 1854 with his wife, Gertrude, a brother and a sister. All of them settled in the Dutch-dominated community of Clymer, New York. My great-grandparents had two sons, William and my grandfather, John Bernard, who was born two years after they arrived. William's descendants have the name Croscutt, an obvious effort to "Americanize" the name. My grandfather simply changed our name from Kortschot to Korschot.

The two brothers, William and John Bernard, developed a conflict about which of the two branches of the Reformed Church (Christian Reformed and Reformed) was consistent with their beliefs. This conflict caused my grandparents to leave Clymer in 1893 without disclosing their destination to any of the Croscutts. This decision had to have been a difficult one. They had brought nine children into the world with eight of them having lived to go to Chicago. The oldest child was 14 when they made the trip. Two children were born and died in Chicago, one at birth and one at the age of three. Their oldest child also died in Chicago. They lived in poverty in Chicago and, in all likelihood, were probably not too happy to be there. My grandfather was a garbage collector, and my grandmother and the oldest child worked in a factory. In 1898 or 1899, they moved to Lafayette, Indiana, when my grandmother's cousin became pastor of the Lafayette Christian Reformed Church. Two more children were born in Lafayette with one of them dying at three years of age. So out of thirteen children, only eight lived to maturity.

My grandparents made no effort to establish contact with their relatives in Clymer; however, quite by accident, their location in Lafayette was discovered by those in Clymer. My grandfather worked for the Monon Railroad, and, at that time, boxcars were sent on their way with a signature from an authorized dispatcher posted on the outside. Entirely by coincidence, someone in Clymer, New York, saw the Korschot name on a boxcar and traced its origination. A reconciliation was almost immediately accomplished, and since then the descendants have kept in touch with each other. These events told me much more about my grandfather than I learned from him when he lived with us. Obviously he was a strong-minded, stubborn man with great religious convictions.

In recent years, I have devoted a considerable amount of my time to additional research on my father's ancestors, particularly my great-grandfather's departure from the Netherlands and the settlement of the family in Clymer, New York. In the future, I intend to do an equal amount of research on the background of my grandmother who was an Einink. Her family also had its origins in the Netherlands. I am not devoting much of this book to my ancestors, but I believe knowledge of where we come from is more than just fascinating information. In my opinion, it is a window to the past that provides many insights into who and what we are.

CHAPTER 3

◆

Special Insights Into My Family

The deterioration of my father's health from 1932 through 1940 was something I look back on now with some insight, but at the time, I really had very little sensitivity to the seriousness of the situation. I am sure the financial losses, with their accompanying mental turmoil, moving, remodeling, trying to support the family and many other stressful things combined to erode his physical strength.

My father's most serious health development during the late 1930s was headaches that gradually increased in their severity and duration. My mother shielded me from this. After he died, she told me there were mornings when he would wake up with a headache that lasted for hours and was so severe he would crawl on the floor in agony. They hid this problem from me for a long time; however, in 1939, I became aware of the seriousness when I became involved with their search for an answer. My father had gone to the family doctor repeatedly and had gotten no help. Somehow, then, he found a chiropractor who believed his sinuses were the problem. His treatment was to run probes through Dad's nostrils into his sinuses. I would drive him to his appointments because he knew he would be incapable of driving after the treatment. He would not let me go inside with him. After the treatment, he would look as if he had just been through the tortures of hell.

Dad's Death And Some Regrets

My father died as a result of what this chiropractor did when he was called to the house by my mother very early in the morning on August 5, 1940. My father had awakened with a terrible headache. My mother, in desperation, called the chiropractor to see if he would come to the house. I am sure the man had great sympathy for my father, yet at the same time he did something that he should not have done. He administered a shot of morphine, and my father died.

I was sleeping in my bedroom when the chiropractor was called, but I was awake when he came. I did not go into their bedroom and, therefore, did not know that Dad had died until my mother called me into the room. I was devastated. After the funeral, I went to our family physician and told him what had happened. Legal action was instituted against the chiropractor so that, apparently, he was forced to leave Indiana and cease practicing his profession in the state. It is my understanding he went to Florida and was able to resume practice there.

My father's physical shape made it necessary for him to have his suits custom-made by a tailor. This was very expensive, and, because of our poverty, he only owned one suit at a time. The suit had to be made of wool, which was satisfactory most of the year but not in the summer. He never complained about such things. I was sensitive to his physical limitations and weaknesses, such as constant shortness of breath, but I was too much of a self-centered teenager to keep it in mind always. This attitude resulted in my failure to perform some simple chores that were difficult for him. One was that I did not milk our cow every time it was required. Sometimes I did not get up early enough to get it done before school, and other times I would come home late, so he would do it for me. My mother would reprimand me, but he never did. Yes, I was practicing basketball and had a demanding schedule, but I was letting him down when he needed me.

One way that I never let him down was my willingness to work with him in painting houses and hanging wallpaper. I did this every summer and in my spare time until he died in the summer of my junior year at Purdue. But, I am not patting myself on the back, because it was easy to be thoughtful and cooperative when, as a family, we were all struggling together to obtain the simplest needs in life. I really never knew there was such a thing as a vacation until I joined the business world.

My greatest regret is that I did not have as much courage to accept, as I should have, our poor financial status and my father's physical deformities. While it did not happen often, I should never have let these things become a personal embarrassment to me. When I was at Purdue, certain events happened that do not make me proud of myself.

The only way my father could carry the paint ladders was on the side of our Model A Ford. We tied them to the door handles and let them rest on the fenders. Frequently he would take me to the campus in the morning and drop me off on Grant Street in the area fairly close to the Union Building. This major intersection where he always stopped the car was where most of the fraternity fellows and the sorority girls would be crossing. Since I was on the basketball squad and was reasonably well known, I was embarrassed to get out of the car at the intersection in front of everybody, because they could easily surmise what our financial situation was. I am sure many of those students had parents who were no better off than mine. I never lost my courage to the point where I would ask Dad to let me off in the middle of the block. We always went right up to the intersection and I faced the situation; nevertheless, I did not feel very comfortable or proud of our status in life.

An event for which I am ashamed happened in my sophomore year at the close of the basketball season in March 1940. It was at our annual awards banquet when I was given my minor "P" letter. Before dinner, as is usual in these situations, we stood around with the other basketball players and their parents prior to going to the banquet.

During that half hour or so, I did not go out of my way to introduce my father to the other players and to the other players' parents. Now I don't recall that they made any special efforts to introduce their parents to me, so perhaps I really did treat my father reasonably well. I was never ashamed of how he looked, but I was sensitive about his physical deformities. This memory has always bothered me, because, as I think about the last things I did with my father before he died, I think of that one time when we were out together and did not share it in the way I wish now that we had. At that time he never gave any indication he was unhappy about any aspect of the evening. I have always been very proud of him, and in everything I have done in my life, he has been the guiding light. His deformity resulted in a life with physical ailments, but he never indicated he wanted sympathy, and he never indicated he was ever suffering from his condition. It is my recollection that he never raised his voice to anyone. He was always calm and collected and thoughtful about everything he did. He was a very gentle person.

A Christian Environment

I had the deepest respect for my parents because of their approach toward Christian living. We went to church regularly. I went to catechism classes on Saturday morning and attended Sunday school classes until I went to Purdue. We read the Bible after every meal, taking turns reading at least one chapter. We always had a prayer both before and after the meal. We had a piano, and two of my sisters, Ruth and Mary, could play quite well. Frequently on Sunday evenings after church, the girls would bring their boyfriends to the house, and we would gather around the piano to sing hymns as well as other songs popular at that time. I thoroughly enjoyed every part of our family life.

In the middle of the 1930s, my father and mother became very irritated and upset with some of the attitudes that prevailed in the Christian Reformed Church. I was not particularly interested in what was motivating them, but I cooperated more out of curiosity than anything else when they commenced attending another church. Actually, it was a small group that gathered together on Sunday mornings above the Purdue University Book Store. All our relatives were upset about our doing this, and I was happy when it came to an end and we returned to the Christian Reformed Church.

There were many reasons for me to be very impressed with my father's character and Christianity, but one event stands out as a special one because I was directly involved. When I was about 16 years old, I was expected to make my confession of faith and become a regular member of church. James Gysels was the minister of the church from when I was in grade school until the end of World War II. We prepared for our confession of faith and regular membership in the church by attending a young people's class on Thursday evenings. At that time, the Christian Reformed Church expected its members to live by rules that were based, to a great extent, on keeping one from participating in what the church believed were the sinful ways of the world. Some of those so-called sinful actions were going to movies and dancing. I did not share this belief. Dancing, of course, was a normal thing to do at class parties in high school. At one of our Thursday evening young people's meetings when Gordon accompanied me, we got into a discussion with Rev. Gysels as to why dancing was so sinful. His belief was that, when you held another person in your arms while you danced with them, you were doing it with lust in your heart and mind. He talked about going to Purdue University on a Saturday evening, standing in the doorway and watching the young men looking out on the dance floor with lust in their eyes. Gordon and I argued vociferously, but of course, ineffectively, against this attitude. When we made our public confession of faith, we were expected to say that we would not dance or go to movies. I could not do this and told my father, who was on the consistory at that time. I felt badly about the fact it would be embarrassing to him, but I did not see how I could make a public confession of faith and agree to church policies that I believed were wrong. He said I was right and they were wrong. Most of the teenagers in our class agreed with me but still joined the church. That same Sunday night, four of us went to a movie after church. Perhaps I was making a bigger thing out of this than I should have, but it was the reason I did not become a regular member of the Christian Reformed

Church and why I was proud of my Dad. It must have been a very difficult consistory meeting for him when he had to explain my attitude.

As would be expected from this kind of environment, there was no drinking of alcoholic beverages in our family. My father believed one drink wouldn't hurt anyone. His viewpoint was that, he was fearful if he did something like that, others, who might not be as strong-willed, might not be able to control their consumption, and he would be guilty of being a bad influence on them.

My mother's beliefs were different than my father's because she came from a family with an alcoholic stepfather. My mother never wavered from her very strong conviction that one should not drink. As might be expected, she was a member of any organization that took that position. Her attitude and conviction from which she never deviated was something I always respected.

My parents had a very progressive approach toward raising me. They believed the best way to encourage me to go the extra mile was to use praise and compliments. I cannot remember during all the time I was going through school being reprimanded or put down by my parents in any way at all. It was always the opposite. I was always led to believe I was someone special, should have pride in my brains and myself, thank God for them and do my very best with my talents. I was always encouraged to study, read and learn all I could about everything. They could not help me with homework from school. They just said you can do it, and I did. They never criticized or demanded; they just expected me to perform conscientiously.

The Tillotson-Goodman Family

I have not said much about my mother's side of the family, and I should. When I was about 10 years old, I came to realize there was something different in our relationship between her family and my father's family. To be specific, we were not permitted to associate with most of my mother's half brothers. There is an interesting history to this, all of which is extremely important in understanding my mother and why she was such a strong-minded person. Her father was Calvin Goodman. He married my mother's mother, my grandmother, Amanda

Tillotson, in 1889 and he died in 1893 when my mother was three years old. Apparently the cause of his death was typhoid, which he caught while doing some work on a sewer that was being constructed along Greenbush Street. Sometime after he died, my grandmother married his brother, who had a drinking problem. They had eight children, three girls and five boys, and my mother consistently was kept out of school to help her mother. She found this so unfair and unpalatable that she left home and went to work as a maid and live with the Crouches, a wealthy family who lived rather close to my father's parents. My mother was 13 years old and had only spent enough time in school to finish the fourth grade.

With the passage of time, my mother came to know the Korschot family and married one of my father's older brothers, Joshua. Their only child, Alice, was born March 14, 1910. Unfortunately Joshua died on January 4, 1912. He was 28 years old, six years older than my mother. With Alice to take care of, my mother went to live with my grandparents. My father was still living at home, and on August 13, 1913, they were married. Alice was a half sister, but we never thought of our relationship in that way. My father always treated her as his daughter, and we never thought of her as other than a full sister. I did not even know she was not a full sister until I was an adult.

My mother thought highly of her three half sisters, particularly the oldest one, Ethel, who was married to Lloyd Hammel. Aunt Ethel and Uncle Lloyd raised a very fine family, but they lived on the other side of town so we were not with them too often. They had four children; my contact over the years has been Lloyd, Jr., who is two years younger than me. Lloyd is also a Purdue graduate and majored in accounting. After receiving his undergraduate degree, he earned his degree in law at the University of Michigan. This prepared him to specialize in the regulation of public utility companies. Lloyd's wife was Mary Ann Click, my next door neighbor when I lived on Northwestern Avenue. They settled on the West Coast where Lloyd has retired after being the General Counsel for Northwest Pacific Bell Telephone Company. Mary Ann is deceased, and they have several children and grandchildren. One of their daughters, Sharon, visited me several years before I retired to discuss opportunities for her in the investment business. She and her husband, Harvey Rubinstein, are now in the investment business in Seattle, Washington. One of Lloyd's younger sisters, Ruth Amanda, has devoted a great deal of her life to researching the family history of the Tillotson family. The records are quite complete and trace my mother's ancestors to John Tillotson, who came to Boston on June 3, 1635.

Next in age to Ethel was Mary, whom we always enjoyed seeing because of her outgoing personality. She was married at least twice but had no children. The third girl, Dorothy, was married to Ray Hermes, who was responsible for the dog pound in Lafayette. Every once in a while we would see them, and they always seemed to be a very nice family. My mother had no problems with our association with Mary and Dorothy, and her relationships with them were quite meaningful to her. One of my mother's five half brothers, Raymond, was retarded and always lived at home. He worked as a laborer for the city and had a useful life. Over the years, I got to know and respect Raymond.

My mother did not approve of the lifestyle of her stepfather and four half brothers, Clarence, Lester, John and Charles. I have no recollection of our having visited the family, but I believe they lived for some time on the "Plank" road, which ran along the Wabash River, not far from downtown Lafayette. I understood they lived under poverty conditions, which my mother attributed to her stepfather's problem with alcohol and the financial needs related to raising a very large family.

The oldest boy, Clarence, was nicknamed "Peg Leg" after he lost a leg while jumping on a train. I recall some conversations about the probability of his being involved in " bootlegging" in the years when the sale of alcohol was prohibited. Lester's life ended at a police road block where he was shot after having stolen a truck owned by the Smith Candy Company. Since the owners of the Smith Candy Company were members of our church, my mother was not pleased with being associated with a brother she did not respect. I saw John a few times and met Charlie and his wife once when I was a teenager. I have no knowledge of what happened to them or their families.

My mother had always loved her mother, and during the last few years of my grandmother's life, she lived with my mother. My grandmother had several close relatives living near Lafayette, so we frequently visited my mother's uncles, aunts and cousins who were part of the Tillotson family. There were two families in Rensselaer (located about 40 miles from Lafayette) that we visited several times over the years, but from my viewpoint, the relationship never became meaningful. To sum it up, my parents liked and respected the Tillotson side of the family, but it was my father's family, the Korschots, who were the focal point of our family activities.

CHAPTER 4

◆

High School, Purdue And Marriage

My memories of Klondike High School are pleasant in every respect. I was a good student and always near the top of our class of 19 students. I took my school work seriously, but playing on the school's basketball team was the most important thing to me at the time, although I did play baseball in my junior and senior years.

In my freshman year, I was on the varsity basketball squad — too good for the B team and not good enough for the first team. As a result, I did not play very much. In my sophomore year, when I was 5 feet 9 inches tall, I was made a regular substitute for the first team and saw considerable action. When I came back to school at the beginning of my junior year, I had grown five inches. I shall never forget the look on our coach's face when he first saw that I was about 6 feet 2 inches tall. We had a very good team in my junior year and had the best record in the county, but we did not go far in the state tournament. Playing in a small gymnasium (typical of rural high schools) did not enable us to get into the kind of physical condition that was necessary in order to compete with the larger (usually city) high schools, who were accustomed to playing on standard sized floors.

When we came back for our senior year, we thought we could dominate basketball in the county and possibly go to the state tournament. Gordon Robbins and I had played as starters for two years, and we knew we could beat teams from larger high schools. I was 6 feet 4 inches tall, and another senior , Bill German, was 6 feet 3 inches tall, so we were able to control virtually every tip-off because of our unusual height advantage. Bill and I were the tallest basketball players in our part of the Indiana at that time. Unfortunately, between our junior year and senior year, the rules for high school basketball in Indiana were changed. Instead of going back to the center for a tip-off after each basket, the ball was taken out of bounds. This rule change meant we would miss the opportunity to control the ball after every basket. Nevertheless, we had a good team and lost to only one high school in the county. In the state tournament, I fouled out very early in the second half of our first game, and we lost to a team we had defeated 42-19 earlier in the year. Although our year ended in a disappointing way, my four years of high school basketball paved the way for many of my accomplishments later. Bill Chase, our coach and teacher, influenced almost every aspect of my life in a positive way. The players liked each other; the students idolized us; and the community support was unbelievable. Because of my scoring ability and our team's wins, the local newspapers gave us a great deal of publicity. When they put me on the all-county team with words such as being an "answer to a coach's dream," my ego could not have been more inflated.

My parents very seldom came to my basketball games in high school. My father did go to some of the home games, but my mother never attended. Their absence did not bother me at the time because money was scarce, and I knew they were proud of what I was accomplishing. My father's poor health undoubtedly kept him from attending games we played at other high schools. My sister Alice and her husband, Clarence, attended all of our games. My sister Ruth had been the cheerleader at Klondike during her junior and senior years, so it was quite natural for her and her husband, Art, to attend most of the games. Ruth had graduated in 1935 and Art in 1936.

High School

The school teachers at our little country school were very good. The principal of the school for most of my seven years at Klondike was J. H. Baker. Mr. Baker had majored in mathematics at Purdue University but taught physics to us. The girls' athletic director was Bernice Foster, a vivacious and attractive person who also taught typing to my class for two years. My mathematics teacher was William Welch, nicknamed "Wee Willie." He was also a graduate of Purdue, as was the English teacher, Ethan Turley. My basketball coach, Bill Chase, taught history and social studies. One of his clever teaching techniques was to write a different "saying" that had a special meaning on the board each day, and I looked forward to coming into his class to see what he had written on the board. He was instrumental in my playing basketball at Purdue, and he influenced me to major in history. Those four teachers, Baker, Welch, Turley and Chase, made sure we had the knowledge we needed to be competitive at Purdue.

A most important extracurricular activity for me in high school was participation in the junior and senior plays. The play was a big event during the school year, and in both years I had a lead role. In my junior year, I shared the lead with Gordon, but in my senior year, I was the sole lead.

My social life at Klondike was unusual in many ways because of an age gap. I was from one to two years younger than the other kids in my class, and, as might be expected, this age gap influenced my participation in social activities. We had some school dances and some class parties that I always attended; however, I usually dated girls who were in classes behind mine. I'm sure that was because I felt more secure with the girls who were my age. One time I did have a date with a girl who was older. This was when I was a sophomore and went to the senior prom with a junior. With this start, I participated in five proms, including three years in high school and my freshman and sophomore years at Purdue. My primary interest in dating during my last three years in high school was with Cecilia Koning, a girl my age who also went to the Christian Reformed Church. Whenever we dated, it was a double or triple date and was almost always on Sunday nights after church. Sometimes I took her home after the Thursday night young people's meeting at church. I was so infatuated with her I would use any excuse I could create to drive by her house with the remote possibility I would see her outside. I took her to a few of the class parties at Klondike, so the girls in my class, as well as other classes, knew we were dating steadily. This all came to an end one Sunday night during the summer following my graduation from high school. Cecilia told me she was tired of our not doing anything new or different. I was shocked because I had thoroughly enjoyed our being together. My reaction was to decide not to date her in the future. About two months later, Gordon Robbins and I double-dated to a party at his fraternity — Cecilia was his date. A few months later, she married Menlo Pridemore, a friend who also belonged to our church.

Purdue

The decision to go to college, specifically Purdue University, was almost a routine decision as a result of our moving to West Lafayette. In the fall, the sound of the Purdue Band practicing not more than a half mile away made you feel as if you were already a part of the school. We never missed climbing a tree next to the stadium to watch the football games. Listening to the Purdue basketball games on the radio took precedence over everything but our high school games. I admired people like Professor Fred Robbins who had money, status, responsibilities and prestige. Gordon was always talking about going to Purdue in a way that made it seem as natural as going to bed at night. To my parents, having a college education was the most important goal I could possibly have. Two of my older cousins, Lawrence Dunnewold and Martin Galema, had already graduated from Purdue. So when I started high school, I enrolled in the college preparatory program without even considering any other approach. I did not worry about the cost because I knew I would live at home and work to pay my other expenses.

The likelihood of playing college basketball did not develop until I began to receive favorable publicity in my senior year. My coach said I should begin to think about it and arranged for the coach of Wabash College, located in Crawfordsville about 40 miles from home, to come to see me play. He offered me a very attractive scholarship, but I did not consider it seriously because "Piggy" Lambert, Purdue's coach, had watched me play and was interested in me. My coach and I met with him, and, although he would not give me an athletic scholarship then, he thought I could make the squad and said the scholarship would be offered to me at that time. His encouragement, even without a commitment, was all I needed, because I had great confidence in my ability, and I also realized our small high school had not had the competition a Big Ten coach needed to justify a scholarship.

During the summer of 1938, before entering Purdue, one of the concerns Gordon and I had was not only whether we would pass the orientation examination, which Purdue required for all new freshmen, but also whether we could do well enough with the English test to get into either a regular credit course or a double credit course for the first semester. If you did not get into either one of those two courses, you had to take a non-credit course in your first semester. While we were preparing for the exam, we decided a probable requirement would be to write an essay on some subject such as an important experience. So that we would have a pretty good chance of doing well, we wrote our papers during the summer, took them to our high school English teacher, Ethan Turley, and asked him to check our punctuation and grammar. Having done that, we memorized them. My subject was the trip we made to the Chicago Board of Trade. Gordon qualified for the double credit course. I was happy to get into the regular credit course.

After I made the basketball team, several fraternities became interested in me. I had developed a negative attitude toward fraternities and sororities as a result of a very unpleasant experience while I was still a senior at Klondike getting ready to go to Purdue in the fall. The fraternity I visited was the one for which Professor Robbins had the responsibility of being the sponsor. When Gordon and I arrived shortly before noon for lunch, I entered into an environment that was completely foreign to me. After lunch Gordon was invited to a meeting with some of the fraternity fellows, but I was excluded. I knew then they had invited me simply as a courtesy to Professor Robbins and regarded me as a nobody. The experience left me with a very unfavorable attitude toward fraternities. That they later wanted me because I was a member of the basketball team solidified my negative attitude. In my thoughts at the time was my belief that the only justification for a fraternity would be the contacts that might be of a beneficial nature in the business world. Since I was planning to coach and teach, I saw no need for fraternity life.

Making The Team

As soon as I was acclimated to the schedule at Purdue and felt comfortable about what was going on, I began to go to the gymnasium after my last class to practice basketball in anticipation of the tryouts for freshmen, which were to start sometime around the middle of October. It was not long before I identified the ones who were lined up for the squad and had been offered scholarships as a result of recognition they had achieved in high school.

As we approached the middle of October, I believed I had a reasonably good chance of making the team. Piggy and Mel Taube, the freshman basketball coach, were usually in the gymnasium, and, although they were not allowed to coach, they were observing all of us. When the tryouts commenced, there were somewhere between 150 to 200 fellows who were trying out for the team. The cutoffs began quickly because Piggy and Mel knew what they were looking for. After two weeks, they had the squad cut down to the 12 people they wanted on the freshman squad. It was then I discovered there were only two of us on the squad who did not have scholarships in hand before we actually arrived at the campus. Both coaches congratulated me and gave me my athletic scholarship.

At that time at Purdue, one of the requirements for the freshman and sophomore boys was to be a part of the Reserve Officers Training Corps (ROTC) program; however, one of the policies of the university was routinely to excuse athletes from the ROTC. When I went over to the ROTC headquarters to ask to be excused, I was surprised when they acquiesced in a very grudging manner.

For the most part, my freshman year at Purdue was uneventful. Basketball was very demanding as were all of my courses. I believe that coming from a small high school was not particularly disadvantageous. However, my greatest challenge was chemistry, a required course for freshmen. Most of the students had come from larger schools where they had taken chemistry in their junior or senior year.

There were 15 players on the varsity basketball team, and I was happy to be one of them in my sophomore year. Our team was a very good one, and we won the Big Ten championship. As a matter of fact, that was the last time Purdue won the Big Ten championship for 29 years. I played in quite a few games, but most of the time I played when the game was coming along pretty well and it looked as if we were going to win. I was happy to receive a minor letter.

At the end of my sophomore year, it became apparent to me as well as to the basketball coaches that my stamina was something less than it needed to be. I had just finished growing and was only 18 years old. Piggy's style of basketball was a fast break that had enabled him to win or share the Big Ten title in 11 of the 20 years from 1921 to 1940. The medical staff at Purdue recommended having my tonsils and adenoids removed. Since I could not handle the cost, Purdue assumed the expense. Unfortunately the operation was not helpful, and lack of stamina continued to be a problem. I could only be effective for a few minutes, which automatically put me in the role of substitute.

Making It Financially

My father died on August 5, 1940, just before my junior year at Purdue. For financial reasons, we began to sell off some of the 13 lots we owned as a result of sub-dividing the five acres of land on which our house was located. Dad had commenced working on dividing the property about a year before he died. It became apparent that I needed to earn more money to help with my own expenses as well as some of the family's living expenses. During my freshman year at Purdue, I had found a job (at 30 cents per hour) working for the agricultural school under the National Youth Administration program.

This program had been developed by Roosevelt during the Depression years. I worked in a greenhouse and was scheduled to put in an hour between classes and sometimes in the early afternoon before I went to basketball practice. Piggy also gave me jobs at the field house where, for performing various tasks, I was able to earn 10 dollars a week.

In my junior year, Piggy gave me the privilege of selling the advertisements for the program that was passed out at the basketball games. This program was simply two sheets of statistical information with a lot of advertisements. All I had to do was contact all the merchants who advertised the previous year and try to develop some new advertisements. As a result of selling the advertisements, I earned about $300.

In my junior year, I worked for the Purdue newspaper called the *Exponent*. My job was to deliver the newspapers in an area that included many fraternities and sororities. This was a time when I was very active with the basketball team, practicing every afternoon and making all the basketball trips out of town. I still had the job with the National Youth Administration and the two jobs in the field house that took about 15 minutes each day. I also had a full load of courses, so when I got home in the evenings after basketball practice, I had to study fairly late. In the morning I had to get up at five o'clock in order to deliver the newspapers at the right time. I did not take the job of delivering the newspapers as seriously as I should have and neglected to arrange for someone to deliver the papers when I went on basketball trips. This happened twice, and I was reprimanded by the editor of the newspaper. However, after it happened a third time, I was told that they had given the job to somebody else when I got back from the trip. Piggy was very upset because he was always looking for jobs for his basketball players and I had lost one of the jobs for him. It was a great lesson for me because it made me realize for the first time that one had to have a sense of responsibility toward other people. There was no question I had been completely oblivious to the importance of the responsibility. I did not realize students living on campus were so anxious to receive the paper in the morning. When it did not come, they were rightfully upset, and I was insensitive to this.

The story of my athletic activities would not be complete without mentioning baseball. In my junior and senior years in high school, I had played baseball for Klondike as a pitcher and had done quite well. When I entered Purdue, I was concerned about the amount of time basketball would take away from my studies and decided not to try out for the baseball team. Even though I had not tried out my freshman year, as a sophomore I decided I could do it all. The baseball coach, Dutch Fehring, was quite willing to give me a tryout. After about three weeks of practice, he told me there was a basic flaw in the way I was pitching, and, although I could throw the ball well, he was fearful of what it could do to my arm. Fortunately for my ego, I was a good softball pitcher, so for the next two summers, my evenings were dedicated to that sport. During the summer between my junior and senior years, I was on a team that won the city championship. It was sponsored by the *Lafayette Journal and Courier*, so we received plenty of publicity. In the final game of the tournament for the championship, we beat a team on which two of the players were my cousins, John Bol and Charley Korschot.

Life Begins With Mary Schelle

I do not know when I first fell in love with Mary Schelle. It might have been when I was in the eighth grade and we walked around the school at lunch time holding hands. I dated Mary three or four times when she was in high school — usually when she wanted to talk to me at length about problems she was having with her boyfriend at the time. Between classes I frequently talked and flirted with her, and she never missed the basketball games. I had one date with Mary during my freshman year at Purdue. It was a double date with Gordon and a girl from Rossville, Indiana. Mary had been going steady with a fellow by the name of Paul Senesac, and, as usual, during the date we discussed her concerns. At that time, I still did not realize how much Mary meant to me. The best indication of that is something she later loved to tease about: on the way home with Gordon driving and Mary between us in the front seat, I fell asleep.

The date that really began our going steady and eventually led to us becoming married was one that occurred after the last basketball game in my sophomore year at Purdue. Mary's best friend in high school was Jackie Lemenager. She and Gordon had started dating about the time we started at Purdue. After I had finished playing in the basketball game, Gordon and Jackie joined me at the Union Building. As we talked about what to do the next night, a Sunday, Jackie suggested that if I called Mary perhaps she might be free and interested in going out with me. I called her immediately. She had been listening to the basketball game and had been very happy with how I had played. So we had the date, went to a movie, and from then on, my life revolved completely around Mary.

During the summer after my junior year, Mary and I were seeing each other a good deal. As the summer went along, we began to think seriously about possibly getting married in my senior year before my graduation. We made the decision shortly after my senior year started and were married on October 31, 1941. In making the decision, we knew it could have a serious impact on my participation in basketball. We were apprehensive about Piggy's attitude toward married players, so we decided to be married secretly and endeavor to keep our marriage from being publicized until after the basketball season. Since I was only 20 years old, I had to have my mother's consent in order to obtain a marriage license. She had no objection and gave us permission to keep it a "secret" from her as well as everyone else.

In attempting to keep our marriage a secret, we arranged for the wedding to be outside Lafayette, specifically in Lebanon, Indiana. There was no particular reason for Lebanon, except it was fairly close. We were able to contact a Methodist minister, and after explaining our reasoning, he was willing to marry us the following week. We asked Al and Mary Elizabeth Todd if they would witness the wedding and also keep it a secret. Mary Elizabeth was Mary's cousin, and Al was working on his doctorate degree in electrical engineering. The arrangement was made, and on Halloween night, October 31, we went to Lebanon and were married in the parsonage.

Unfortunately, Al and Mary Elizabeth Todd decided they had too important a secret to keep to themselves. Not much more than a week went by before we learned they had told Mary Elizabeth's mother about the marriage. She immediately talked to Mary's mother, and from then on, it was no longer a secret. We called the newspapers, and because I was a Purdue athlete, we received enough publicity for Piggy to know what had happened.

In the meantime, I had been going through the normal procedure of preparing for the basketball season with long practices every night, every Saturday and sometimes even on Sundays. Shortly after the wedding was announced but before the first game of the basketball season, Piggy called me into his office and said if I wanted to stay on the team during my senior year I could do so, but he wanted me to know he had decided to go with a rebuilding approach and was going to use sophomores whenever possible. I made the decision, then and there, that basketball was not going to be the focal point of my life and I would not stay on the team.

After searching around for an apartment, we found one in Lafayette, not too far from the Christian Reformed Church at Tenth and Salem Streets. The apartment cost us $32 a month, and Mary's income as a sales clerk at Palais Royal was $13.86 a week. This meant we had a few dollars each week to buy food and whatever was necessary to operate the 1935 Plymouth that my Dad had bought for $50 late in 1939. Since basketball was no longer a demand on my time, it was an easy decision for me to look for some part-time work. I contacted the J.C. Penney store in Lafayette and immediately started working with them after school and on Saturdays. Our financial needs were not a problem.

The 1935 Plymouth was instrumental in the first argument we had after we were married. It came about because I told Mary I would pick her up from work after I left the library to come home. Unfortunately, as I was leaving the campus, I noticed a girl who lived in our neighborhood standing on a corner waiting for a bus to go home. I offered her a ride and, in doing so, completely forgot about picking up Mary. As I was driving toward home, I passed Mary, carrying two bags of groceries, walking home from work. She saw me in the car with the girl, but I did not see her. I arrived home a few minutes before she did and was reading the newspaper when she walked in. As you might imagine, she was more than a little upset since she had walked the two miles home in her high-heeled shoes.

Automobiles And Accidents

As a teenager, I was not a very careful or considerate driver. I had reason to regret this just after I got my license, when I was on a Sunday afternoon date with a girl whom I was dating for the first time. Our car, a 1932 Ford, did not have any brakes other than the emergency brake, so after driving around for a while, she began to cry. I took her home and realized I had been fairly reckless. However, the most reckless thing that happened was while Gordon and I were seniors in high school. His folks had just purchased a new 1938 Buick Special, and it was gray, beautiful and high-powered. So one afternoon with Gordon driving, we crossed the Wabash River on the Highway 52 bypass at 118 miles per hour. I still remember the look on the faces of some of the men who were working on the bridge. Another time, when we were with Mary and Jackie, a blacktop, hilly country road enticed me, and as I drove with one arm around Mary, we became airborne at 95 miles per hour. From the back seat came Gordon's comment, "I'm sure glad you had both your hands on the wheel."

The first accident I had with an automobile occurred in the late spring of 1940 when I was coming home from a date with Mary. This happened around 11:00 P.M. as I was going north on Northwestern Avenue toward the Lambert Field House where we played basketball. I fell asleep and did not wake up until the car was halfway through a wire fence adjacent to the field house. I had just missed a tree in front of the field house by about six inches. When the police came, I reported what had happened and walked home, which was about a mile away. The next day, I met with Guy Mackey, the athletic director at Purdue, to talk about the accident. Since I was a basketball player and not well off financially, Purdue did not ask me to pay for the damages to the fence. It cost us $50 to fix the Plymouth.

In the fall of 1940, during my junior year at Purdue, Mary and I had a serious automobile accident while we were driving on the

South River Road to her home. A car coming toward us was slightly on our side of the road, and I did not react quickly enough to prevent my left front end and his left front end from hitting each other. The impact pulled us over to the left hand side of the road and down an embankment. We got out of the car and climbed to the top of the road. Then we noticed that, after the other car had hit us, it had hit head-on into a car following me. The man on the passenger side of the front seat in the car behind had the unfortunate experience of having his face go through the windshield. He was very badly cut, bleeding profusely and had to have plastic surgery. We also learned a lesson from that experience ... namely, that people will take advantage of you if it is financially beneficial to do so. While we were on the highway immediately after the accident, the driver of the car behind us told the police the other car was on the wrong side of the road. Later we learned from my insurance company that the car behind us had put the blame on me. The fact that the owners of the car that had hit us and then hit them head-on had absolutely no insurance, while we were fully covered, was an obvious reason for the change. While we were talking to the police after the accident, they were very sympathetic toward us. They also drove both of us home. Mary lived six miles away and it was another ten miles to my house.

CHAPTER 5

Involvement In World War II

Our marriage on October 31, 1941, was five weeks before the bombing of Pearl Harbor. On that Sunday, we had gone to church and to our house for Sunday dinner with my mother, Ruth, Art, Alice and Clarence. It was sometime after we had finished eating when we heard the announcement on the radio about Pearl Harbor. Mary's recollection was that we got the word about four o'clock in the afternoon.

It was not long before the government began the military buildup needed for a world war. I was very much interested in somehow becoming a part of the war effort. One of the first opportunities that came to my attention was a program developed by the University in cooperation with the U.S. Army Ordnance Department. They encouraged students to take certain classes that would prepare them for jobs in which their responsibility would be to inspect equipment produced for the Army. I was accepted into that program, and classes commenced after the first of the year. I had only one course to take during my last semester and was excused from attending classes. In effect, I had completed the requirements for my graduation in three and one-half years.

Immediately upon completing the training program sometime in March 1942, all of those who were in the program were sent to Cincinnati, Ohio, to receive some instruction for a day or two and receive our orders to work somewhere in the Midwest. Mary and I had very little money saved, and while we were driving to Cincinnati, something went wrong with the car. We found our way to a garage and were told it would cost $270 to have it repaired. I have no recollection of how we paid for it, but we got the car repaired and went on to Cincinnati. While we were in Cincinnati, we had to pay for our expenses. Mary and I went to the cheapest possible places to eat and stayed in a very inexpensive, run-down hotel.

After we were in Cincinnati about two days, I received my assignment. I was to go to Detroit and report to the Ford Motor Company for work in the Highland Park plant. Mary and I left Cincinnati immediately and arrived in downtown Detroit sometime after midnight. We stopped at the first hotel that looked as if it might fit our budget. They had a room that I signed for using only my name, not Mr. and Mrs. We were very naive but still knew what the clerk was thinking when he said "Well, what about her?" Mary stayed up very late that night to iron my suit. I got up about seven o'clock in the morning in order to get to the Ford Motor Company office by about eight. Since I did not know exactly where it was or how long I would be with them, I left her with no idea when I would return. Unfortunately I also forgot to leave her any money. When I returned to the hotel around 4:30 in the afternoon, she was famished and worried about how we were going to find a place to live.

We bought a newspaper, looked for advertisements in the Highland Park area, and around six o'clock, found a place we thought might be satisfactory. A woman was renting out a room in her home and providing some kitchen privileges. The most notable feature of the house was that it was filled with stuffed birds. We stayed that night, got a reasonably good night's sleep, and I reported to the Highland Park plant the next morning. When I got off work and returned to the house, Mary met me at the door with our bags already packed. She said, "I'm not staying here another night! I cannot stand the stuffed birds." We bought a newspaper and only had to look at two places before we found one we could afford with a bedroom and a very tiny kitchen.

It did not take long for me to realize how boring the job was. Ford was just starting up production of aircraft control equipment and had an assembly line of sorts. The assembly line had lots of bugs, and production was virtually nil. I had to look busy when there was nothing to do. All I could do was to try to keep out of sight of the people who were working on the production line.

The most important challenge during that period was to find some way to exist without being paid. My salary of $100 per month would have been reasonably satisfactory if it had been available. The government's excuse was, as usual, "paperwork." Fortunately, we found three other couples who were in equally dire straits and willing to pool resources. Since we did not have enough money to buy food, we used our cash for gasoline and drove to Lafayette almost every weekend so that Mary's folks could give us food to take back to Detroit.

We still had the 1935 Plymouth that was not in the best shape. One night when we were leaving Detroit quite late, we encountered a fog that was so dense we could hardly see what was ahead of us. The windshield wipers did not work, so we had to stick our heads out the windows to see where we were going. Even then we relied upon following the taillights of a truck for a good part of the trip.

Getting Into The Navy

During this time I decided that, if I could become an officer in one of the military services, it would be the Navy. When I visited their recruiting office, they gave me a physical examination and discovered I had a double hernia. I was told I could not be taken into any military service as long as I had that weakness, but if I had an operation to correct the problem, they would send me to school to become an officer. I immediately made the decision to have the operation, and Mary did not object. We contacted our family doctor in Lafayette, arranged a six-week leave of absence and had the operation in August. On our first day back in Detroit around the middle of October, the Navy welcomed me back, gave me a physical examination and approved my application. They said I would be sent to either Northwestern University in Chicago or Columbia University in New York for the indoctrination program for officers. At that time, those who went through the program were sometimes called "90-Day Wonders."

I was not back for much more than a week or two when I received an increase in pay from an annual salary of $1,200 to $1,400. That evening we splurged and went out to eat. Later that evening, I received my orders from the Navy to report to the Columbia University midshipman school on December 7. I immediately resigned from my job with the U.S. Army Ordnance Department. We packed up our few belongings and went back to Lafayette for a vacation before I reported for duty in New York City. In the meantime, I was healing slowly and wondered if they would want to take me into the Navy when I was still experiencing such discomfort. When I arrived at Columbia, they looked at the record and said enough time had passed for me to heal. This convinced me I could do whatever I wanted to do. Since the midshipman school had a basketball team, I joined it and also the choir that sang every Sunday morning in the Riverside Church, one of the most beautiful Protestant churches in the world.

My experiences at midshipman school were quite rewarding in every respect. I did very well and ranked in the upper 100 in a class of 960. The basketball games were most enjoyable because I was playing with fellows who had played in college. We played all kinds of teams in the New York area, and it proved to be a pleasant diversion from a very tight and difficult schedule.

We became Ensigns in March 1943, and, since this was a very important event in our lives, Mary made the train trip to be present. She arrived at the Biltmore Hotel ahead of me, so as soon as I arrived, I took the elevator to her room. Almost immediately there was a knock on the door. It was a woman saying no visitors were allowed on the floor. We did not know what she was talking about, but we soon learned I had not registered to stay that night, and they were not about to let me visit. So I registered and solved the problem, and nine months later we had our first child.

Following the graduation ceremony, one of the men with whom

I had become acquainted invited several of us to his home, which was located a few miles north of the University. As might be expected, alcoholic beverages were available, with most of those present drinking beer. Neither Mary or I had ever tasted beer, so we decided we should at least discover what it tasted like. In our society today, it may seem strange that a 22-year- old man who had played basketball at Purdue could have had such a sheltered life. Both Mary and I had the same reaction to our first taste of beer. We did not like it. I do not believe Mary ever tried beer again, and I have placed it near the bottom of my taste for beverages.

To The U.S.S. Knapp, DD653

Since I ranked rather high in my graduating class at midshipman school, I was given the assignment I had requested, a destroyer. I had also indicated a preference for Pacific Ocean duty. My assignment was to report to Bath, Maine, to be on board the U.S.S. Knapp DD653 for the completion of its construction and the commissioning of the ship in Boston, Massachusetts. In preparation for joining the ship, I was sent to Norfolk, Virginia, for a basic training program. Mary and I were together in Norfolk and lived in an apartment not too far from the Navy base. This was followed by six weeks of additional schooling in Alexandria, Virginia, near Washington, D.C. While there we lived with Al and Mary Elizabeth Todd, the couple who could not keep our marriage a secret.

The schedule worked out so that we arrived in Bath in the early fall. The ship was well along under construction, so our challenge was to learn how its systems operated and make sure all the equipment and materials we needed were delivered aboard ship.

While we were in Bath, we had the privilege of staying off the ship at night. Our evenings were usually free and provided the officers and their wives the opportunity to get to know each other. One interesting experience for us was a shore lobster party one of the officers arranged on the beach. They bought live lobsters, took them to the beach and cooked them in huge vats filled with seawater and seaweed. Mary and I had never eaten lobster and did not have the slightest idea how it tasted. We did try it but did not like it. We decided we would try to learn to like lobster, because it seemed to us if people enjoyed it so much there must be something special about it. I was reasonably successful, but Mary never learned to like it.

Mary lived with a Mrs. Hill whose deceased husband had been the president of a bank in Bath. She had decided she would open her home to two officers and their wives while ships were under construction. So we lived there, Mary all the time and I part of the time. The other couple was Eli Vinnick, the executive officer of another ship under construction, and his wife, Barbara. We had kitchen privileges at the house, and, on one occasion, Mrs. Hill permitted Mary and Barbara to have a cocktail party for all the officers and their wives from the two ships.

The U.S.S. Knapp was launched in early October, and we immediately went down the Kennebeck River and to Boston for the commissioning. We were not in Boston long, but even so, one evening a group of us went to Sculley Square to see a burlesque show. This was the first time Mary and I had ever seen one. At the end of the show, they released pigeons, which flew all around the auditorium. With our distrust of live birds flying above us, we were not very impressed with this part of the performance.

Prior to going to the Pacific Ocean, newly built ships were sent on a shakedown cruise to Bermuda. Accordingly, we left Boston immediately, and Mary went back to Lafayette. She was six months pregnant, so we had to assume there would not be another chance for us to get together before our first child was born. The shakedown cruise to Bermuda was vitally necessary. We had to learn everything about running the ship and preparing to fight. I was an assistant gunnery officer (the machine gun officer to be specific) in charge of the 40mm and 20mm guns. One of the responsibilities this gave me was to take a crew of men ashore every day for training at the firing range, which was located on a cliff looking out to the ocean. This was in November; the weather was beautiful; and the sun was shining every day. After a while, I became very familiar with the routine, so I would deliver the enlisted men to the firing range, walk around the countryside and do some sightseeing in Hamilton, which was within walking distance.

Also during this period, I had one of the unfortunate experiences that occur when you are trying to handle a large number of men who have had too much to drink. We established a schedule to provide liberty from the ship for the enlisted men so they could spend a few hours in Hamilton. Most of the men were young, unaccustomed to heavy drinking and unfamiliar with rum and how to handle it. One time, coming back from such a shore leave, I was the only officer on board one of the motor launches when two of my gunner's mates who had had much too much to drink started fighting each other. They had knives, but, with the help of some of the enlisted men, I threw them overboard. This cooled them off, and we got the knives away from them so no harm came from the experience.

To The Pacific

When we completed our shakedown cruise in Bermuda, we returned to Norfolk for one day before we headed through the Panama Canal to the Pacific Ocean. As soon as we arrived in Norfolk, I got off the ship so I could call Mary. We were trying to agree on a name for the baby if it were a boy. We had decided on the name for a girl, Barbara Elaine, but the name for a boy was still up in the air. During our half-hour conversation, we decided if we had a boy his name would be Kenneth Calvin. Neither of us was too happy with Kenneth but we had been trying out names for months, and a decision had to be made.

The trip through the Panama Canal Zone was an interesting experience, and I looked forward to arriving at the west end of the canal, where I might have the opportunity to look up Gordon, who was stationed in the Army Signal Corps at Panama City. We were permitted just enough time off the ship for the two of us to spend the better part of one day and an evening together. Panama City was an eye-opener for me, especially the red light district. We walked through this district in the afternoon. The women were visible in rooms with doors like those on a barn. Sometimes they would be standing out in front and sometimes just behind the lower half of the door with the upper half open. Even when they had sexual intercourse with men, it was not unusual for them to leave the upper half of the door open.

When we left the Panama Canal Zone, we learned that, instead of going straight to Pearl Harbor, we were going to stop in San Diego for some special orders. When I learned this, it was obvious that I ought to see if I could go ashore to call Mary. The Captain, Frank Virden, was the only one allowed to leave the ship, but although it was against his orders, he permitted me to go ashore with him, with the understanding I would stay within the naval base to make the telephone call. When I found a telephone, I called the hospital in the belief Mary might still be there. When the people at the hospital learned I was calling long-distance to find out about my baby, they did everything they could (against the orders of one of the Sisters) to make sure I talked to Mary. The only way they could get Mary to a telephone was to wheel her down to the office. They also brought Barbara to the office so I could hear her jabber or cry. She would not make a sound even when they spanked her.

Barbara's birth was a very difficult one for Mary. She was in the hospital from December 9, when Barbara was born, until December 24, and when she did go home to her parents, it was a very uncomfortable period because she had needed about 60 stitches. The telephone call was fortunate since Mary's letter telling me about Barbara's birth did not get to the ship until the middle of February.

Our Role In The Task Force

On the way to join the task force to which we had been assigned, we stopped at Hawaii for additional training and supplies. We then joined a task force stationed at an island atoll named Eniwetok in the Marshall group, one of the first groups of islands the Allied Forces invaded on the way to Japan. We were in Halsey's task force (which was called the Third Fleet) as one of the destroyers in a protective circle around the cruisers, battleships and aircraft carriers to ward off submarine and aircraft attacks. Most task forces had one or two battleships and one or two very large carriers in the very center. These ships were surrounded by perhaps four cruisers. In another circle about five miles in diameter, there were usually from 10 to 20 destroyers.

With our sonar equipment, we were able to detect submarines before they could get close enough to torpedo the aircraft carriers, battleships and cruisers. Also, as airplanes approached, we were in position to fire before they could get inside the task force and attack the aircraft carriers, which were their primary targets. Our role was to support various landing operations, including Kwajalein, Palau, Guam, Saipan, Tinian, the Philippines and, ultimately, Okinawa.

The primary role of the Third Fleet was to stay offshore and provide air support for our troops who were making the landing. Some of the destroyers, along with the battleships and cruisers, would go close to shore and participate in the bombardment of the island while others would stay with the carriers. We would approach to within 5,000 yards or so of the beach, and, using our 5-inch guns, manually pinpoint targets as we supported the invasion. The Japanese always had airplanes on the islands; however, our air support usually destroyed them before we landed the troops.

Life on board a destroyer at that time could be exciting or boring. When nothing was going on, we always had to make sure the ship was manned to protect itself against a surprise aircraft attack. This meant we had men on duty for four hours and then off for eight hours at all times. This did not change even when we went into a harbor or atoll for supplies and fuel. We rotated the schedule, which meant I was sleeping at odd times because I was never on duty the same four hours. When off duty, if not sleeping, we spent most of the time in the ward room. We played a lot of backgammon and all kinds of card games. We conducted drills with the guns every day to make sure we were fast and ready. Most of the drilling took place while we were on duty. My duty station was in the fire control tower that was on top of the ship. With our radar we could pick up airplanes up to 150 miles away, track them and commence firing when they were about four miles away. With the kinds of shells we had, which exploded when they were close to the aircraft, we were very effective in bringing them down. These shells were a great development, because, even with the sophistication of the fire control equipment, it was difficult to make a direct hit.

We Sank A Ship

The battle for the Philippines in late 1944 was the beginning of the end of the war, as we won both sea and air battles associated with MacArthur's landing on Luzon, the northernmost island in the Philippines. The Japanese made an all-out attempt to attack our ships when we were in the midst of landing; therefore, we went through a long period of time when we were under constant attack. During this period, the Japanese sent a task force of carriers and other ships north of Luzon toward Japan. Halsey recognized this as a great opportunity, and we all began to sail northward in pursuit. Our airplanes dominated the skies and sank numerous ships in the Japanese fleet. For reasons that I never understood, our ship was assigned to chase one destroyer that was escaping to the north of Luzon. This was our first and only ship-to-ship combat, and fortunately we had the advantage over it. Our 5-inch guns had a longer range than their guns, so, as we were chasing them north, we were able to sink their ship from a very safe distance. When we reached the site where the ship sank, many men in the water begged us to pick them up. We were fearful of being torpedoed so we stopped just long enough to pick up four of them for interrogation purposes. It was not a very pleasant feeling to leave the other men in the water, knowing their chances of survival were minimal. We had no alternative because we had no capacity for taking prisoners.

Halsey And The Typhoon

On December 17, 1944, we were part of a huge fleet of five separate task force groups under Halsey's command when we ran into one of the worst, if not the worst, typhoon ever experienced by so many ships at one time. One of the five groups was entirely British and, in total, there were probably over 100 destroyers, 8 or 10 aircraft carriers and a similar number of battleships and cruisers. All of us were on course to rendezvous with a fleet of tankers and refuel when we began to have severe weather warnings. We were concerned because it seemed to us that Admiral Halsey was completely ignoring the storm warnings, and even with our limited forecasting ability, we were quite sure our heading would take us where the storm was going to be at its peak. All the officers on our destroyer believed Admiral Halsey and his staff were making a very bad decision. It was apparent to us that we should change direction and make no attempt to rendezvous until the storm passed. However, Halsey kept us on course for the tankers, and we got there just about the time the typhoon hit around noon on the 18th. We disobeyed the order to de-ballast, that is, to pump out the seawater we had pumped into our tanks after we had used up our fuel. Since we retained the seawater in our tanks, we were riding fairly low in the water as if we had a full load of fuel on the ship. We did not see any possibility that we could refuel.

Unfortunately, some of the destroyers and some of the other ships did not act so wisely. There were several destroyers who did not protect themselves by keeping the ballast on board ship. As the typhoon hit, all the ships in the task force turned in the direction the wind was moving. By moving with the wind and with the waves, we kept the ship from rolling as much as it would have otherwise. Even then, in the midst of the typhoon with the winds well in excess of 100 miles an hour, we were rolling as much as 60 degrees one way and 45 degrees the other. This meant that, as the ship rolled, you either held on to something or else you went flying across to the other side of the ship.

Three destroyers sank; of those, two were in our group with one of them stationed immediately off our starboard bow. For reasons we did not understand, this destroyer was given instructions to change its position in the task force. When it moved, its rudder became caught right-full-rudder just as it turned into the storm. With the rudder caught, there was no way they could straighten themselves out. Their ship soon flipped over on its side and eventually sank. There were no recoveries from that ship.

The other destroyer that went down in our task force was the Hull, and she had only two survivors. Our ship was fortunate enough to come across them the next day after the survivors had been in the water for 24 hours. The two who survived talked to us at great length about what had happened. It is interesting to know what people do in circumstances like that in order to live.

The officer we rescued was stationed in the combat information center, which is in the center of the ship and above the main deck. When their ship went over on its side — and it went over because they did not have enough ballast — he got off the ship and into the water almost immediately. At first he was fearful of being hit by the mast, which was lying flat in the water but flopping around. He managed to keep out of the way of the mast but was almost sucked into the two smokestacks. When he got to the fantail of the ship, he thought the ship would stay afloat and tried to climb aboard. He could not do that but managed to get into a life raft that had broken loose. He could not stay in it, so he tried to wrap his arm around the circular balsam sides of the life raft. This he found was also impossible, so he floated away from the ship. He decided all he could do to survive was to keep his back to the waves and, as the waves came over him, try to get enough air in his lungs so that when he was underwater he would simply fight his way to the top again to try to get some more air. He battled the waves all day and all night. When we picked him up around noon, he was lying flat on his back and unconscious, with the K-pak life jacket holding his head out of the water.

In the midst of that storm, we lost three of our sailors who had ignored the instructions from the captain not to go on deck. We learned later there were similar experiences on other ships.

Another interesting sidelight was that one of the carriers in our task force reported that, in the middle of the storm when we were rolling 60 degrees, they were suffering from extreme rolls of 20 to 25 degrees. For a carrier, that was a severe roll, but it certainly was not for a destroyer. The aircraft carriers lost a tremendous number of aircraft, because they could not fasten them down tight enough to keep them from colliding with each other.

On January 3, 1945, about two weeks after the typhoon, a court of inquiry heard the testimony of 54 witnesses and concluded that Admiral Halsey was at fault for not broadcasting danger warnings to all vessels early in the morning of the 18th. The report went on to say that, on that morning, courses ordered by him brought the fleet closer to the storm and contributed to the disaster.

Captain Frank Virden had left our ship early in the fall of 1944 and was replaced by Captain W.B. Brown. Virden was a tough, strict and disciplined leader. He handled the ship exceptionally well in combat conditions and made sure we knew our individual responsibilities. It is my belief we survived during the year we had with Captain Brown, because we had been so well trained by Captain Virden.

I Almost Drowned

My first tour of duty in the Pacific almost ended in tragedy, not because of the war, but because of something that happened when I was flown back to Pearl Harbor ahead of the ship, which was coming back to the States for an overhaul. I had been given the responsibility of being the gunnery officer, and the six-week training program fit the ship's sailing schedule. I completed the program about two or three days before the ship was to arrive and discovered I could take advantage of a rest area located on the opposite side of Oahu from Pearl Harbor. I took the bus, arrived late one evening and checked in. Early the next morning, I decided to go for a swim in the ocean. There were no lifeguards, but it looked completely safe and peaceful. As I swam out from shore, I was caught in an undertow that was dragging me down at a tremendous rate. I had never been told what one should do in a situation such as this, but I had the presence of mind not to fight the power of the undertow. Instinctively, I swam down and with the water pressure as it was moving out to sea. As I swam with it, I used all my strength to swim upward and break away from the undertow. I surfaced a long way from the shore and was completely exhausted. I decided the safest thing for me to do was to dog-paddle ashore — and not in the direction from which I had come. As soon as I was ashore I went to my room, dressed, and at eight o'clock that morning, I was on a bus back to Pearl Harbor. That was the end of the rest period.

Home On Leave

The first time I saw Barbara was in late April 1945, approximately 17 months after she was born. Our ship went to the naval base at Long Beach, California, for the overhaul, at which time Mary joined me on the West Coast. After a week or two, we went back to Lafayette for about two weeks. In that short period, Barbara could only look at me as an intruder. In those days, the way to get back and forth across the country was by train. Mary had no particular difficulty in getting out to the West Coast to meet the ship when it came in, and we had no difficulty in going back to Lafayette. However, when we returned to the West Coast, we went through Chicago and had a most unpleasant experience. The only accommodation available was one Pullman upper berth. Since they were only about six feet long and I was six feet, four inches tall, it was a very uncomfortable trip. On that train trip, the enlisted men were allowed to eat aboard the train, but the officers were not.

The decision for Mary to return with me to the West Coast was not easy to make, because we did not believe the ship would be in Long Beach for more than two or three days. It did not seem to make much sense for her to go with me, but when you do not know how long you are going to live, you treasure time together.

The night before the ship was to leave, one of our enlisted men, who obviously did not want to return to the Pacific, decided that by damaging the ship he could keep us from going permanently, or at least temporarily. He got into the radar equipment room and did enough damage to delay our departure for two extra weeks. After this delay, Mary and I had two extra days together, because when we were leaving port, they discovered the propeller drive shaft was out of round. This extra time together was important to us because we simply did not know what the chances were of my returning. I never mentioned to Mary that we were going to Okinawa to support the invasion and confront the kamikazes. She had no difficulty with the train ride home and immediately went back to the factory where she worked a night shift until the end of the war. During all of this period, Mary lived with her parents, which meant that for all practical purposes they were Barbara's parents until the war was over.

The Kamikazes Missed Us

As we crossed the Pacific, we heard of numerous destroyers being hit by the kamikaze pilots as the ships were attempting to support our troops on Okinawa. On the way to Okinawa, our only stop was an atoll in the Pacific called Ulithi. I was the gunnery officer at this time, and one of the ideas of our chief gunner's mate, Williams, was to see if we could obtain some 50-caliber machine guns while we were there. Captain Brown agreed to mounting them on the ship wherever we could and use the men in our repair party to fire them. When we arrived in Ulithi, we went ashore with some of the gunners' mates to see what we could find. The Air Force agreed to give us the guns, but the problem was that they were constructed to fire electrically instead of mechanically. Chief Williams said he could change them with the help of the men in our machine shop, so we brought about 20 of them on board with enough ammunition to sustain us for some period of time. In doing this, we were violating numerous U.S. Navy regulations. For one thing, there was so much ammunition that it filled every available space on the deck of the ship. Worse yet, our new guns were mounted without the mandatory device that prevented them from firing into the structure of the ship. The guns on a destroyer, that is the 5-inch, 40mm and 20mm guns, each had a cam device that prevented them from firing into the ship. Nevertheless, we mounted the machine guns all around the ship, on top of the torpedo deck, on the bridge of the ship and on the fantail by the depth charge racks. There was no way you could prevent them from firing into the ship itself. The risk was there, but we thought we were better prepared for the kamikazes.

Upon arriving at Okinawa on May 26, we anchored in an island harbor, Kerramo Reto, which was perhaps 30 miles from the landing area. Badly damaged destroyers were everywhere. My guess is that there were 30 or 40 waiting to go back to the United States for repairs. Before the battle for Okinawa ended, 30 of our ships (mostly destroyers) were sunk, and 368 were damaged. As soon as we refueled, we were on our way to our picket station.

There were 16 picket stations with three destroyers and three small ships assigned to each station. The three small ships were there to pick up the survivors from the destroyers when they were sunk. We were on nine different stations with the one closest to the main islands of Japan being about 100 miles directly north of Okinawa. Our primary responsibility was to track the kamikazes on our radar and direct aircraft from the carriers to the incoming planes before they could get to us or Okinawa. The Japanese pilots understood that, if they could not get to the ships in the harbor providing our troops with their support material, they were to dive into the destroyers on the picket stations. Consequently, we were under almost continuous attack. This assignment lasted for about a month, and during that period, we never deviated from a program of being on duty for four hours and off for four hours. Accordingly, you slept most of the time right at the station to which you were assigned. We had many close calls. Our group knocked down several kamikaze pilots as they were diving toward our ships. Three destroyers with us were hit, but we were always the fortunate one. Some of our good luck was due to our having the 50-caliber machine guns. When a plane was coming at us, we were throwing up a tremendous amount of firepower that the kamikaze pilots could see from the tracers. From my position as the gunnery officer in the fire control tower at the top of the ship, I could see the faces of some of the pilots who just missed us.

When we were released from picket station duty to rejoin our task force, we immediately dumped all of the 50-caliber machine guns and ammunition overboard. We had used them successfully in violation of naval regulations, and there was no longer any justification for having them as part of our armament. The task force then moved north to patrol east of the main islands of Japan. It was obvious we were preparing for an invasion of the mainland. We were about 300 miles offshore when the first atomic bomb was dropped on Hiroshima at 9:15 in the morning on August 6. The second bomb was dropped on Nagasaki on August 9, but the Japanese did not surrender until August 15. Even then, the military leaders were not ready to capitulate, and it was the Emperor who made the decision. On the morning of the 15th, Japanese planes were still attacking us, and our task force had to shoot down six kamikaze planes.

Our reaction to the surrender was one of great relief. We were convinced that, since the Japanese were committed to the kamikaze approach toward sinking our ships, it would be very difficult for us to last the war without getting hit. There were simply too many aircraft, and as we came closer to the mainland, they would have the protection of the land just before they attacked. Those of us who were close to the scene were convinced it would have been a difficult fight and the loss of ships would have been tremendous. The loss of infantry men who would have done the fighting on land is too horrible to contemplate. I did not, and do not now, believe we were wrong in ending the war this way.

Our task force was located just offshore from Tokyo when the Japanese surrendered. When our group was given the order to enter Tokyo Bay, we met a Japanese destroyer to pick up charts that identified the location of minefields near the entrance to the harbor. The task force then followed us into Tokyo Bay to anchor and wait for the signing of the peace treaty. Our ship was anchored about 2,000 yards off the port side of the U.S.S. Missouri, where the signing of the peace treaty took place on September 2, 1945.

Not long after we were in the harbor, we were allowed to go ashore to see what it was like to be on the mainland of Japan. Our ship was anchored in the harbor at Yokosuka, a Japanese naval base that we began to use. We allowed about half our crew to go ashore the first time. Not many Japanese men and women were visible. Most of those on the streets were younger boys and some older people. I am sure they were very apprehensive as to how we would conduct ourselves ashore. It was not long before they realized their concerns were unwarranted.

Trying To Get Home

Within a few days after the end of the war, the Navy announced the procedure to be followed for releasing people from active duty. This was a very complicated assignment for those who had that responsibility, because you could not abandon equipment and dismiss the personnel who took care of it unless it was done in some organized manner. At the same time, those who had been on active duty away from the United States and had families were given the greatest consideration and, therefore, the earlier dates for release from active duty. I was one of those given an early release date.

I was anxious to return, not only to get back to Mary and Barbara, but also to go back to school and obtain an advanced degree. My objective was to go to a graduate school where I could major in economics and work toward a doctorate. I had the idea of teaching in a university or possibly obtaining some kind of a job where I could use my knowledge of economics. With this in mind, I wanted to be back in time for the start of the second semester shortly after the end of the year. We had no idea when our ship would return to the United States. Another way to get home was to try to find out when the larger ships were returning to the States. This was not easy to accomplish, because not many ships were being sent home. As September and October passed, I also became more and more concerned about how soon I was going to be released. For that to happen, I had to get the approval of Captain Brown, and his great concern was how to keep enough people to man the ship properly.

Since I was the officer in charge of all of the gunnery equipment, Captain Brown decided he was not going to let me go any earlier than he had to. That in itself, however, was not the focal point of my problem with him. The problem arose when I reported on the Title B equipment we had lost during the war. Title B equipment in the Navy was equipment that was not used up and could be moved around. Title A equipment was equipment that was fastened down aboard ship. Title C equipment was expendable or used up and, therefore, not watched over as carefully as Title B or Title A equipment.

Specifically, what happened is that, as we were leaving Long Beach after we had completed our overhaul, we had to remove all of our ammunition and place it on a barge in the middle of the bay. This was when we had to have our propeller shaft repaired. While the ammunition was on this barge, 6 of 12 shotguns we had taken on board were stolen. Not long after we left Long Beach, I reported it to the captain. He just shrugged his shoulders. However, when it came to reporting the condition of all our Title B equipment after the war, he remembered his training as a regular naval officer, which said that, if you could not account for all of your Title B equipment, you could be reprimanded rather severely for not having done a good job as the captain of the ship. When I wrote my report, which was necessary in order for me to be released, I stated that we were missing these shotguns and had reported the loss to the captain. The captain said he could not release me unless I changed the report to indicate that the loss of the shotguns had not been reported to him. This would have been a lie, and I was determined not to change my report just because he did not want to report what had actually happened. To me, the idea of his being concerned was ridiculous.

During the latter part of October one or two large ships left, but I could not get space on any of them. I also knew that there was no possibility of my being released unless I changed my report on the shotguns to his complete satisfaction. Early in November, I learned on a Saturday morning that there was a cruiser anchored about 1,000 yards off our port beam that was going back to the States early on Sunday. All I needed to do to get on that ship was to be released by Captain Brown. I modified my report in the way I thought the captain wanted, but I was mistaken. He looked at the report and said, without any explanation, he would not release me.

About noon John Lindquist, a very good friend, was going ashore, and I decided to go with him to the officers' club in Yokosuka. This was the first, last and only time I ever consumed so much alcohol I did not know what I was doing. We stayed until they closed the officers' club and a motor whaleboat came to pick us up. In the meantime, the weather conditions had deteriorated, and a bad storm had developed with wind blowing at a tremendous velocity. When we got to the ship, it was rolling so heavily the only way we could get on board was with a rope ladder that was hanging over the side. The challenge was to grab the rope ladder when the motor whaleboat and the ship came together at a certain point. This would have been hard enough to do sober. Somehow I made it, but as soon as I was aboard, I knew I had run the risk of losing my life, all because of the problem with the report. I got up about six o'clock in the morning, changed the report again and took it to the captain. It was about seven o'clock in the morning, and the cruiser was leaving at eight o'clock. I told him what had happened the night before and how close I had come to losing my life. Without any comment, he signed my release; a motor whaleboat was waiting, and I boarded the cruiser just before they were underway.

The trip back home on the cruiser was uneventful. There was nothing to do except wait for the passage of time. When I arrived at the coast, airplane transportation to Chicago was available so my trip was a quick one. My release took place at the Great Lakes Naval Air Station. I had been able to get in touch with Mary, so when I left the Naval Air Station with my release, she was waiting for me at the Drake Hotel in Chicago. I had hoped we would have a beautiful room, but we soon saw that the Drake was in need of extensive repairs. Almost eight months had gone by, so it was truly wonderful to be together again and have the war behind us. There was no way that some plaster falling from the ceiling could take away the pleasure of that evening. The next day, November 27, 1945, we took a train home to the beginning of a new life.

My Shipmates

When you spend more than two years of your life aboard a destroyer in the Pacific Ocean during World War II, you naturally have the opportunity to develop friendships that can last a lifetime. This is what happened to me, although not everyone became a close personal friend. It was my experience that the closeness of the friendship depended to some extent upon whether under peace time conditions we lived in proximity to each other.

There were six of us who settled in the Chicago area and, for that reason, saw each other rather frequently. They were John (Jack) Eagan, Donald (Jamie) Keigher, John (Link) Lindquist, Horace (Hocky) Whitehouse and Betty Westbrook, the wife of Vern Westbrook, who was on the ship at the time of the launching but died prematurely. Betty, along with Lois Lindquist and Mary Lou Keigher, had spent a great deal of time with my wife, Mary, during the war. They started their friendship when the Knapp was built in Bath, Maine, stayed in contact while the ship was at sea, and shared each others' company when the ship was being overhauled in April 1945.

Link became a lawyer, specializing in employee benefit plans, so the two of us had a common business interest in civilian life. He had also played football for Northwestern while I was at Purdue, which meant that the Big Ten was always a part of our conversations. Don (Jamie) Keigher was an engineer and while aboard ship became our Chief Engineering Officer. In civilian life he worked for the Atomic Energy Commission in Chicago, Hanford, Washington and NASA headquarters. Jamie and Mary Lou continue to be an important part of my life. Jack and Hocky had business careers that kept us from having much contact with each other.

Besides our Chicago area friends, my shipmates included Captain Virden and three other regular, career Navy officers aboard our ship: Emory Huff, our Executive Officer; John (Sully) Sullivan and Louis Fields. Their careers kept them on the move, but two of them and their wives (Virden and Sullivan) seldom missed our reunions and always exchanged Christmas communications with Mary and me. Other shipmates were: Alden Clayton and Malcolm Thompson; they both settled in the Boston area; Robert Trudell spent most of his business career in the East; Robert Buck, a lawyer, spent most of his career in the banking business in the state of Washington; Alex Baker stayed in the Navy for 20 years, and after earning a Ph.D. in Education enjoyed a teaching career in California; our medical doctor, (Doc) Margolies, returned to Pennsylvania; Leslie (Les) Johnson became a medical doctor in Alabama; and John Morton, our chief engineering officer when the ship was placed in commission, has lived in California since the end of the war.

The chief gunnery officer, and my boss aboard ship, was Robert (Bob) Hoag. Bob was well liked and respected by all of the officers and enlisted men on the Knapp. Our executive officer, Emory Huff, was not the best communicator I have known in my lifetime, and every once in a while, something would happen that made it possible for Bob to become our "Mister Roberts." There was nothing serious about this, and I always felt that anything that brought some humor into our lives was very constructive for the mental health of about 325 men who were confined to a relatively small home in the Pacific Ocean. After Huff was transferred off the ship to another assignment before we returned to the States early in 1945, Bob became the executive officer, and I took over his responsibilities as chief gunnery officer.

The Knapp has had a reunion every second or third year since shortly after the end of the war. Mary and I attended them whenever my business responsibilities did not interfere. When we were together in 1992, we decided to have a special reunion for those of us who had been present when the Knapp was launched in Bath, Maine, on September 16, 1943. We named this our "Plankowners Celebration" and gathered together in Bath and Boston from September 14 - 16 in 1993. There were six officers who attended: Bob Buck, Alden Clayton, Jamie Keigher, John Morton, Malcolm Thompson and myself. Betty (Westbrook) Cotsonas has never missed a reunion of the ship and was also present. It was a very special event in our lives. I have included in this book a photograph of the six of us sitting around a wardroom table (on another ship identical to ours) that brings back the kinds of memories that are easy to treasure. Three of the original group could not arrange their activities to be with us: Alex Baker, Louis Fields and Robert Trudell. We were also missing 10 officers who were there when the Knapp was launched but are now deceased: Joseph Corcoran, Robert Hoag, Emory Huff, John Lindquist, Leslie Johnson, "Doc" Margolies, John Sullivan, Vern Westbrook, Horace Whitehouse and Frank Virden, the captain of our ship. The U.S.S. Knapp DD653 was dismantled after having been reactivated during the Korean War. However, the bridge of the ship was preserved and is on display at the Columbia River Maritime Museum in Astoria, Oregon.

◆

CHAPTER 6

Graduate School, First Job And First Home

My immediate concern was to decide which university I should attend for my graduate work and, also, to see if I could be admitted by the second semester of the year. I wanted some advice from someone who had an insight into excellent business schools as well as universities where one could receive a highly regarded doctorate in economics. I met with Dr. Rollin Thomas, one of my professors who had written a book on money and banking. I told him I wanted to be able to change my credits to a business school. He recommended giving consideration to three universities where I could have that privilege. The three universities were Indiana, Michigan and the University of Chicago. I decided the University of Chicago was the right one for me. The fact that Chicago was a little closer than Michigan eliminated Michigan, and I had just enough prejudice against Indiana as a Purdue rival to decide against Indiana. So I decided to go to the University of Chicago, applied for admission and was admitted.

Next, Mary and I had to find a place to live. Since school was to start right after the first of the year, we did not have much time. However, with the help of the University, we rented a one-room apartment on the second floor of a three-story building.

Immediately after the first of the year, Mary, Barbara and I settled in this small apartment. We were there for about two weeks, during which time we realized the apartment's size made it an impossible situation. The solution came when the man who owned the apartment building offered us the responsibility of managing the building. In so doing, he gave us the privilege of living in an unfurnished apartment on the first floor, where we would have a living room, bedroom, kitchen and our own bath. This looked great to us even though it would be necessary for us to use some of our savings to buy furniture. We ended up paying him about $30 a month in addition to my taking care of the furnace and removing the garbage, while Mary had the responsibility for taking care of the shared bathrooms and hallways on the three floors.

This was quite an adjustment for us. As a naval officer I had enjoyed many of the niceties of life. Now we were in a situation in which we had a relatively small amount of money and the necessity of staying in school for at least two years. We were going to have to live a fairly frugal existence, but it was a small price to pay for something we both knew I should achieve.

Mary Goes To Work

This was also a difficult period inasmuch as Barbara and I were trying to adjust to each other while I was trying to handle four very difficult courses in economics. The stress on me was great; the stress on Barbara was great; and Mary was in between. We solved the problem for a few months by having Barbara stay in Lafayette and going back to see her on some weekends. This made life much better for Barbara, and I was able to concentrate on my school work. We also had to supplement our income, so Mary looked for a job and found one at the Bismarck Hotel in downtown Chicago. She worked at the mail desk in the hotel and traveled back and forth to the downtown Chicago area on the elevated trains. This neighborhood around 6450 Maryland, one block east of Cottage Grove Avenue and two blocks south of 63rd Street, was an area in transition from one that had been predominantly white to one that eventually became predominantly black.

Mary worked at the Bismarck Hotel for five or six months until one night, when she left the hotel around midnight to walk to the station to catch the train home, a man grabbed her and started to pull her toward an alley. Mary recognized him as someone registered at the hotel and told him she knew him; he let go of her. We decided she should stop working at night.

She looked for another job and found one with a Packard Motor Car Company dealer located on the south side of Chicago. The location was just south of the downtown area and not far from where she could pick up the street car to go home. By this time, Barbara was back with us and, during the day, attended preschool in a Catholic church located about a block away from where we lived. After Mary had worked at Packard for a few months, she was waiting to be picked up by the street car when two men standing nearby began to fight each other with knives. Fortunately the street car came by just then; the motorman opened the door, grabbed Mary by the arm, pulled her in and left the area. Mary then left Packard and took a job at the University of Chicago's publishing office, adjacent to the campus. At that time, we enrolled Barbara in a nursery school located close to the campus. Eighteen months after we arrived in Chicago, when I received my degree and had a job, Mary quit working and began to take care of Barbara full time.

Some Big Decisions At School

One of the first important decisions I had to make at school came toward the end of the first quarter. The University of Chicago was on a four-quarter system so you could attend all year if you wished, which is what I did. As I approached the end of the first quarter, it seemed to me the education I was getting in economics was going to leave me, ultimately, with only two career alternatives. This was perhaps a fairly narrow view of the alternatives; nevertheless, I was convinced the approach to economics that was in vogue at the University of Chicago would limit my opportunities. One of the alternatives would be to teach, which was fine with me. The other would be to work for the government or a rather limited number of other organizations. In order to satisfy my concerns, I talked to the administrators of the business school to see if they could give me some insight into what I might do. It did not take long for me to come to the conclusion that I should transfer to the business school, as I had guessed I might want to do even before going to the University of Chicago. If I wanted to teach, I could certainly teach business subjects, but, if I did not want to teach, I would have the alternative of going into the business world.

Accordingly, at the end of the first quarter, I transferred my credits in four economics courses to the business school and embarked on the MBA program at the University of Chicago. During the first quarter, I took the basic courses that were required. These included such courses as accounting and statistics, which I had not taken at Purdue. During that period, I also began to search for a major in the business school because it was obvious that I should attempt to concentrate in some specific area. After talking to several department heads, I had the good luck to meet with Marshall Ketchum, a professor specializing in investments. His suggestion turned out to be one of the most important things that ever happened in my life. Specifically, he loaned me a book by Badger and Guthman on investments and suggested I read through it simply to see if it might have some appeal. I only had to read parts of the book, for it was obvious to me that this was where I should be in the financial world. I shall never forget the wonderful feeling of knowing what I was going to do with my life. The reason I felt so good was that I could see that investment analysis required a reasonable facility with numbers, the ability to read fast and an interest in everything that was going on in the world. I knew this was for me.

Basketball continued as an important part of my life at the University of Chicago. There was an intramural league, so several of us graduate students who had played in college got together to form a team and participate. We never lost a game, even against the varsity of the University. We also played Sunday afternoons in a league on the south side of Chicago. By that time I was mature and physically stronger with more stamina than I had ever had. I was the high scorer on the team.

Looking For A Job

I completed my graduate work at the end of June 1947, and as I approached that date, I began to interview with the numerous corporations visiting the campus to recruit new employees. I was sure I wanted to go into the investment research department of a bank but thought I should at least investigate other opportunities just to understand what the differences might be. As a result, I gave some thought to three opportunities. One was an offer from the FBI; a second was the opportunity to join the training program at Eastman Kodak; and a third was to join the Studebaker Corporation in South Bend, Indiana. The Studebaker Corporation was willing to pay a higher salary than any of the others, and for that reason, I made the trip to see them in South Bend. This interview was very disillusioning because the treasurer asked me to take a test that they required of all people joining the organization. The test was a simple mathematics test one would have expected to take for a clerical position. I knew that any company treasurer who was asking someone with an MBA degree from the University of Chicago to take that kind of a test did not really understand the world around him. I was not surprised when the company went bankrupt a couple of years later.

I had offers from the three largest banks in Chicago, Harris Trust & Savings Bank, Continental Illinois National Bank & Trust Company and the First National Bank of Chicago. All the offers were for $225 a month to work in an investment research department. However, all three of these banks had as part of their hiring plan a training program that lasted for one year, which required one to move through the different departments of the bank in order to have a broad understanding of them. Since I was then 26 years old and believed I knew all I needed to know about what a bank did, I had absolutely no interest in such a training program. The Northern Trust Company had interviewed me on the campus and told me they had no such program.

Whomever they hired would go to work directly in their investment research department. However, after my interview on the campus, I heard nothing further from them. After some time passed and I knew I wanted to go to work for them, I went to Fred Stone, one of the professors at the University under whom I had taken two classes, and asked him whether he had any suggestions as to what I could do. He immediately called a man by the name of Robert Kneebone, who was working for the American Banker's Association, and asked for some guidance.

Kneebone learned The Northern Trust Company was interested in me, but for some reason or another, they thought I did not have any interest in them. An interview was arranged, and this became a very important day in my life because it was the day my name was changed. The personnel officer, Don Olson, who had interviewed me on the campus, spent most of the day taking me to the different departments and introducing me to the various department heads so I could find out what they did and they could evaluate me. The first person to whom Don introduced me was Art O'Hara, the head of the investment research department. The name Don used when introducing me was my first name, Ben, instead of Cal, my middle name and the one I had always used. I said to myself, "Maybe they're not going to offer me a job, so why make an issue of it." After the day was completed, they came through with an offer of $225 a month, which I accepted and started to work on July 7, 1947. I believed I had no alternative but to go to work for The Northern as Ben instead of Cal. In retrospect, I know I was willing to make the change to my father's name because of my respect and love for him.

My First Three Years At The Northern

A few weeks after I became a member of the team of investment analysts in the research department, Art assigned me to the railroad industry, where I was taught to be thorough and detailed in my analytical approach. I was in Art's department for only two years, but it provided me with the opportunity to become knowledgeable on a large number of industries and companies being closely followed by

Art and the other investment analysts in the department. I also did most of the analytical work on a stock market "timing" program for our largest pension fund, the Retirement System for the Federal Reserve Banks (RSFRB). I was given that assignment because, while at the University of Chicago, I had developed as a research project a "formula timing plan," which produced impressive investment performance. The plan we developed for the RSFRB was not used, because developments in the economy and the stock market in the postwar period were beginning to indicate a strong upward trend in stock prices and the advisability of a policy of just buying and holding common stocks.

I wanted to stay with Art O'Hara in investment research for a long time so I could be assigned over time to many different industries and learn them from the bottom up; however, in the summer of 1949, I was asked if I would accept a transfer to the trust investment division and begin my career managing investment portfolios. This was always my long-term goal, and for that reason, I readily accepted the promotion.

The head of the trust investment division was Henry Bodwell, another great investment man. Henry was broadly based in every phase of investment management: common stocks, bonds, preferred stocks, mortgage-backed private placements and the portfolio strategy to be followed in every imaginable kind of account. Art O'Hara's strength was in the selection of common stocks, so as a team they provided the best possible leadership for investment management in the country.

My specific responsibility was to work on personal trust accounts with Wade Ringenberg. Wade had been with The Northern for a long time and had developed a satisfactory and rewarding way of working with personal customers, so it was a good experience to work with him. My responsibility was to meet with his customers and discuss investments whenever he needed someone who was working on a day-to-day basis with investments. Also, in any kind of communication with a customer when it was necessary to discuss investments, I was expected to write the letter for his signature. Wade had his own style of writing, so I had to learn how to write letters that would not have to be rewritten. It was an excellent experience, and the letter writing I did in that period was a basis for developing some skills in dictation and correspondence that were unbelievably beneficial to me over the years. It taught me how to communicate investment ideas effectively, how to dictate efficiently and how to turn out a great deal of work. It is still amazing to me how many investment people I worked with over the years found it necessary to write their letters in longhand, a much more cumbersome procedure.

Mary, Barbara and I continued to live at 6450 Maryland, but we had some concerns as the neighborhood deteriorated. Actually, with the passage of time, we became fearful for our lives. A variety of events gradually brought our fears to a head. One morning, when Barbara and I walked out the front door, we saw a man running down the street and another man coming out of an apartment building across the street firing a gun at him. Another time we walked out of the apartment building and found a pool of blood on the sidewalk.

The situation with the apartment was resolved early in 1949 when I went to the office of Mike Symonds, the head of the investment department, to see if the bank could provide an apartment for us in a building that the bank managed located at the corner of 54th and Ellis Streets. The building was close to the University of Chicago campus and in a more secure and satisfactory environment. I had learned of the building because some of the new men who had joined The Northern had been given apartments there. We were fortunate in being allowed to select one of the larger and better apartments. It was a corner apartment on the first floor and a paradise compared to what we had before. It had six rooms, a large living room, a very nice dining room, three bedrooms, an old-fashioned kitchen and one bath. The building, although fairly old, was still much newer than the one in which we had been living, and the neighborhood was no comparison. When we moved into this apartment, we had to buy new dining and bedroom furniture, and I hung new wallpaper in four rooms. Some of my associates who lived in the apartment building became very good friends of ours, especially Bill and Clara Jane Hill, and Lowell and Ruth Thompkins. Both of the men were in the investment research department with me, having started at about the same time. The move into the new apartment coincided with Barbara starting kindergarten at Kozminski, a grade school that was located just a block away. Needless to say, Mary was delighted to no longer have the responsibility for cleaning the bathrooms in the apartment building on Maryland Avenue.

During the time I was doing my graduate work at the University of Chicago and during my first 20 months at The Northern, we never owned a car. We were very happy when we moved to 54th and Ellis Streets and Mary's parents gave us their 1938 Plymouth. The car was 10 years old, burning oil and not in good condition but, after three and a half years with no transportation of our own, it was a gift to be appreciated. I had not needed a car for work because I could walk about ten blocks to the South Shore train station, which was right along Lake Shore Drive, and take it into the loop.

Mary was well along in her pregnancy with Lynne, and we were quite concerned as to whether the car would start when it was time to go to the hospital even though it was only about two miles from our apartment. However, we had no difficulty and arrived at the hospital fairly early in the morning on May 11, 1949. Shortly after we arrived, Mary casually walked to the delivery room, and, less than a half an hour later, they told me we had a baby girl. When the office opened at 8:30 in the morning, I was there because there was nothing else for me to do since Mary had come along fine and just wanted to sleep.

Teaching At Night

Since the $225 per month was not the most fabulous salary in the world, I decided to see if I could get a job teaching at night. I found a teaching post at De Paul University's downtown evening school of business, where they employed teachers who were occupied during the day with full-time business positions. My only concern was whether I would be too nervous to do a good job of teaching a class of college students. I was not worried about my knowledge, just my ability to speak before them with the kind of confidence a teacher should have. This feeling of concern was brought to a head shortly after I joined The Northern when they held a dinner so that all of the new MBAs could spend an evening with their bosses and get to know each other. We had a very fine dinner, but, at its conclusion, one of the senior officers said he would like each one of us to speak for about five minutes about ourselves. All of a sudden, I was filled with concern and apprehension and broke into a sweat. This made me realize that, if I were going to teach school, the fear of speaking in front of a group had to be solved. This realization led me to enroll in a Dale Carnegie course.

The decision was one of the wisest ones I made in my business career. I shall never forget the pleasure of knowing there was nothing to fear when talking in front of a group. One of the techniques used to build up one's ego and introduce a bit of competitiveness was to award a fountain pen to the person whom everybody in the class voted as having made the best five-minute speech. I still have the pen and vividly remember the thrill when they voted for me as having made the best speech that night. My five-minute talk was about the typhoon our task force had experienced late in 1944. My teaching experience at De Paul was completely satisfying. Most of the time, it was three evenings each week on either the "Analysis of Financial Statements" or "Portfolio Management." They were on a two-semester system, and I taught for three years.

The banks in downtown Chicago had a basketball league, so for three more years my desire to play basketball was satisfied. We won the league every year (1947, 1948 and 1949), and I received a trophy each year for having scored the most points of any player in the league. Frequently one or more of my bosses, Henry Bodwell, Art O'Hara, Mike Symonds and other senior officers, would stay after work to watch the games.

A New Car And The Suburbs

Early in 1950, we decided to start looking for a house in the suburbs. I had a good job with great people in a great company and believed there was a good future ahead of me. Furthermore, we had bought our first car, a new 1949 Ford, shortly after Lynne was born. It was a great pleasure to have that car, because it was the first time we had ever had good transportation. Mary, with her exceptional ability to recall names, reminded me about 35 years later that we had bought the car from a man with the name Muumaa.

Some of the difficulties one faces when trying to move out of the south side of Chicago into a suburban area is to find the time for house hunting. We had to drive to the area we liked, contact a real estate agent, look at the available houses and do so often enough to make a good decision. We were convinced we wanted to live in either a western or a northern suburb of Chicago. We decided against the northern suburbs of Chicago because of the time it would take us to get there from the south side and begin to look at houses. So, in the summer of 1950, we contacted a real estate agent in Wheaton to help us find something in that area. During that summer and before we made the decision to buy a house in Wheaton, one other development impacted my future.

The Organized Reserves

The U.S. Navy had a program for its organized reserves in Chicago that changed the course of our lives. The unit in Chicago met evenings at the foot of Randolph Street on what is called Navy Pier. Two of my officer friends from the Knapp, Don Keigher and Jack Eagen, had enrolled in this program fairly early after the end of the war and were on a pay basis throughout 1947-1949. Both families lived on the south side and were good friends. Every time we were together with them, they talked about how logical it was to go there once a week and add it to your period of service in the Navy. After giving it considerable thought, I decided we needed the money and I should try to get into the program. Unfortunately, I had to do it on a voluntary basis and hope for an opening on a pay basis. Accordingly, I went for one night a week for almost a year on a non-pay basis, always with the hope that right around the corner would be the opportunity to be on a pay basis. Finally, it came in the spring of 1950.

In that program, I was required to spend two weeks each year on active duty. We wanted to fulfill that obligation during the summer, so we selected the naval base in Key West, Florida, as our location and July as the time to go. We drove our car to Key West and enjoyed the trip, even though it was a lot of driving. We left Barbara and Lynne with Mary's folks in Lafayette.

While we were in Key West, we received a telephone call from Mary's brother, Jacob, in which he said her father was in the hospital hemorrhaging from a stomach ulcer. The situation seemed serious enough to justify her flying back to Lafayette. It proved to be a long, difficult and unnecessary flight in rough weather in a small propeller-type plane. In the meantime, I invited three other men to ride with me back to Chicago, share the driving of the car and do it without stopping.

Before I left Key West, I experienced a severe sunburn. Mary had already gone back to Lafayette when I decided I would wash and polish the car. Foolishly, I did so in the bright sunlight without keeping track of how long I was exposed. I believe my skin problems since 1964 date back to that bad experience.

The four of us started home as soon as we were released from duty at midnight. We agreed upon a rotating system in which we were driving for about an hour or two before changing drivers. One of the men had a heavy foot, so, every time he got behind the wheel, we were concerned as to whether we were going to be arrested for speeding or have an accident. The concern came to a head when we were in southern Georgia and were stopped by the state police for excessive speed. Rather than run the risk of him driving again and to avoid any problems, I decided to drive the rest of the way myself. This was a very foolish decision, because I had to fight sleep as I had never fought sleep before. We arrived in Lafayette about noon the next day, which meant I had been awake for 36 hours.

Shortly after we returned from Florida, Mary and I again looked for a house and found one in Wheaton that we felt was just right for us. The house was at 726 Michigan Street and cost $13,500. We borrowed $1,500 from Mary's folks, and with that money as the down payment, we moved into the house on the first day in September.

One of the big decisions we made immediately was to buy our first television set. This was three years after they had come on the market, and we were ready to enjoy life to the fullest. However, bad news was around the corner. The Korean War had started on May 26, 1950, and I immediately knew that, by having joined the organized reserves, I was now vulnerable to being called back into active duty. Columbus Day is a banking holiday, and on October 12, The Northern, as was usual on that day, had a golf tournament at one of the clubs in a northern suburb of Chicago. When I arrived home that night after dinner, Mary met me at the door with a set of orders for me to return to active duty in the U.S. Navy. The orders were for me to report to Guantanamo Bay, Cuba, on November 1 to the U.S.S. Harold J. Ellison, a destroyer with the number DD864. It was very difficult for me to believe I was being removed from my business career at a very crucial time. I had been with The Northern for a little more than three years and was approaching the time when I would be made a junior officer. By being absent for two years, it was apparent I might be at a competitive disadvantage to those who would join the organization after my departure, as well as to those who had joined with and before me.

There was some justification for my hoping I could get the orders rescinded, for I learned immediately that none of the services were recalling those who had four dependents, that is, three children and a wife. John was to be born in January; therefore, it was obvious that before long I would have the number of dependents necessary to prevent them from calling me back to active duty. I talked to the Navy office in Chicago to see what could be done and was told I had no alternative but to report to active duty. The rest of that week was spent in the office, and in the next week and a half, I painted the outside of the house. On October 31, our ninth wedding anniversary, Mary, Barbara and Lynne took me to the airport, and a two-year period of great frustration began.

My grandmother Gertrude Einink Korschot and my grandfather John Bernard Korschot.

My father (standing) with his brother Jess.

My mother (Myrtle Pearl Goodman) before she was married.

With my dad at 9 months

The house where I was born on Morton Street. This picture was taken in the 1940s. Dad built the house when he and Mom married in 1913.

With my family when I was 6 years old. (From left to right) Mom, Mary, Ruth, Johanna, Alice, me and Dad.

In front of our home at 1924 Greenbush in January 1929 when I was 8 years old. (From left to right) Jane Bol, Johanna, Mary, Ruth, Chuck and John Vanderweilen and me.

Christian Reformed Church.

With Johanna in 1929.

I was 10 when we moved to this 100-year-old farmhouse on Northwestern Avenue. Here I am in 1931 on the lawn with Johanna, Buster and Spot.

At about 14 years old with Spot at the house on Northwestern Avenue in 1935.

My mother and father when we moved to Northwestern Avenue.

My grandfather in our front yard in 1935.

My mother with her mother and sister, Ethel.

(From left to right) Alice, Mom, me, Ruth, Mary, Dad and Johanna when I was 16.

*My 1938 graduation photo from
Klondike High School.*

*Mary's 1940 graduation photo
from Klondike High School.*

*Our Klondike 1937-38 team. Three of us went on to Purdue - I'm in
the first row, center; Bob Arvidson, to the left of me on the end; and
Gordon Robbins, to the right of me. Bill Chase, our coach is on the back
row at the far right.*

I'm pictured here as a sophomore on the Purdue team in 1939-40 when we won the Big Ten Conference Championship.

Lafayette's 1941 Softball Champions – J-C Club. (From left to right) front row, Johnny Smith, Johnny Conrad, Joe Dolan, Bob Chester. Second row, Harry Olds, Bud Stamm, Jim Prien, Bud Shively, Bob Stump. Third Row, Walter Nelson, Bob Riley, Cal Korschot, Dick Shively, Bob Johnson.

Mary and I soon after we were married on October 31, 1941.

The U.S.S. Knapp (DO653). I reported for duty in September 1943 in Bath, Maine.

An ensign in the Navy in April 1943.

With Gordon Robbins in Panama City in December 1943.

With my four sisters in July 1943. (From left to right) Johanna, Alice, me, Mary and Ruth. I had my orders to report to the U.S.S. Knapp (DO653) in September.

Mary and her mother, Ethel Rubright Schelle in 1944.

Home on leave in April 1945. I held Barbara for the first time. She was 16 months old.

Mary and me on the beach at Norfolk in 1952.

We lived here and managed the building to reduce our rent from 1946 to 1950.

Our first house, Wheaton, Illinois, September 1950.

Back in the Navy, October 1950, with Barbara (6-1/2) and Lynne (1-1/2).

Lynne (3) and Barbara (8) in front of our apartment in Norfolk in 1952.

Out of the Navy in 1953. With John and Lynne.

Fishing group from the Glen Ellyn, Illinois Kiwanis Club. Going to Lake of the Woods, Canada, in 1955. (From left to right) Gordon Glaysher, Owen Zapel, Emerson Lacy, Jim Dolansky, Henry Rosenthal, Howard Hansen, Rolly Davis and me.

On a Kiwanis Club fishing trip to Canada in 1957.

Our Home in Glen Ellyn, Illinois, from 1952 to 1964.

Trip west in 1960. John (9), Barbara (16) and Lynne (11) at Petrified Forest.

Mary on one of our vacation trips in the late 1950s to Lake Metonga at Crandon, Wisconsin.

CHAPTER 7

---◆---

Back In The Navy

As soon as I reported for active duty at Guantanamo Bay aboard ship, I had an experience that , in hindsight, still seems almost unbelievable. The ship left the harbor almost immediately after I came on board. Our assignment was to go with an aircraft carrier to provide plane guard duty. This meant that our ship, the U.S.S. Ellison, took a station about five degrees and 1,500 yards off the starboard quarter of the aircraft carrier. Our task was to pick up any pilots who might have a bad landing or miss the ship while they were landing. This particular trip was designed solely for the benefit of training pilots to land aboard an aircraft carrier.

After unpacking, I went up to the bridge just to look around, see what was happening and talk to whomever might be up there. Not unexpectedly the captain was in command. We had already taken our position behind the carrier. To my great surprise, around noon the captain said he would like for me to take over command of the ship while he went to the wardroom for lunch. I had not been on the bridge of a ship since late in 1945 and had not been thinking of how to give orders to the helmsman or talk with other ships over the communication system, the TBS. Not long after I took command of the ship, the aircraft carrier came over the TBS with a voice signal to change our course and reduce our speed from 20 knots to 15. The mistake all of us on the bridge made was to believe we were to reduce our speed. Actually, the order was to increase the speed to 27 knots. Since the carrier was turning more quickly than we were (because she was going faster), we came closer and closer to her stern. I realized I should not have reduced speed and began to increase the speed as rapidly as I could. I first moved it up to 20 knots and finally to flank speed, which was as fast as we could go. We slipped under the stern of the carrier by not much more than 100 or 200 yards. It could have been a catastrophe. After we cleared the ship and regained our position at the stern of the aircraft carrier, I was convinced we would receive a serious reprimand. Instead, there were no voice transmissions from the carrier. Obviously they had not paid any attention to what happened to us during that maneuver.

Another disturbing and dangerous experience developed about five months later when we were in the North Sea between Great Britain and Norway. We were in column formation between two other destroyers on a bitterly cold winter night in a driving rainstorm. I was in command of the ship during the watch between midnight and four o'clock. With the heavy seas and stationed only 300 yards astern of the ship ahead of me, I did not have complete confidence in relying on our radar to maintain our position. I had no alternative but to position myself on the open bridge and do my best in the rain and cold with water streaming down my binoculars and glasses. It was a most dangerous position to be in and caused me to question seriously the Navy policy at that time of demanding good eyesight when one enlists and disregarding it when one is responsible for lives and ships.

726 Michigan Without Me

We left Guantanamo Bay in December and returned to the ship's base in Norfolk in time for me to be in Wheaton, Illinois, with the family for Christmas. Our orders were to leave for Europe on January 1.

Since the ship would not return until May, Mary had a rough situation to handle. It was a very severe winter with lots of snow; we had two small children, not much money, another child on the way and no friends to help her. We had a great deal of apprehension as to how the circumstances around John's birth could be handled, since she had to get to the hospital in Aurora, Illinois, which was about 20 miles from Wheaton. Her doctor said she should call him when the pains started; he would then take her to the hospital so that she would be under his care the entire time. This sounded as if it was a pretty good arrangement based on the assumption he would be available.

When Mary's pains came, it was a terrible winter night, in effect, blizzard conditions. The doctor did not come immediately when she called but finally did arrive. My mother was there to take care of the two kids. On the way to the hospital, the doctor decided he was hungry and stopped at a restaurant despite the fact that Mary was in the midst of her pains. He ordered a meal that took some time to arrive. Mary did not eat. Then, after he finished his steak dinner, he ordered a hamburger because he said he was still hungry. Mary was experiencing frequent pains and was more and more concerned about getting to the hospital so she would not have to give birth in the car. She also knew the doctor had a record of having births occur in automobiles on the way to hospitals. On the way to the hospital, the only way they could see the highway in the blizzard conditions was for Mary to stick her head out of the window on her side of the car while he looked out the window on the other side.

When they finally arrived at the hospital's emergency entrance, Mary was shaking all over. After this ordeal, John's birth, in contrast to Lynne's, was very difficult for Mary. Needless to say, after that experience, when we moved back into the area after I was released from the Navy in September 1952, we had absolutely no interest in having that doctor as our physician!

My mother only stayed with Mary for about two weeks after they got home from the hospital. Mary recovered her strength quite rapidly and was happy when she could let my mother go home and take care of the three kids on her own.

We knew the ship would be returning to Norfolk in May 1951; Norfolk would be the base for the ship during the two years I expected to be in the Navy. Accordingly, it was easy to make the decision to sell the house in Wheaton and rent an apartment in Norfolk so that we could be together as a family when the ship was in port.

Prior to the time we sold the house, we had not been able to accumulate much money. The reasons were obvious. My salary at The Northern increased in 1948, 1949 and 1950 but was still only $300 a month when I was called into the Navy.

While making arrangements with a real estate agent to sell the house, Mary was also very busy taking care of the three children and getting ready for the trip to Norfolk. Since we did not want the house to be empty while it was on the market, she made arrangements to rent it to tenants. The people to whom we were renting knew we were going to put the house on the market and they would be expected to move. Nevertheless, they gave us an extremely difficult time when the house was finally sold in September 1951. Mary left Wheaton on May 11 and drove to Lafayette to leave the kids there. Then she drove to Norfolk by herself to meet the ship, which came in around May 20. Making this long drive took some courage, and it was uneventful except that a man followed closely behind her for about 200 miles. When she met me at the ship, we had no place to stay; however the Navy immediately made a one-bedroom apartment available to us. It was in an apartment complex where all the occupants were Navy officers and their families. By the time we sold our house in September and moved our furniture, we were able to move into a two-bedroom apartment.

The Mediterranean, Europe And England

My experiences during this tour in the Navy were both educational and entertaining. We left Norfolk early in January in both years and returned around the middle of each year. We were assigned to the Sixth Fleet with the primary objective of creating goodwill in cities bordering the Mediterranean Sea, the western coast of Europe and the major ports of Great Britain. The Navy's idea of how this should be accomplished was simple: the ship was to show the flag in a port for anywhere from three days to a week, travel for a day or two to the next port and do the same thing all over again. In almost every port, we gave liberty each day to one-third or one-half of our people, and, since they had more money to spend than the majority of the people in most of the countries we visited, they usually created more ill will than goodwill.

In addition to numerous ports in Great Britain, some of the places we visited were Gibraltar, Tripoli in North Africa, some of the ports of southern Spain, the island of Sicily off the southern coast of Italy, Naples, the island of Malta, Athens, small ports in Greece (such as Volos, Salonica and Alexandroupolis), Istanbul, Turkey, and other islands in the eastern part of the Mediterranean, such as Crete and Rhodes (a stopping place for the Crusaders as they went to the Holy Land).

Some of my more interesting experiences were in places like Istanbul and Tripoli. The bazaars were their shopping areas, where everything was jammed together in narrow streets with small shops. The salespeople bargained with their customers, which is typical in that part of the world. The worst thing you could do was to take the first price they asked because they would be disappointed. They would expect you to bargain them down to a reasonable price, but we did not have the slightest idea what a reasonable price should be.

The three small towns in southern Greece that we visited (Volos, Salonica, Alexandroupolis) were arid and barren with very few automobiles. In fact, in most of the small coastal cities, an automobile was a rarity in 1951. One of the most impressive features of the way of life throughout the Mediterranean was the evening promenade along the waterfront, a practice followed in most cities. It was the big social event of each day. Husbands, wives and children walked up and down on sidewalks along the waterfront, sometimes visiting with friends, neighbors and relatives. We do something slightly comparable in the United States by going to a shopping center.

On the island of Malta, the churches were most impressive sights, with their costly fixtures made of gold leaf and solid gold.

Five years had passed since the end of World War II, so our experiences in the different ports in Germany were fairly friendly, although once in a while we would run into situations where it was obvious they disliked Americans. We also visited Holland, Norway, Denmark and France, but most of our time was spent in England. I was in London several times and enjoyed every visit because there was so much to see. It was while visiting ports around England that I came to realize the importance of soccer games between cities.

The most interesting port in England was Bristol, the home of Harvey's Bristol Cream and Harvey's Milk, two sherries that are popular in the United States. When we pulled into the port, the mayor came aboard to welcome us, accompanied by Mr. Harvey and his two daughters, who were blonde, unmarried and very attractive. Mr. Harvey and the mayor invited us to two separate parties. Since the mayor was the senior dignitary, the captain took about half the officers to his party, and I, as the executive officer, took the other half to the party Mr. Harvey provided for us. First we went to a restaurant where he served his sherries before dinner and wine during dinner. Afterward we visited the facilities for the production of his two products. They were very close to the restaurant and under the streets of Bristol. His bottling process was simple. He brought the sherry over from Spain in huge casks and bottled it in a very small bottling operation in a room probably not bigger than 20 feet square. The storage was fascinating. He had apparently leased or owned areas under a good many of the streets throughout Bristol. He had racks installed in these viaducts, and the Harvey Bristol Cream and Bristol Milk were stored in racks on either side of a walkway. I learned from him that sherry is aged in the bottle before it is shipped.

One of our more unfortunate experiences was in Glasgow where our sailors were extremely well received by the girls in the town, with the result that numerous young fellows in Glasgow decided the only thing to do was to fight our men. The police separated them and no one was injured, but it was an unpleasant experience and indicated we were not creating very much goodwill.

A Search For Ancestors

The highlight of my two tours was the trip to Amsterdam in 1952, when I had the opportunity to learn where the Korschot family had come from in the Netherlands. As the ship was coming into Amsterdam, the pilot came aboard with several reporters. In a conversation with one of the reporters, the question of my ancestry came up and I told him I was hoping to find where the Korschot family had come from in Holland. He recognized this as a good newspaper story, so the next day his newspaper, the *Trouw*, had a picture of the ship on the front page and printed a rather big story around the ship's arrival and my search for my ancestral home. The article included a picture of me. As soon as the ship arrived, I also made contact with a relative of Neal Grond, my brother-in-law. Neal's relative and his wife were delighted to see me, and I spent some time in their home. They could speak English and had been active in the underground during the war. Their friendliness toward the United States was unbelievable.

As the result of the newspaper article, the *Trouw* was contacted by a student at the University of Amsterdam who had read the article and wanted to meet me. They made arrangements for him to visit the ship along with the newspaper reporter and my brother-in-law's relatives. This student, with the last name of Te Kortschot, came from a town named Winterswijk, which is in the eastern part of Holland. He said there were two families in that town with the name Kortschot and one of them had the *Te* in front of it. He said perhaps hundreds of years ago, it had been the same family, but, for one reason or another, they were now two distinct families. Arrangements were made with the relatives, the newspaper reporter and myself to drive to Winterswijk to see if the Kortschots were my relatives. The newspaper had made arrangements with a high school teacher who could speak English to meet us when we arrived in town. He took us to the city hall where they maintained complete records of the names and dates of those who had emigrated to the United States. The city hall had been given the names I had with me. They were able to match them up, and in that way, I learned what had happened to the family. The farm where the family lived was small, and there had been six children in the family. In August 1854, two brothers and a sister had come to the United States, probably for economic reasons, but no one knew for sure.

Since none of the members of the family could speak English, the high school teacher accompanied all of us to the house. It was obvious this was a big event in the lives of these people. They really had no idea who I was or what it was all about. Later, they told me that, when they first saw me with my U.S. Navy uniform, they thought I was a member of the royal family of Holland. I learned the farm (about 20 acres with two large houses and attached barns) was called the Kortschot-Rensink Farm and had been in the family for centuries. It is located about four kilometers from the city limits. I have visited it several times since then.

I will end my comments about my travels by emphasizing that it became quite boring on the second trip. Most of the time when we arrived at a port (especially those we visited more than once), I would stay on board ship and watch a movie rather than go into town and spend money. During that trip, Henry Bodwell sent me huge amounts of reading material on the investment environment so that I could be up to date on everything when I returned to The Northern Trust Company. I was also doing my best to save money because we were anxious to buy a larger house when I was released in the fall of 1952.

Living In Norfolk

The sale of our house in the summer of 1951 produced a very nice profit. We had owned it a little less than a year and made about $4,000. At the end of the summer when we returned to move out of the house, we left Barbara with Navy friends so that she could start school in Norfolk. The Navy moved the furniture and everything else we wanted to Norfolk.

One of the nice things about being in the apartment complex was that several of the officers on board the ship had brought their wives and children with them to Norfolk. This meant the wives were not left without friends or a social life while we were gone.

Just before the ship left for the Mediterranean in 1952, we had an unfortunate experience. Shortly before the end of 1951, my mother wrote to say that a son of one of her half brothers was in the Navy, in Norfolk and wanted to visit us. She had never met this man, and she did not ask us to initiate contact with him. Without calling us in advance, a couple of days before we were ready to go back to the Mediterranean in January 1952, he came over to the apartment with another enlisted man. We spent the evening visiting with them, and I mentioned the ship's departure for the Mediterranean. After they left, we discussed the visit and concluded Mary might be seeing more of them after the ship departed.

The next morning, when we were dressing John, I caught the skin of his chest with the zipper of his coat very close to his throat. We tried to get it out by pulling down from the direction we had zipped it up but without success. We took him to the emergency room at the naval base, and all they did to release it was to zip it up all the way. I was supposed to leave the next morning for the Mediterranean but, for one reason or another, the ship did not leave and I had another day in Norfolk. Not unexpectedly our visitor from the night before came again, but by himself. We made him welcome, entertained him, talked to him and watched television. Finally we had to tell him to leave because I was going to leave the next day, and we wanted a little time together.

Two days after the ship left, the two sailors again appeared at the door. This time Mary had one of the wives, Carolyn Swift, and her two children with her. Carolyn stayed, long after she otherwise would have gone home; as a matter of fact, she stayed until after midnight. Finally, Carolyn said she was going home and would take them to the corner where they could catch a bus to the naval base. Not many days later, they again appeared in the evening; this time Mary was by herself. Barbara stayed up with her until they left. Once again, they were insensitive about how long they were welcome. That night they asked if they could use our car. Mary said no. Not too much later they made another visit. This time the kids had chicken pox so Mary did not invite them in. That was the last time she saw them. We do not know how they reacted to this series of events, and no comments were made to my mother. We have surmised they were lonely for a home environment and probably could not understand why Mary could not provide it.

During the winter, the weather at Norfolk is reasonably nice, so almost every night Mary took the kids for a walk. During both summers when the ship was in port ,we spent a fair amount of time going to the beach and parks. Virginia Beach was not too far away so we took full advantage of the sand and ocean.

Mary had quite an experience with a Peeping Tom the second summer. One evening she saw someone looking through our bedroom window and walked over to pull the shade down. As she pulled it down, it did not hold and instead ran all the way to the top. This probably frightened the Peeping Tom as much as it did Mary. On that particular occasion, the ship was out a few days so I was not at home. Later the Navy discovered who he was.

When I was called back into the Navy, it was understood that it was to be for two years, ending in the first part of November 1952. During the summer, I requested an early release so that Barbara would not have to transfer schools after just a few weeks of school in Norfolk. They accepted my request, and I was released from the Navy in the early part of September 1952. Then we faced the problem of finding a house in the Glen Ellyn-Wheaton area as quickly as possible so Barbara would not miss too much school. The Navy was obligated to move our furniture back to the Chicago area and keep the furniture on a truck, or at least in storage, until we could give them a permanent location. We bought the first house we saw and never had the furniture in storage. It was at 356 Turner in Glen Ellyn, with three bedrooms, one bath and a one-car garage. Since it was immediately available, in a good neighborhood and with a price we could afford ($14,500), it was an easy decision.

CHAPTER 8

The Northern Trust Company

My conversations with Henry Bodwell while I was away led me to believe that, as soon as I returned, The Northern Trust Company would welcome me back. I also believed there was a very good chance I would not lose too much forward progress as a result of my two-year absence. I was not disappointed, and as of January 1953, I became an assistant secretary with the salary of $6,000 a year. Henry also gave me the responsibility for managing all the employee benefit accounts. This business was the fastest-growing part of the trust business and the most challenging type of account to manage.

One of the first accounts assigned to me when I returned was the account for the Retirement System of the Federal Reserve Banks (RSFRB). As I mentioned earlier, it was the largest account we had at The Northern, with the assets amounting to around $300 million. It was a prestigious account for The Northern because it was a powerful endorsement of the superiority of our investment capabilities. The company did not lose the account until after Art died, I left and Henry retired. I suspect the decision was based on something other than investment performance. As was expected, we gave it a great deal of attention and endeavored to get the very best investment results. Our contacts and working relationships with the people in the Federal Reserve System were most rewarding. We worked with a committee of four people; three of them were presidents of Federal Reserve Banks and the fourth was the Chairman of the Open Market Committee, which was headquartered in the Federal Reserve Bank of New York. During the period I worked on the fund, from 1952 to 1964, the chairman of the Fed's Open Market Committee was a man by the name of Bob Rouse. Managing this account and working closely with Henry Bodwell in that responsibility was one of the most valuable experiences I ever had. We held quarterly meetings that lasted all day and normally were held at the Federal Reserve Building in Washington, D.C. Once a year they held a meeting somewhere else, usually at the Federal Reserve Bank in Chicago, but once in a while we would go to some other Federal Reserve Bank, like Minneapolis or Richmond. Since it was an all-day meeting and we used charts extensively, it was necessary to plan ahead and decide in great detail what we were going to present. There were always four of us making the presentations: myself, because I had the responsibility for the day-to-day management of the account; Henry Bodwell, who had the responsibility for the overall management; John Wills, our economist; and Art O'Hara.

It was Art O'Hara's responsibility to present charts on industry studies and individual companies. John Wills presented charts having to do with the economic outlook, and Henry and I shared the responsibility for presenting the charts on the fund and separate studies we made from time to time. We had at least 30 or 40 charts just on the fund, showing every aspect of our investments.

Some of the management techniques I learned as a result of this responsibility deserve comment. One was the importance to the RSFRB investment committee of active management of a bond portfolio. It was beneficial to know and work with this group of people who was probably as knowledgeable about what was going to happen to interest rates as any group in the country. They had the sincere belief the bond market was inefficient. Therefore, opportunities would be presented to take advantage of this by reacting to the changes in the spreads between the yields of different types of fixed income securities. We had numerous charts that enabled us to watch very carefully the yield spread from A1 corporate bonds to government bonds; from A1 corporate bonds to B1 bonds; and from industrial bonds to public utility bonds, etc. Accordingly, I followed a very active program of managing their bond portfolio.

The RSFRB's approach to investing fixed income money also emphasized the need for call protection, that is, the purchase of only those fixed income securities an issuing organization could not refund prior to their normal maturity dates. Whenever interest rates moved up, the RSFRB expected us to buy bonds selling at a discount from their par value, so there was no possibility of those bonds being called away from us. As a matter of fact, I conducted studies proving that, in 1953 and 1954, if one owned bonds with a coupon greater than 3.5 percent, every single issue outstanding at that time was called away from investors simply as a result of a decline in interest rates of not more than a half percent. This desire for protection against bonds being called away from them also influenced the RSFRB in a policy of investing in direct placements of nonmarketable obligations of corporations and mortgage-backed securities. Therefore, we got into the financing of different kinds of projects, such as apartment buildings, in which we had a combination of sufficient income to protect the interest payments as well as the value of the property itself. Knowledge of how to do this proved to be very valuable later in my investment career.

Since the pension fund business was growing rapidly in the 1950s, The Northern was determined to be aggressive in developing business. In preparing for each sales presentation, we used our charts and developed a booklet in which we set forth in detail the different kinds of information an organization should have in order to evaluate us. We also invested heavily in developing computerized reports that provided, in a very readable manner, all the information our customers needed, on an ongoing basis, to see and understand the results of our investment management. We were successful because our highly professional approach was significantly superior, at that time, to our competition. Today, The Northern is a very important factor in the business of being master trustee of employee benefit business in the United States. Our early efforts laid the groundwork for that success.

A most important experience was to learn how to conduct meetings with the leading businessmen of Chicago. Not only did these men meet with us to review the investment portfolios of their employee benefit funds, but we also met with them as members of a finance or investment committee that had the responsibility for supervising the management of the investments in the endowment fund of a school or hospital. Specifically, in addition to all of the employee benefit funds, I had the responsibility for the institutional-type accounts such as the Presbyterian-St. Luke's Hospital, the Art Institute of Chicago, the Field Museum of Natural History and many others. In these meetings, I was always accompanied by Solomon A. Smith, Chairman; Solomon B. Smith, Vice Chairman; or Edward Byron Smith, President, because the accounts were so important to the prestige of the bank. My approach toward handling the meetings with the committees responsible for the management of this money was very similar to the one we used for managing the money of the RSFRB.

I believed I was progressing very well at The Northern, but my confidence was severely shaken when we received our first paycheck in January 1954. When I opened my envelope, I had an increase of $25 a month and felt very good. One man came over to my desk and said, "Say, do you mind telling me what kind of an increase you got? I got a $50 dollar a month increase." I was concerned, so I decided to talk to Henry Bodwell. Henry did not hesitate to tell me the reason was that my associate and his wife had six children. It was a logical explanation and was no reflection on me. From then on, I was always sensitive about letting anyone know how much of an increase I had received or asking anyone else what kind of a pay increase they had been awarded for their endeavors.

Measuring Investment Performance

In the '60s, '70s and '80s, measuring investment performance was universally accepted and recognized as an integral part of portfolio management. But when I began to manage pension fund money in 1952, it was an unknown part of the investment business. The management of personal portfolios had never demanded or expected performance measurement in anything other than some simplistic calculations. The difficulty of evaluating investment results in employee benefit accounts was due to the variable flow of additional dollars from income, contributions, distributions, and also to the impact of capital gains and losses in tax-free portfolios.

Quite early in 1952, I recognized the need for some method of making the calculations on performance so the results could be compared with other accounts, different in size and growing at different rates. One of my customers, the Northern Illinois Gas Company, was helpful because they had heard of a system developed by Cleveland Electric Illuminating Company. This approach compounded the rate of return, taking into consideration the flows of money, but it meant laborious hand calculations. We only followed this method for a year or two because it did not enable us to compare accounts with different growth rates and size. I then was successful in developing a procedure called a "time weighted rate of return." Others were attempting to do the same, and there was a great deal of conversation among pension fund managers as to how to accumulate the data and make the calculations. We had confidence in our approach and began to make the information available to our larger corporate accounts. In the late 1950s, A.G. Becker (a brokerage firm) led the way in developing a measurement system they could sell across the country. I was pleased with the opportunity to advise them on the kind of data they needed to obtain in order to make the calculations. Developments such as this in the employee benefit area made the business even more fascinating and challenging.

Pioneering In Pension Fund Management

Prior to the 1950s, most pension fund money was managed by insurance companies with less than 10 percent of the assets in common stocks. As soon as I had the responsibility for managing this kind of money, I was determined to prove it was logical to have more than 50 percent invested in that category. In The Northern's personal trust accounts, the normal proportion of stocks and bonds was 65 percent stocks and 35 percent bonds. In pension accounts where there were no taxes on capital gains and income and no risk of needing cash for pay-outs for a long time in the future, common sense said to place most of the assets in common stocks where one could obtain a much higher total return on the investment, that is, the combination of income and capital appreciation.

Accordingly, my first project, which was completed in 1955, calculated the total return from common stocks in comparison with bonds going back to 1900. The results proved many things, such as, on average during the 55-year period, common stocks produced a total return of about 9 percent each year compared with under 5 percent for bonds. Furthermore, during any period of time longer than five years (beginning and ending in any year), common stocks outperformed bonds.

During the next few years, I had our research department con-duct a variety of studies designed to prove there was virtually no risk associated with investing larger proportions in common stocks. It was not an easy assignment to convince the management of The Northern and some corporate officers of the logic of this policy; however, I was successful, and in the early 1960s, our common stock position in most portfolios was around 65 percent, with the remaining 35 percent in bonds and some short-term reserves.

Other pension fund managers around the country were also moving in this direction as the superior performance of the stock mar-ket in the '50s and '60s proved the validity of this policy. In the early '50s, the senior officers of corporations did not pay much attention to how their pension funds were being managed. However, as the cost of their pension funds became more important to their company's earn-ings, the management of pension funds became a top priority. Unfortunately, this led to some corporate officers placing too much emphasis on the investment results over periods as short as two or three years. This quite naturally resulted in money managers worrying about short-term performance as they strived to retain accounts under their management and obtain new business. It has always been my belief, and it is widely shared, that those who manage common stocks should have approximately five years in which to prove their capability. This length of time normally includes both up and down periods in the stock market. The question of diversification between stocks and bonds continues to be one of the greatest challenges faced by money managers as well as those responsible for public and private retirement funds. More than 40 years have passed since I first began to evaluate the relative attraction of stocks and bonds as long-term investments. In recent years bonds have provided good performance at times, but nothing has changed the fact that common stocks over longer periods provide better results. The assets in retirement accounts are a logical place to take advantage of that fact.

The People With Whom I Worked

The two most senior men in the investment research department when I joined Art O'Hara were Carl Lambrecht, the assistant manager, and Frank Hausmann, Jr., a senior analyst. Both had been with Art for many years. Needless to say, they were very helpful to those of us who were just getting started in the business. Carl eventually moved over to the portfolio management area, and Frank left in 1951 to become the chief investment officer at the National Bank of Detroit. Frank was quite active in the Financial Analyst Federation, and over the years we have been in frequent contact with each other. Frank was president of the Financial Analysts Society of Detroit in 1967-1968. Another very capable investment man was Bill Erickson. Bill had started in the investment research department, stayed there longer than I and became the assistant manager of the research department under Art O'Hara. In the late 1950s, he came over to help me in the management of institutional accounts. He left The Northern about two years before I did to go to the trust department of the American National Bank across the street. Later he transferred to the banking department and eventually ended up as the president of the bank. Unfortunately, Bill died prematurely.

Also working with me in the 1950s in the management of employee benefit accounts was Jim Nelson. Jim left in the late 1950s when he was making about $8,000 a year and was offered $10,000 a year by Loomis & Sayles to work in their Milwaukee office. Jim's father and mother needed financial help. Jim became head of the Milwaukee office and has been very successful.

The individual who worked with me most closely and for a longer period of time than anyone else was Dean Coleman. I had hired Dean as a summer employee while he was doing his graduate work at Stanford University. Dean was a very thorough investment analyst and an excellent portfolio manager. He was a very youthful-looking person but handled his accounts in an extremely professional manner. After customers had the chance to listen to Dean talk and observe his investment results for a relatively short period of time, they were convinced that he was a true professional. Dean was eventually transferred to a new subsidiary of The Northern in Miami, the Security Trust Company, to manage investment portfolios. One time I endeavored to hire Dean away from them; however, Dean was conservative in his personal affairs and also very loyal, so I was not able to entice him away. A Thrift Incentive Plan, which I had been responsible for encouraging The Northern to develop, was one of the reasons he stayed.

I also had the good fortune to work for six years with our assistant economist, Charles (Chuck) Partee. He left in 1961 to head up economic research at the Federal Reserve Board and later became a governor of the board. Chuck and I worked together quite closely, particularly in the latter part of his employment when he became the representative of the economics department in meetings with our larger pension and institutional accounts. Chuck would join me in the meetings at which I would present the investments and he would present the charts covering the economic outlook. I came to have a very high regard for him during that period.

The head of the trust department during most of the time I was at The Northern was William Turner. Bill was a good friend and had a sincere interest in me as an individual. During the 17 years I was at The Northern, I also worked very closely with our senior economist, John Wills. John was very sound, dependable and highly regarded by his peers and others such as the members of the investment committee of the RSFRB.

I mentioned Mike Symonds earlier and had one experience with him that was important in the early stages of my career. It happened in his capacity as chairman of the investment committee. When I had concluded my first industry report (it was on the railroad industry), Mike looked at me and said, "Don't you have something else to say?" I said, "No, that's the end of my report." Everyone smiled as he reminded me about the necessity of recommending what we should do with our investments. Obviously I was still thinking as a student rather than somebody who had responsibility for money. I had just simply lost sight of what was really important in my desire to impress the committee with the depth and breadth of my knowledge of the railroad industry.

Art O'Hara

In my opinion, Art was one of the great investment men of the '30s, '40s and '50s. In analyzing companies, Art stressed the need for having direct contact with the officers. He believed in a calling program where the investment analyst spent enough time with the officers of the corporation to have a good feel for their abilities and what they were likely to accomplish. As a result of this kind of research (and he was always looking for younger companies), he was one of the first analysts to discover the potential of Texas Instruments. Art called on them in Arlington, Texas, a suburb of Dallas, and gained the insights that enabled us to take large positions in the company.

I also learned from experience how important it was to be objective about what one learned as a result of calling on a company. Quite frequently the worst thing one can do upon returning from a visit with a company is to decide immediately to purchase its common stock. The reason is one tends to become overly influenced by the management. It is a good idea to sit back, examine the figures and keep them in perspective before beginning an aggressive acquisition program. An analyst must not let emotions become a dominant factor in making an investment decision.

Another lesson was the importance of concentration. The old story of "putting all your eggs in one basket and then watching it very, very carefully" is the basis for great success. Whether it is one egg or a few, concentration contributes to superior results. In my personal investments over the years, I have used a combination of leverage and concentration in three or four individual issues. This approach is applicable primarily to individuals who wish to build an estate by investing in the stock market. Also it is suitable only for those who can take above-average risks and have the ability to evaluate thoroughly and continuously supervise their concentrations. It also does not apply to managing employee benefit accounts or any situation in which one must act prudently while fulfilling fiduciary responsibilities.

Art did a great deal of public speaking for The Northern and was a good storyteller. One of his speaking techniques was to "romance" a common stock that the audience could understand. I used the same approach for discussing portfolios with customers. Instead of making dull comments about 30 or 40 stocks in a portfolio, I would build stories around a few holdings where something different or unique was happening.

Art had one true-to-life story that he used many times in his talks. This investment situation showed me that having the courage of your convictions and the willingness to back them will work when you make the decision to stay with a concentration in an individual security ... as long as you know exactly what you are doing. This was the situation. A man had died and left his assets in trust with us at The Northern. He had been an employee with Acme Steel Company, which was located in Chicago. On the date of his death, his estate owned approximately $600,000 of Acme Steel common stock and also a holding of about $800,000 in Minnesota Mining and Manufacturing Company. The investment in Minnesota Mining and Manufacturing position had come as the result of a $1,500 investment shortly after it had been established in Minneapolis, Minnesota, in 1903. In this particular instance, the man held the stock through World War I and saw it appreciate somewhat in value. But he did not make much money on it until the late 1920s and then saw a good part of the value disappear in the 1930s. Eventually, he saw it increase above his original investment, and, by the time he died in the late 1950s, it was worth about $800,000. Under the terms of the trust agreement, we were allowed to hold the Acme Steel stock; as a matter of fact, we were encouraged to hold the Acme Steel stock because of the way the trust agreement was written. This request was made because the grantor had acquired this position as a result of being a senior officer in the company. Our research showed conclusively that Minnesota Mining was a very attractive company, whereas Acme Steel had limited attraction. In this particular case, there was no need for income and the widow had great confidence in us. The decision we made was to pay for the estate taxes of about $600,000 out of the holding of Acme Steel and continue to hold Minnesota Mining. By the time I left The Northern in 1964, we had diversified out of Minnesota Mining to some extent, but the shares we had retained had increased in value to $12 million. The diversification had produced another $3 million that was largely in tax-exempt bonds. The decision to maintain the concentration was extremely important and difficult, and it indicates why The Northern is so successful in the management of personal accounts. I understand they now have the largest personal trust department in the country.

Another aspect of Art O'Hara's training was the importance of developing a sincere interest in the personal lives of employees. He never hesitated to sit down to talk to a person. As a result, people knew they had a personal relationship with him. As I mentioned earlier, when I was playing basketball on the bank team in the bank league, he would frequently stay downtown in the evening to watch me. I was just one of about 15 people in the research department, and in one way or another, he gave others the same feeling of being someone special.

After I left the research department and was working for Henry Bodwell, I continued to have a great deal of contact with Art because he would join me in meetings we held with some of our larger institutional and pension accounts. Art was a great believer in charts, and to this day, I think it is one of the most effective ways to communicate investment ideas. I do not know how many charts we had at The Northern, but they numbered in the thousands. We had a series of charts on every industry, which the analysts updated as a way of presenting their ideas to the investment policy committee. These same charts, as well as charts on the individual companies in the portfolio, were also used by the portfolio manager to show the customer the status of the particular account, historically as well as currently. Our chart inventory required three full-time chartists.

Early in 1963 Art developed a prostate problem, had surgery and was making good progress until a blood clot in his lungs caused his death. Mary and I had a very pleasant visit with him in the hospital the day before he died, and there was no indication of the impending tragedy.

One of Art's responsibilities away from the bank was his representation on the faculty of the Southwestern Graduate School of Banking at Southern Methodist University in Dallas, Texas. This school was in session two weeks each summer, with the curriculum also requiring that the students work on case studies submitted to them during the year. The management of The Northern asked me to take over Art's job, so for the next 12 years I was very involved in this program.

The students were officers in banks located in the southwest, with most of them coming from Texas, Louisiana, Oklahoma and Arkansas. This school and several others scattered throughout the United States were sponsored by the American Bankers Association. My responsibilities included supervising the trust investment program and teaching the students how to manage investment of the assets in the trust departments of the banks. Many of the students came from relatively small banks where one or two people, in addition to making investment decisions for each trust account, had to be involved with business development, tax laws, legal considerations, customer contacts and the routine administration of the accounts. Other students came from large banks where they specialized in the investment area. Accordingly, one of my many challenges was the need to help all types of students. This experience reinforced my conviction that the larger trust departments with many trust accounts differing in size and objectives are more likely to have the kind of expertise necessary to make good decisions and produce superior results. However, I am well aware of the fact that some small trust operations are successful and produce competitive investment results.

The Decision To Leave

I never seriously considered making the decision to leave The Northern until after my mother died in February 1963. I could utilize my talents only in big cities, and, because of my mother's poor health, we needed to go to Lafayette whenever we could get away on weekends. The trip took less than three hours.

My only concern about my future at The Northern was based on one very minor problem Art O'Hara had with Edward Smith, the president. I believed that much of the success of the trust business was the result of Art's investment decisions and leadership. Two or three times I was with Art in his office after a session with Ed in which something had come up where Ed did not agree with what Art was recommending. I believed I would not be able to accept this nearly as easily as Art did; therefore I was concerned about my future. At the same time, I had a very high regard for the leadership the Smith family, who controlled the company, had provided since the inception of the company. They managed with a high level of ability and integrity, and, the reputation of The Northern in Chicago and nationally could not have been better. They surrounded themselves with intelligent, aggressive and dedicated people and provided an extremely satisfying working environment. I had thoroughly enjoyed being a part of the team and knew I was highly regarded by the senior people on the banking as well as the trust side of the business. In retrospect I know there was no justification for my concern. But, when the headhunter for the St. Louis Union Trust Company approached me and asked if he could interview me, I was vulnerable because I was unhappy with my salary increase in January 1964.

The interview was at the Chicago Club with Roland Behrens and Eugene Williams. Roland Behrens was the chief investment officer at the St. Louis Union Trust Company, and Gene Williams was the executive vice president. It was a satisfactory discussion and resulted in my trip to St. Louis to visit the company and meet Dave Calhoun, the president and chairman of the board. When I flew to St. Louis for this meeting, I did so with the feeling that I probably would not accept their offer. I liked living in the Chicago area and was apprehensive about joining a company that had somewhat fewer trust assets under its management than we had at The Northern. The St. Louis Union had about $3.2 billion of assets under its management, and The Northern had about $4.5 billion under management. I was also in line to take over the senior investment responsibilities at The Northern in about three years when Henry Bodwell retired.

Anyway, when I came into the downtown area and the taxi drove up to the St. Louis Union Trust Company, I had a very negative feeling toward what I saw. St. Louis looked run-down; the buildings were old and the St. Louis Union Trust Company facilities were not very attractive from the outside. However, Dave Calhoun drove me to the airport and had a great influence on me. Their offer was $35,000 to be the chief investment officer in an environment very similar to The Northern's in that the St. Louis Union Trust Company was the dominant trust company in the city. The Trust Company controlled the First National Bank in St. Louis, and the assets under management were three times as great as any of the other trust operations in St. Louis. They managed about 50 percent of all the trust assets in the city and were the largest trust company west of the Mississippi River. Roland Behrens was considered the number one investment man in the community, and I knew I could be recognized in the same way. An increase of salary from $22,000 to $35,000, with a membership in a country club of my choice, was too much to resist.

It was a very, very difficult decision, but I did make it and announced it to Henry Bodwell. The Northern hated to see me go. I believe that from the bottom of my heart. All the key people attended a farewell gathering and presented me with a very nice pen and pencil desk set that says, "From his friends at The Northern Trust Company." I shall never forget the emotions of that moment. I said to them, after they gave me the gift, that, when Mary and I had settled in the Chicago area and accepted the offer at The Northern, we decided to dig our roots in very deeply. We had done this in Glen Ellyn as well as at The Northern. It was with a sincere sense of loss that I left the company. Even now, after being retired, I would hesitate to say it was a good decision. Yes, I believe I accumulated more money with the changes I made, but if I had remained, I would have ultimately achieved a senior position in a great company. A good friend, Robert (Bob) Reusche, took over my responsibilities when I left and later became the officer in charge of the trust department.

CHAPTER 9

◆

Glen Ellyn

Dubefore the time Mary was in Wheaton, she went to a Presbyterian church located near the center of town. While we were in Norfolk, we attended a Methodist church, which made us receptive to the idea of joining a Methodist church when we returned to the Glen Ellyn–Wheaton area. Henry Bodwell lived in Glen Ellyn and talked to us about an organization in the First Methodist Church called the "60-60 Club" and what it had meant to him and his wife, Marian. We were attracted to the idea and accompanied Henry and Marian to a Sunday evening church supper that was an important part of the 60-60 Club approach toward getting everyone involved.

Henry asked Lester Springer, the pastor of the church, to come to the house and invite us to become members. We told Lester we wanted to check out some other churches, but we liked him and what Henry had been saying. We immediately made the decision to join the First Methodist Church. It was an important decision because the church became the focal point of the close to 12 years we lived in Glen Ellyn.

Lester made arrangements for us to join the church the following Sunday. John had not been baptized, so we all joined the church and had John baptized the same Sunday. Both Barbara and Lynne had been baptized in the First Presbyterian Church in Chicago, located on the South Side near the lakefront, not very far from the University of Chicago campus. This is where I made my public confession of faith.

Mary and I were pleased to get settled and looked forward to becoming a part of the community. The 60-60 Club of the Methodist Church was one of the first ways we became active in community life. It was there we developed friendships that proved to be the most enduring ones of our lifetime. The 60-60 Club was organized with a well-thought-out approach toward getting couples together, active in the church and interested in each other. The Club had some special rules. One was you were supposed to be under 60 years of age. There was another club in the church (called the Tandem Club) for people who were over 60; however some of the ones over 60 belonged to the 60-60 Club. A dozen committees, each of which had a certain responsibility, ran the Club. One committee was in charge of the program for the once-a-month Sunday evening supper; another was responsible for the food; another set up the tables. An important committee was the one responsible for service; that is, if adversity struck any family in the church, the service committee members would be the first ones to step in and make sure the 60-60 Club would help the family. Another committee was responsible for an annual fund-raising program put on in the parking lot of the church. The committees met once a month prior to the Sunday evening meeting. Each committee was comprised of 10 to 12 couples and met in individual homes on a rotating basis throughout the year.

The evenings in the homes were important in enabling us to develop friendships. Usually some time was available during the evening for games, such as playing cards. There was never any liquor served. The host furnished dessert and coffee, and after we were through with business, the rest of the evening was entirely social. This was when we first met Rolly and Virginia Davis, who became our closest friends. This was also how we met the Hansens, Howard and Maxine, and other couples who became good friends, such as the

Rosenthals, Scates, Bergstroms, Wallaces, Coopers, Bergers and many others.

Not too long after we became involved in the activities of the church, we became aware of friction in the congregation regarding Lester Springer. It seemed to revolve around whether he really believed in Jesus Christ as the Son of God. We never knew for sure what the disagreement was, but we knew it was a fairly deep-seated one and was dividing the church. We liked Lester and Ruth Springer and enjoyed his sermons. Mary and I believed he was sound in his religious beliefs, and we did not interpret his sermons as indicating he did not believe that Jesus Christ was the Son of God. In any event, Lester eventually left the church, and Jim McKelvey became the new minister.

Shortly after Jim became minister of the church, a decision was made to build a sanctuary. Prior to building the sanctuary, the Sunday services were held in the gymnasium of the church that was part of the original building built in 1929. The gymnasium worked out quite well as a sanctuary but still was not satisfactory. Mary and I were very enthusiastic about building the sanctuary and gave money to its construction on a sacrificial basis.

When John was about eight years old, I initiated a program to teach the fundamentals of basketball to the boys of different ages at the church on Saturdays. My first class started with those between eight and nine years of age. A second class was for ages 10 and 11, and the last class was for the 12 and 13-year-olds. John and I were there from eight o'clock in the morning until lunch time.

During our 11 years as members of the church, I accepted several different responsibilities. One of the first ones was to be the head usher for a period of two or three years. That meant very regular attendance, and it posed some problems because we were trying to go back and forth to Lafayette as frequently as possible to visit my mother and Mary's parents. I was on the finance commission for several years, including the period we did the fund-raising for the new sanctuary. One of my more demanding responsibilities was acting as the chairman of the pastor relations committee at the time when there was a controversy between Jim McKelvey and an assistant. It ended with both men leaving; Jim moved to the Park Ridge Methodist Church. I had the responsibility of participating in the selection of a new minister as well as an assistant. This took a great amount of time and occurred just before we moved to St. Louis.

Founding The Glen Ellyn Kiwanis Club

Sometime late in 1953, Rolly Davis approached me to see whether I would join with him in establishing a Kiwanis Club in Glen Ellyn. Rolly's father was active in the Hinsdale Kiwanis Club, and that club, along with the one in Wheaton, was interested in starting a Kiwanis Club in Glen Ellyn. I had never considered being active in a service club, much less starting one, but Rolly's enthusiasm and my respect for his father persuaded me to participate. Rolly knew more people than I, but I contacted a few in the Methodist Church. We were able to develop a group of about 15 initially, and with their help, we were up to about 30 men when we received our charter from the National Kiwanis Organization in 1954. This club became an important part of our lives during the time we were in Glen Ellyn. Rolly was president from April, when we were organized, until the end of 1954. I succeeded him as president in 1955. It was a rewarding experience, but I made the mistake of getting involved in too many activities in addition to the tremendous demands on me from my investment responsibilities at The Northern Trust Company. Late in 1955, I came to realize I might be damaging my health by putting too much pressure on myself, so I began to slow down, but not much. One change was Mary's and my decision to resign from the Wheaton Drama Club. I had been the treasurer and also had participated in two performances. Mary was the advertising chair, participated in one performance, and we both assisted in the preparation of scenery. We had joined it because of friendships Mary had established during the nine months she lived in Wheaton.

The Kiwanis Club was a very active organization, which was probably a reflection of the age of the members. Most of them were about my age and were very interested in the community. One of our activities was annual participation in the Fourth of July parade. Every year we built a float. This parade was a major event in Glen Ellyn and was climaxed by fireworks that people watched from across the lake behind the high school. After the parade, they always had activities at the park around the lake, such as pony rides for the children. It was a nice kind of community in which to raise children.

An important fund-raising project we started when I was president was sponsoring a series of travelogues (usually six) presented at Glenbard High School during the winter months. Another project of the Kiwanis Club was to raise money by selling peanuts. It was a project sponsored by all of the Kiwanis Clubs in the Chicago area. We sold peanuts all day on Friday and until noon on Saturday. On Friday we stood on street corners and stopped cars on the way to and from work. On Saturday we would be stationed all over the downtown part of Glen Ellyn. John, Lynne and Barbara helped me, and in that way we could cover a corner without help from others. The Club also started a "pancake day" and held it in the Methodist Church. We organized a bridge club, and even though Mary and I were never card-playing enthusiasts, we did our part. We also had a bowling team, so one night a week during the winter months, I had another way to develop some great friendships.

Not long after we organized the Kiwanis Club, one of the members came up with the idea of a fishing trip to Canada. Since I had thoroughly enjoyed fishing when I was in Lafayette, it was easy to become an avid supporter of such a trip. It immediately became an annual affair with about 12 members usually participating. Normally, it was a five-day trip with three days of fishing and two days of driving. We always left work on a Friday and drove all night with four or five of us in each station wagon. We would take turns sleeping in the back and riding in the front seat. When we arrived, we would have enough rest to enjoy fishing the first day. We always used guides, usually Indians, with two men fishing in each boat. The guides always had us fishing for wall-eyes in the morning, so we could have them for a shore lunch. Those lunches were unforgettable experiences, and the friendships that developed from the trips have been very important to me. I made about 10 trips, but only one after I left Glen Ellyn.

Krebiozen

About the time we were organizing the Kiwanis Club, Mary and I became very deeply involved with the use of Krebiozen as an effective drug for certain types of cancer. Rolly's father, John Davis, became familiar with the drug when it was effectively used with one of his employees. Andrew C. Ivy, M.D., from the University of Illinois believed in the drug, and because of his stature and reputation, we became very interested. We attended meetings during which testimonies were given that confirmed its value both to relieve pain and slow the spread of the disease. A book written by Herbert Bailey entitled *A Matter of Life and Death* documented the history of the drug's use and the turmoil surrounding its acceptance. We participated in fund-raising efforts and knew of one personal situation where the drug was effective. The American Cancer Society and the American Medical Association vigorously fought its use and, in the end, won.

When it was used, the physicians who prescribed it did so at great personal risk and only in terminal situations. The basic problem was that the drug had been developed by two physicians from Yugoslavia who lacked credibility. The Ivy Cancer Research Foundation was founded by Rolly's father, and as late as 1965, we were active in raising funds for Dr. Ivy. Eventually, as a result of legal action, the organization fell apart; use of the drug was completely halted. If one read Bailey's book, one would wonder why the American Cancer Society fought the drug so vigorously. To this day, I find myself having great difficulty supporting the American Cancer Society. In justification of our support for Dr. Ivy, it is important to mention that George D. Stoddard, president of the University of Illinois, also wrote a book in 1955 on the controversy entitled (*Krebiozen: The Great Cancer Mystery*).

The 6259 Investment Club

Early in 1959, some of my friends in the Kiwanis Club urged me to start an investment club. I liked the idea, so we managed without any difficulty to put together a group of 15 people. I was helped by Howard Hansen, who was an investment analyst with Duff & Phelps, a research firm headquartered in Chicago, and who had access to information about investment clubs. My neighbor across the street, Al Kornhauser, was also interested in the idea. Al had been with an investment research firm before he became treasurer of Controls Company of America. The three of us were responsible for getting the investment club organized. We met once a month after our first meeting, held on June 2, 1959. Without controversy we named it the 6259 Investment Club, simply by giving it a name that related to the date of our organization meeting. It is still functioning today. During my four and a half years in the club, the members leaned on me almost entirely for investment ideas. Between Al, Howard and myself, we taught them how to go about the investment decision-making process. We did pretty well during that period, and I hated to give up that association when I left Glen Ellyn.

Family Life

Prior to my return from Korean War naval duty, I had only played golf a few times. When we moved to Glen Ellyn and got involved in the Methodist Church, the Kiwanis Club and the Investment Club, it seemed everyone we knew was playing the game. The Kiwanis Club had a Father's Day golf outing; The Northern had its Columbus Day outing; and opportunities to play began to develop. In the late 1950s, Mary and I played golf with three other couples during Sunday afternoon outings that always started after three o'clock at the Arrowhead Golf Course in Wheaton. We played Arrowhead because the green fee was very low after three o'clock, and there was almost enough time to play 18 holes. The four women would play behind us. The men, regardless of how much daylight remained, would usually get in a few more holes than the women were willing to play. Mary and I also found a little nine-hole course in Downer's Grove where we played once in a while. Our serious involvement with golf commenced when The Northern Trust Company provided a golf membership for us in the spring of 1962 at the Glen Oaks Country Club in Glen Ellyn. We had two summers, 1962 and 1963, when the membership in the Glen Oaks Country Club enabled us to play more often. This was when John and Barbara got started. Lynne was not interested. Once in a while, John caddied for me on Saturday mornings. It was a way he could make a little extra money, and I paid him the same amount a regular caddy received. One of the very pleasant memories I have of that membership was the decision I made to have a lesson with the pro. I had a very bad slice that everyone with whom I played tried to solve for me without success. The pro at Glen Oaks, with one lesson, changed what I was doing so that I was able to hook the ball. The slicing habit still comes back once in a while, but it was great to realize that I could play golf without slicing the ball on every shot.

The Glen Oaks Country Club membership was not as pleasant as it might have been. The Northern Trust Company was not paying me the kind of salary that enabled us to participate the way one should in the activities of a country club. I do not recall exactly what my salary was in 1962, but it was around $18,000 a year. The company was picking up all our business expenses, so that was not a problem. However we did not have enough money to eat at the club as frequently as we would have liked. Also, when Mary and I played, we would pull a cart instead of riding a golf cart or hiring caddies.

In the '50s and '60s it was not as customary for families to eat out as it is today. Our frugal habits meant we dined out infrequently. When we did eat out, more often than not we went to McDonald's. McDonald's had first come into the Glen Ellyn area when the company opened a restaurant on Roosevelt Road not too far from our house. It was inexpensive, quickly accessible, and we liked the food. We permitted the children to spend 35 cents on each meal. Usually they would have a hamburger, french fries and a Coke. If they gave up the french fries and Coke, they could have a milk shake. This experience and favorable attitude toward the company led Mary and me to purchase the stock on March 1, 1967, just two years after it first became a public company.

In the third chapter of this book, I mentioned that, at our evening meal when we were all together, it was customary for Dad to pray before the meal and thank God for our many blessings. Also, we always read a chapter from the Bible, and Dad made sure we knew the meaning of the passage. I did not mention then that, as a serious student of the Bible, he was always studying the six-volume set of Mathew Henry's Commentary, which was written in 1706 and that I have retained. Mary and I decided that, with our children, reading a Bible storybook would be a more efficient way to teach them. Accordingly we concluded our evening meal by taking turns reading from Egermeier's illustrated book of Bible stories. I also said the prayer at the beginning of the meal. Today, my grandchildren participate in our meal-time prayer.

We liked the house in Glen Ellyn enough to remodel it several times during the 12 years we were there. The first addition was the closing-in of a porch on the back of the house. Following that I finished off the basement by putting the paneling up by myself. After that we closed in the breezeway between the garage and the house in order to provide a breakfast nook and an enclosed entrance way. Our major addition was to put in a new kitchen, and we added a master bedroom and a bath upstairs above the garage. We also put in a half bath on the first level. We were never terribly unhappy with the house on Turner, but, even with all the remodeling, we never thought of it as an ideal house.

As our financial situation improved, we began to look at other houses in Glen Ellyn. In 1962 we came very close to buying a house in Glen Ellyn Woods that was priced at $64,000. We have wondered whether we would have left Glen Ellyn if we had moved into that house.

One of the interesting sidelights of our continuing attempt to upgrade our housing was the experience we had with paying increasingly higher interest rates on our mortgages. We started with a $3^3/4$ percent rate on the house in Wheaton and moved up to a $4^1/4$ percent rate when we bought the house in Glen Ellyn. The first addition raised the rate to $4^3/4$ percent, and when we put on the big addition, which was just a few years before we left, the rate went up to $5^1/4$ percent. These changes in rates were all due to the impact of a higher rate of inflation.

The school system in Glen Ellyn was outstanding. All three

kids went to Main Street School, which was four blocks away from where we lived. Barbara graduated from Glenbard High School, but Lynne finished only half of her freshman year. John was interested in basketball and played on the junior high school team. One of the bittersweet experiences we had as a result of our leaving Glen Ellyn occurred when we left on February 14, 1964, and John was in the midst of the basketball season. I was anxious to see his last game, so I left work early and got to the school in time to see the game and watch John be carried out of the gymnasium on the shoulders of his teammates. This was a proud event for us.

Barbara's interest in painting became obvious when she was quite young. The Northern sponsored a contest that Barbara won when she was 10 years old. A teacher in the Main Street Elementary School also noticed her talent and called it to our attention. The Art Institute of Chicago conducted classes on Saturdays for younger people, so we enrolled her when she was a freshman in high school. She made the trips to downtown Chicago on the train by herself for three summers.

During the summer between Barbara's junior and senior years in high school, we devoted weekends and some of my summer vacation to visiting a variety of colleges and universities in the Midwest. We were very selective, and after a visit to Boulder, Colorado, her choice was the fine arts program at the University of Colorado. After a disappointing freshman year (the size of the school was largely responsible), we decided she should transfer to a small liberal arts college. That summer we visited at least a dozen campuses in Missouri and Iowa, and she chose Simpson College in Indianola, Iowa. Our visits to numerous colleges and universities provided insights to Lynne and John, so when the time came for them to choose a college, it was easy.

The Little League program in Glen Ellyn was well organized and open to boys when they were eight years old. I coached John's team for a few years and managed it for two years. Despite the demands on me at work, I found a way to get home early on workday afternoons whenever they practiced and played during the week. On one occasion, I demonstrated the same weakness most parents have when their children are participating in competitive sports. We were playing for the championship of our age group and were defeated, but the manager of the other team committed a rule violation. I let emotion get in the way of reason and appealed to the governing board for a replay of the last inning of the game. The board agreed to a replay and we won the game, but in the process, I received a great deal of antagonism from the parents of the boys on the other team. I was guilty of very poor judgment.

Often a child or an adult is thought of as accident-prone. John was such a person. One of his first mishaps happened at night after he had gone to bed. He got up to go to the bathroom with the wooden stick end of a pinwheel in his mouth. He fell down and the stick cut through his throat. He pulled it out and ran back to his room. Mary heard the noise, and when she went in his room to ask what was wrong, he answered with blood pouring from his mouth. A year or two later, when he was in the second grade, he fell off an eight-foot cement wall onto a depressed driveway at a nearby neighbor's house. He and some of his school friends were coming home for lunch when he jumped from the wall and landed on his face rather than his feet. When I arrived home, his face was black and blue, although nothing was broken. When he was a year or two older, he ran into a wire used to brace a telephone pole in the front of our house. The wire cut his finger, which required three stitches. When he was in the sixth grade and I was managing his Little League baseball team, he was hit in the face by a pitched ball, while I was holding a meeting at our home with all of the parents. One boy, one of my pitchers, had come along with his parents, and the first ball he threw to John, who was batting, hit him in the nose. From then on, John was never as good a batter. When he was in the eighth grade, he was visiting at a friend's house, and while running in their basement, he ran into a cold air duct. The resulting gash in the top of his head meant an emergency trip to the hospital and a number of stitches. Also, in the eighth grade, he fell while walking through a neighbor's house under construction and severely bruised his face and ribs. At the beginning of the basketball season in his freshman year in high school, he broke a bone in his foot and missed the first few games. I had the good fortune never to have seen any of these things happen.

Lynne was a very studious child. As soon as she could read, it was almost impossible to satisfy her desire for books. Most of her after-school and weekend activities were with her girlfriends, so my involvement with her was minimal. I did teach her the fundamentals of basketball and baseball, so that she spent many hours playing ball with the boys in the neighborhood. However, as a family we did a great many things together. Visits to the Brookfield Zoo on Sunday afternoons were important to us as were our summer vacations for two or three weeks at a resort on Lake Metonga at Crandon, Wisconsin, a six-hour drive north of Chicago.

Having a dog as a pet was a high priority for me, but not for Mary. When she was growing up on the farm, dogs were treated as outside animals and never entered the house or became personal pets. The kids were anxious to have one, because their friends were always saying how much having a dog meant to them. We made three attempts to find the right one for the family, but all were failures except one that was a partial success. He was a little black dog we named Spooky, who never created a problem but just did not appeal to any of us. When my mother asked if she could have him, it was a unanimous decision to make her happy.

Our first dog was Buzzy, a male German Shepherd, whom we obtained from an animal shelter when John was about three years old. Buzzy was smart and friendly, but in our small house, a big, energetic dog was in the wrong environment. He was taller than John and always knocking things over, including John. Our biggest problem was leaving him alone in the house when we were gone. We would leave him in the laundry room in the basement, where he would never stop clawing at the door. This led me to the decision to borrow the cattle control, electric fence system used by farmers. My brother-in-law, Don Schelle, mounted wires on the inside of the laundry room door, and for a few days the idea seemed to work. However, it did not take long for Buzzy to start scratching sideways on the door, thereby avoiding being shocked. That ended the battle; the wires were removed. His end for us as a pet came one day when he pulled up the stake to which he was tied in our back yard and ran away. Mary was home alone, and, when she saw he was gone, she began to search the neighborhood. Mary found him, just as he jumped (playfully) on a lady walking down the street behind our house. When Mary caught him, the chain wrapped around one of her legs and left a large painful bruise. When we came home that evening, Buzzy was gone and the property of the animal shelter. The kids agreed with us that he belonged on a farm or some-place where he had the room to run and play.

That bad experience did not deter us from trying again. This time it was a beautiful, white Samoyed. When we answered the adver-tisement and took her home with us, we blithely ignored the fact that Mimi, the name the previous owners had given to her, was hyperac-tive. We soon found out that Mimi enjoyed spending the day running from one window to another, barking continually. We also soon learned what shedding is like when a dog has long, white, fluffy hair that a vacuum cleaner cannot handle. My fastidious wife could not have been more unhappy. Once a week, at least, all of us got down on our hands and knees on the floor and, starting at the front door, with masking tape in both hands, collected the hair as we covered the furniture and every inch of the first floor of the house. Lynne, in particular, was fond of Mimi, but Mary was persistent and placed an advertisement in our local newspaper. It was answered immediately by a lady who could not have been more excited about the prospect of having this beautiful, pedigreed Samoyed. About six months later, she came by the house to tell Mary how happy she was with Mimi and still could not understand why we had been willing to give her away. Mary said the woman's clothes were covered with long, white dog hair.

In 1960 when John was 9, Lynne 11 and Barbara 16, we made a month-long trip west to visit my sister Ruth and her family in Arizona and my sister Mary and her family in Norwalk, California. The most exciting part of the trip was our attempt to drive to the top of Pike's Peak. Before we approached the mountain, I neglected to fill our tank with gasoline. When we were about two-thirds of the way up, the motor began to misfire and use excessive amounts of gasoline. The car was a pink 1957 Oldsmobile with lots of power and, even under normal driving conditions, gave us only 12 miles per gallon. When we were about 1,100 feet from the top and the gas gauge was showing empty, we came to a small place where we could turn around. I took a vote, and there were no objections to going back. The carburetor was so fouled up we averaged only five miles per gallon from there to Tucson.

In 1963 all of us made a trip to the Washington, D.C.–Williamsburg area, and in 1966, John, Lynne, Mary and I visited Civil War battlefields and New Orleans. Both trips proved to be timely from an educational viewpoint. The only other trip we made as a family was to Florida in 1969 with John and Lynne (Barbara was married and a mother) while Lynne was a sophomore in college.

How I Began To Acquire Some Assets

The first opportunity I had to invest some money was in 1953 when I bought five shares of Merck at a cost of about $100. It is important to keep in mind that my salary at The Northern was always very low, and we had three children to raise. We also provided a great deal of financial support for my mother and traveled to Lafayette at least once a month. To accumulate money, it was necessary to save nickels and dimes and live a very frugal life. Also at this time, we were giving 10 percent of my salary to the First Methodist Church.

Even with a small amount to invest, I could have made a great deal of money if I could have participated in the hot new-issue stock market. I had the opportunity to purchase the shares of new companies that were just coming to the market, buy them at the opening price and sell them immediately for a profit. I could not take advantage of these offerings because of my fiduciary responsibilities. Brokerage firms were very willing to make shares available to me, and I would not have had to put up any money. I could have simply bought and sold the same day. Opportunities to make money easily in this way were always available to me during my lifetime in the investment business. Since they were not ethical, they had to be ignored.

At the end of 1956, I owned the common stock of two companies having a market value of $740. During the next few years, my investments had values at successive year-ends of $2,147; $3,044; $4,565; $8,560; and by the end of 1961, they totaled $25,270. My shares in Combined Insurance Company of America alone were worth $20,640. My approach was to invest a few hundred dollars, borrow from the bank and buy a few more shares. I always concentrated on a handful of companies I knew very well. When I borrowed money from the bank, I always made sure that, in a market decline, I never had so much invested that I would be forced to liquidate any of my holdings.

In 1962 we were in the midst of a severe decline in common stocks, so my portfolio of four stocks was down to $21,482 at year-end. By the end of 1963, all but $1,000 of my portfolio of $23,500 was in two companies, Combined Insurance Company of America and The Northern Trust Company.

When raising children, it is very difficult to accumulate and save money. Most of the $23,500 had been created by appreciation in the value of Combined Insurance Company. On March 22, 1964, I was 43 years old. The equity in our house in Glen Ellyn, that we sold for $32,500, was $16,500. Accordingly our net worth was about $40,000. We were making headway in accumulating some money and could not have been happier with how life was treating us. If it had not been for the stock market, our progress, except for the equity in our home, would have been minimal. It is vitally important for those who can save money to realize the importance of utilizing the stock market as the way to invest money.

Our Attitude Toward Money

The accumulation of money was never a goal in itself for Mary and me but, having lived through the Depression years, we certainly wanted a comfortable standard of living. Beyond that I wanted to enjoy what I was doing, accumulate knowledge, have the respect of my peers and gain public recognition of my business status and expertise. About one year after I had joined The Northern, an insurance company in Chicago, Continental Assurance Company, offered me a job as an analyst in which I would have doubled my salary. I did not give any consideration to a change because I knew the experience of continuing to work with Art O'Hara and Henry Bodwell would be invaluable to me in later years. I also rejected an unsolicited offer in 1962 to double my salary to $40,000 per year by joining a nationally known investment advisory firm in Chicago.

When I accepted my new responsibilities in St. Louis, everything I had sacrificed in terms of money had prepared me for what I knew I could do in the future. I had grown up in a family where the spiritual side of life was dominant. I had experienced poverty in a way that taught me to be conservative and careful in all of my financial affairs. By playing basketball, I became dedicated to the importance of a team in attempting to be successful. My two years as the executive officer on a destroyer gave me some important insights into how to supervise those with whom one works. The MBA degree from the University of Chicago was highly regarded in the business world, and along with the knowledge I had acquired, it provided me with a stepping stone and a door opener to greater responsibility. The 17 years at The Northern Trust Company had prepared me to manage all kinds of investment portfolios with firsthand experience in all of the securities available to a manager of other people's money. I was ready for the future.

CHAPTER 10

The St. Louis Union Trust Company

I had about one month to find a house before I joined the St. Louis Union Trust Company on February 15. It only took us two weekends with a real estate agent, looking for properties available immediately and concentrating on the area west of downtown St. Louis along U.S. 40. Specifically, we concentrated in Clayton, Frontenac, Ladue, and Town and Country. At the end of the second weekend, we bought a house at 12943 Woodlark Lane in Town and Country and in a new development called Colony Woods. It was a beautiful area, and the house was immediately available. The developer and the bank worked quickly on both the permanent and bridge loans so we could move in on the weekend before I reported to work.

We had never had a second car during all the time we were at The Northern Trust Company because I rode a train back and forth to work. Now we needed one, so we bought a used 1960 Ford.

On the trip to St. Louis, Lynne rode with me and John with Mary. It was snowing in St. Louis, and when we were about two miles from the new home, Mary and John slid off the road, across the front lawn of a house and bumped a tree — fortunately with no damage or delay. When we got to the house, we had to wait about three hours before the moving van arrived. The snow was about seven inches deep and slippery. This caused the moving van to get stuck at the end of the cul-de-sac. The moving van finally got unstuck, and when everything was unloaded, we discovered to our great unhappiness that not everything had been put aboard the van. Virtually none of Lynne's and my clothing had been brought along with the van. Fortunately, we did find a pair of pants and a suit coat that matched, so for the first four days, I had to wear the same suit to work. The moving company had used two vans, and since the second van wasn't completely filled, they had unloaded the stuff and put it in storage until they could get a full load to St. Louis. My telephone call changed their plans.

The senior officers of most corporations in the St. Louis area did business with, or were affiliated in some way with, either the St. Louis Union Trust Company or the First National Bank in St. Louis. Each of the two organizations had boards of directors of about 30 members, so that most larger corporations were represented on one of the two boards. A few companies were represented on both boards. The St. Louis Union Trust Company was the dominant manager of pension assets, so I immediately came to know the chief executive officers, other senior officers and the chief financial officers in most of the larger and many of the smaller corporations in the St. Louis area. The St. Louis Union

Trust Company dominated the personal trust business in the city, which gave me the opportunity to meet many of the members of the wealthier families in the area. As a result, Mary and I quickly became familiar with what was going on in the community.

The senior officers at the St. Louis Union were a friendly group, and before long, they were making us feel very much at home. Roland Behrens and his wife, Ruth, made sure we met people, and one of his first acts was to sponsor a dinner with about 20 of the senior officers and their wives at his country club, Old Warson. Some of those attending, in addition to David Calhoun and Eugene Williams, were:

Sam Davis; Harry Miller (personal new business); Oren Miller (probate department); Roy Ozment (administration of personal trusts); Fred Shepherd (general counsel); Ken Eggers (privately owned corporations); Hugh Logan (pension new business); Hord Hardin (corporate transfer and custodian department); and six of the more senior men in my investment operation. With the passage of time, we came to know all these men and their wives on a social basis. This had never happened at The Northern Trust Company

When a new chief investment officer joins a company in which he has responsibility over other very capable people, one of whom had aspired to that responsibility, it is vitally important for the new officer to gain respect as quickly as possible. Carl Beckers had been Roland Behrens' right-hand man for many years and was several years my senior in age. Quite obviously, it was an unpleasant situation for him, for his investment capabilities were superb and he was highly regarded by financial analysts in St. Louis and nationally. If there was animosity toward me, it never became apparent. I believe it was because my training and experience enabled me to handle my responsibilities in a way that gained his respect and that of everyone in the company.

In the year prior to my departure from Chicago, I had taken and passed the first of the two tests it was necessary for me to take in order to become a Chartered Financial Analyst (CFA). This is a program our national organization, the Financial Analysts Federation, had developed as we moved toward gaining national recognition as investment professionals. My final test was in June 1964. Obviously, the passing of this test was vitally important, not only for my investment stature in the company but in the community as well. My feeling of relief when I received a letter confirming my success is not difficult to understand. I was the 552nd person to become a CFA. Today there are 21,000 CFAs, and over 29,000 people will take one of the three tests in 1996. A CFA has also become a prestigious accomplishment for foreign investment analysts and portfolio managers.

When I took over my responsibilities at the St. Louis Union Trust Company, it was apparent to me that some of their investment policies were quite conservative for that particular period of time. They were still operating their pension accounts with about 30 to 35 percent in common stocks, and we were in the midst of a great bull market. We immediately moved to a more aggressive equity position, raised the percentage of common stocks in our pension accounts and became much more active money managers. They had been limiting their universe of companies to follow to about 125 big, well-known blue chip companies, most of which were growing slowly. Accordingly, one of my challenges was to broaden the list of common stocks so that we could operate more effectively and get better investment results over a period of time. The St. Louis Union's computer capabilities had some deficiencies, particularly as I compared them with The Northern where they had spared no expense to be completely up-to-date. For example, the St. Louis Union did not show the cost of securities on the reports that were shown to their customers. Dave Calhoun and Gene Williams agreed with my suggestion to update and authorized spending whatever money was required to improve our computer capabilities.

I had a good investment policy committee that functioned effectively and achieved good investment results. The members were: Carl Beckers, who headed up the investment advisory accounts; Ted Boswell, who headed up the personal trust accounts; John Weil, who headed up investment research; Harry Johnston, who was the number two man to Ted Boswell; and Tom Henson, who was the number two man in investment research. The only people on the committee were investment people, a policy I believed was mandatory if we were to be successful. One reason our committee achieved good investment results was simply that we had the leeway to do what we wanted to do without being thwarted by the lawyers and administrative people who, however well intentioned, were not trained to manage money.

In the early fall of 1964, I accompanied about 100 other investment analysts for a Financial Analysts Federation-sponsored trip to Europe. The St. Louis Union also had investments in companies located in Europe. Therefore, it was an opportunity for me to acquire more knowledge of investments in that area. The trip turned out to be a very important one for me because I developed contacts that proved to be quite valuable in later years. Some of the men and the companies they were with at the time were: Walter Stern (Burnham & Co.); Walter Oxley (Arnold S. Bleichroeder & Co.); Joseph Refsnes (he had his own firm in Phoenix, Arizona); Al Winter (Mercantile Bank & Trust Co.); and George Norton (The Continental Illinois Bank and Trust Company).

Family Life

One of the first decisions Mary and I had to make was about membership in a country club. Gene Williams believed we should join either Old Warson or Bellerive. Since our new home was only about a seven-minute drive to Bellerive, Mary and I opted for that club.

Membership in Bellerive Country Club meant a great deal to me because I wanted to play golf frequently. Since I knew so many corporate officers in St. Louis, it was very easy for me to find the opportunities to play golf with one or more people and use the club as a way of entertaining customers. For Mary, it was an entirely different situation. Most of the people whom I met from a business viewpoint already had established social relationships, so it was not easy for us to move into their social environment. At the same time, we never had the desire to push ourselves into social relationships. The membership in Bellerive during the nine years I was with the St. Louis Union Trust Company did not mean a great deal to Mary, although we did play together about once a weekend and ate at the club quite often. John got some use out of Bellerive, but there was a limit to how frequently he could take his friends to play with him. Accordingly, they also made good use of the public courses in the area. John and Lynne tried to develop friendships at Bellerive, but it simply did not work. One of the reasons was that they were going to Parkway (a public high school) while most of the kids whose parents belonged to the club either went to private schools or they lived in the Ladue or Clayton area and went to those schools.

We never seriously considered sending either John or Lynne to a private school. In John's case, we believed membership on the basketball team of a large public school would provide him with the opportunity to receive an athletic scholarship when he went to college. We also knew the Parkway school system was good and believed each of them would graduate with a good education.

The decision to buy the house in Colony Woods on Woodlark Lane was a very good one. We soon discovered there were several kids the same age as John and Lynne living in the neighborhood who were going to Parkway. There were three girls in the neighborhood in John's class, and Lynne developed a good friendship with one girl who lived about a half mile away. Mary and I soon came to know the people in Colony Woods as well as the parents of some of John and Lynne's friends. The Holekamps, Carl and Barbara, our next-door neighbors, were the greatest people in the world. Next to the Holekamps were Tom and Mary Evans, and directly across the street were John and Mary Dean Vickroy. Not long after we moved in, Frank and Sue Maddox became our other next-door neighbor. The Holekamps had a very good and close relationship with George and Marybill Andrews, who lived about a half mile away. Their daughter was in John's class, and before long, their family became an integral part of our neighborhood. They never missed seeing John play basketball. The Vickroys had a daughter in John's class and were good friends with Harry and Fran Hillary, who lived nearby and also had a daughter in the same class. Another couple we got to know very well was Jan and Elmer Boehm, parents of Barry, who was in the same class as John. Later, John and Barry went to DePauw University and were fraternity brothers and roommates.

Our neighbors became unbelievably meaningful to us, a situation that has never been duplicated. It was probably so special because many of them had children the same age as John and Lynne and several of the kids were in the same class together. Since we lived in the same neighborhood and had kids in the same school, it was a natural thing for the adults to get together periodically at someone's house for a wonderful evening or weekend afternoon.

Another part of our life in St. Louis was the church affiliation that we developed with the DesPeres Presbyterian Church, located not too far from where we lived. As a result of our membership in that church, we got to know some other couples, particularly Don and Betty Thomas, who had two daughters about Barbara's age. The church was a disappointment to us because it never became as meaningful to John and Lynne as we had hoped that it would. We had no good explanation except the belief the first minister (Richard Huey) lacked the ability to relate effectively to teenagers. When he left our church, he became the sales manager for a local automobile dealer.

Sometime in 1966 or 1967 when I believe Huey was still the minister, our church experimented, along with other churches in the St. Louis area, with a project aimed at bringing the inner city black churches and the suburban white churches in closer contact with each other. The idea was to alternate having volunteers from each church attend the other church ... and in that way, get to know each other better. One part of this program was for a work party to spend a Saturday providing maintenance help in an inner city apartment complex where many from the congregation lived. Accordingly over 100 of us spent the day painting hallways and repairing broken windows and doors. John accompanied me, and we spent the day painting hallways with many black women working alongside us. When you paint a door, it is necessary to leave it partially open until the paint dries. After painting many doorways, John and I became aware that black men were in almost every apartment watching television as we and the black women worked. Afterward, John and I concluded that something was fundamentally wrong with this project if the black men did not feel as if they were an integral part of the program. Since then, I have been very apprehensive about the advisability of white people doing the work that black people (or people of any minority) could and should do for themselves.

We terminated our membership in the DesPeres church after we had been members about six years when a new minister, Robert Tabscot, was brought in. Tabscot, a tall man about 6 feet 7 inches, had been a basketball player in college and was pretty effective from the podium. He encouraged and permitted different kinds of music, ecumenical services and various approaches to conducting a service. One time he had everybody walk outside on the lawn to have communion. Some of those things were interesting, but what turned us off was his political thinking. It became evident when McGovern was running for the presidency and Tabscot wore a McGovern button. At about the same time, Jim McKelvey, the minister of our church in Glen Ellyn, came to St. Louis as the minister of the Webster Hills United Methodist Church. The decision to transfer churches was easily made and implemented. About the time we left, several families (about 20) transferred to another Presbyterian church in the area.

Having been deeply involved in Kiwanis activities as president of the Glen Ellyn club in 1955, I continued my dedication to the organization in St. Louis. Other service organizations were providing answers in other areas of need, so in 1968 I joined the board of directors of Junior Achievement. During 1971 and 1972, I also served on the board of governors of the Deaconess Hospital Foundation.

Mary became quite active in the "Freedoms Foundation of Valley Forge" as vice president. She was prominently portrayed by *The St. Louis Globe Democrat* on February 3, 1968, when the newspaper devoted a full page to the cotillion sponsored by the organization. Most important to her was "SINAWIKS," an organization of Kiwanis wives. She became very active in their charity program and was president one year. However, it was the activities with our children, our friends in the neighborhood and in the office that enabled her to be completely satisfied with our way of life.

In the summer of 1967, we used two weeks of my vacation to see if we wanted to buy a farm within one hour's driving time from St. Louis. I was convinced farmland was a real bargain. Our search was thorough, and we found an ideal situation, about 170 acres at $80 per acre, for a cost of $23,600. One hundred acres were tillable, and the house was old, but well kept. Mary's prejudice against farms came through at decision time. We would have made some money with the farm, but that was irrelevant. Mary convinced me we would never spend a vacation or weekend at the farm.

The decision to buy a house at the Lake of the Ozarks was made in September 1967. In the summer of 1965, we had vacationed for one week down at the Lake with Lynne, John and Barbara, and we enjoyed it very much. Ken Eggers, a very good friend and a vice president at the St. Louis Union, mentioned to me that a house next to his at the Lake of the Ozarks was on the market. The owner was in bad health, and his wife wanted to sell and get the money out of the house. The real estate agent had been told to sell it, no matter what the price. This was on a Friday. On Saturday we went to the real estate agent, looked at the house and bought it for $22,000, including three boats and a rickety dock.

Not long after we were settled in St. Louis, a small, brown dog who looked as if he was starving and had probably been abandoned, wandered into our yard. Mary felt sorry for him, and, after he was fed, he claimed us as his new family. We named him Dutch even though Mary wanted to call him Dummy. At some time in the past, he must have been treated badly, for any sudden movement of your hands would scare him away. The only person he seemed to like was Mary, probably because she was the usual source of his food. His one great enjoyment was playing with the Holecamp's dog. He was only with us for two or three years, when he disappeared and never returned.

Even before we put up our St. Louis mailbox, John and I built a field goal for basketball along our driveway. There was no eighth grade team, so John had to wait for the ninth grade to play. He was a starter for the varsity team as a sophomore, junior and senior. In his senior year, Parkway's team won their way to the state tournament with a record of 25 wins and 5 losses. Unfortunately, they were eliminated in the quarter finals by the team (Sumner) that went on to win the tournament. Those three years of basketball were, for Mary and me, the most enjoyable years we had ever experienced since our marriage. Both of us loved watching basketball games, and there is nothing quite like watching your son excel in a sport that had always meant so much to you personally.

Another very special pleasure for us was having my nephew, Leonard Rhoda, as the assistant basketball coach of John's team at Parkway. Len had graduated from Calvin College in Grand Rapids, Michigan, where he had played basketball and majored in physical education. Len and Lee, his wife, had bought a house about five miles from where we lived, so we were in frequent contact with them.

John was an all-around team player. He was very good on

defense and on offense averaged about 12 points a game during his senior year. He had the opportunity to go to two medium-sized colleges on a scholarship basis but decided to go to DePauw University in Greencastle, Indiana, as a walk-on without a scholarship. He liked the size of the school and the idea of being with his friend Barry Boehm, who had decided on DePauw. Mary and I were disappointed, but nothing could change his mind. John and I met with the coach, and afterwards John believed he could make the team. He did accomplish that, and we were able to see three games, one of them being against the Purdue freshmen. The Andrews' daughter was at Purdue, so they accompanied us to Lafayette to see the game. We were thrilled and impressed with John's performance, which resulted in his being the high scorer in the game with 22 points.

The next summer he worked for Goldman Sachs, a leading investment banking firm headquartered in New York, in their downtown St. Louis office that was located near mine. We traveled together and, on the way home at night, stopped at the YMCA for a workout. He was playing well, and Mary and I were confident we would be traveling to Greencastle frequently during the next three years to see him play on the DePauw team. However, sometime in November of his sophomore year, we received a phone call from John telling us he had been cut from the team. We were shocked and disappointed, but, to our surprise, it did not seem to matter to him. He said he would be very happy playing on his fraternity's team and making sure he had good grades. During his senior year, John spent the first semester in Greece, following a summer touring Europe. If he had been on the basketball team, he could not have done this; so, as a result, he was probably better prepared for the future than he would have been by playing basketball.

Barbara graduated from Simpson College in May 1966 and was married on June 18, 1966, to Craig Carver, a fellow she had met in her sophomore year. Jim McKelvey had become pastor of the Methodist Church in Park Ridge, Illinois, after he left Glen Ellyn, and, since Barbara thought so much of him, we were willing to make the arrangements and somehow overcome the logistics in order to have the marriage in Park Ridge. It meant several five-hour car trips and many telephone calls to have a large wedding and nice reception. Craig was interested in becoming an investment analyst, perhaps to some extent through conversations with me and visits to the St. Louis Union Trust Company prior to graduation. They were both attracted to St. Louis, and I was in a position to assist him in finding a job in investment research with a highly regarded brokerage firm.

Their only child and our first grandchild, Mischelle Marie, was born December 16, 1967. They lived in a duplex until they bought Len and Lee Rhoda's house in the summer of 1969. Len and Lee were leaving St. Louis to move to Sioux Center, Iowa, where Len had accepted the opportunity to coach basketball and other sports at Dordt College. Mary was able to spend a great deal of time with Mischelle, whom we called Schelle since it was her grandmother's maiden name. Barbara, Craig and Schelle frequently joined us for weekends at the Lake of the Ozarks. Unfortunately for Mary and me, in the fall of 1971, Craig accepted an offer to be an investment analyst with Piper, Jaffery and Hopwood, a brokerage firm located in Minneapolis.

Lynne finished Parkway High School in 1967 and was accepted for admission to Southern Methodist University in Dallas, Texas. She had accompanied us to SMU several times during the years I was teaching there and had no difficulty in making the decision. During her freshman year, Lynne returned to St. Louis to make her debut in society. Shortly after we settled in St. Louis, I had joined the "Veiled Prophet" Organization, an exclusive yet rather large group of men who had inherited wealth or achieved some success and recognition in their careers. The group met monthly and sponsored two well-publicized functions. One was a Fourth of July parade, and the other was an annual ball for the debutantes who were daughters of members. The presentation to the "Prophet" was an elaborate and spectacular formal occasion followed by a very sumptuous late-night dinner. The committee selecting the "Queen" for the ball, as well as the Veiled Prophet, was an exclusive group whose membership was not disclosed to most members. The "Queen" when Lynne participated, was the daughter of my boss, Gene Williams.

During her sophomore year, Lynne decided to transfer to the University of Texas at Austin. She also decided her major subject would be Radio, Television and Film. Lynne liked the idea of being independent, so between her sophomore and junior years, we bought her a slightly used 1965 Ford Mustang, and I found a job for her that summer at the Bankers Trust Company in New York City. She worked in the foreign department and shared an apartment with a girl working at Time Inc. She climaxed her summer in New York by attending the "Woodstock" rock concert, which has received a tremendous amount of publicity over the years.

After she received her degree in 1971, she interviewed with several radio and TV stations but did not receive a job offer. She remained in Austin working on two different entrepreneurial endeavors begun while at the University of Texas. The first was the development of a comic book in cooperation with two other students. This project failed, although they did print one issue. Lynne had become interested in health foods and tried vegetarianism. Subsequently, when she was unable to find employment in her field of study, she decided to participate with some friends in a business venture baking and selling a natural bread that appealed to some people. This business failed when she came to the conclusion that her efforts, which included delivering the bread as well as finding a market, would not be successful without a more concentrated effort by her partners. Eventually, she was able to work for the Austin Community College in their media department.

Lynne was in school during the Vietnam War and, like so many other students, protested our country's actions. Mary and I, like so many of our generation, tended to believe our country could never be in the wrong. Accordingly and unfortunately, our relationship with Lynne was strained in many ways. We remained in contact with her when she was at the University of Texas and afterwards, but it was a stressful situation for several years.

After she abandoned her efforts in the bread business, Lynne and two girlfriends traveled to Mexico and later hitchhiked up the West Coast and visited my sister, Mary Grond, and other relatives in Oregon. When John graduated from DePauw University in May 1973,

Lynne was with us, and that summer she lived at our house at the Lake of the Ozarks. Late in the fall, she went back to Austin and while there renewed her friendship with Stephen Gooding, a student she had come to know at college. They were married on January 19, 1974, in Houston, Texas, his hometown. Barbara, Schelle, John, Mary and I attended, as did his parents and his brother, Scott.

In March 1967, Lynne had savings of $822.60, which I invested in the common stock of McDonald's. I was convinced the company would grow rapidly because we believed in what they were doing, and at that time, it was obvious the shares were greatly undervalued. When Lynne wanted a car after her sophomore year at SMU, we bought it with money from her McDonald's stock. Her McDonald's stock also paid for her two years at the University of Texas. She needed about $1,000 to print the comic book produced in the business venture with her friends. After she and Steve were married, they bought a truck for about $2,000, and again, the funds were provided from the investment in McDonald's stock. She and Steve decided to buy a house in Austin, Texas, in 1975, and fortunately she still owned about $4,000 of McDonald's. The house was priced at $20,000, and her remaining shares of McDonald's provided the down payment. Less than two years later they sold the house for $36,000, which meant the $4,000 had become approximately $20,000. That $822.60 investment of Lynne's savings had worked very hard for our family in the eight-year period beginning March 1967.

John's savings in March 1967 when he was a sophomore in high school amounted to $1,105.36, all of which was invested in 27 shares of McDonald's. On January 31, 1972, the value of his investment was $14,580. McDonald's stock was then selling at $90 per share and he owned 162 shares. At this time, John had completed the first semester of his junior year in college. Twenty shares of McDonald's, or $1,800, paid for the cost of his second semester. In June 1972, McDonald's split and distributed two shares for each share held. John then held 284 shares that had a value of $23,040 at the beginning of his senior year. Eighty-four shares covered his expenses during his senior year so, upon graduation in 1973, John owned 200 shares. He then entered into a hotel-resort management training program at the Lodge of the Four Seasons. He liked the idea because he could live at our house at the Lake of the Ozarks. Within a few months, he was quite disillusioned with the ethics of the business, so in September 1974, he returned to St. Louis and entered the graduate business program at St. Louis University. The bear market from January 1973 to September 1974 had reduced the value of his 200 shares of McDonald's to $60 per share and a value of $12,000, but it was enough to pay for his two years at St. Louis University.

In May 1976, he received his MBA degree and married Mary Susan Skipton on June 11, 1976, in Susan's hometown of Pontiac, Illinois. It was a large church wedding with several of our relatives and friends traveling some distance to be with us. Susan had earned her M.S. degree in speech therapy from Illinois State University, and when they decided to live in St. Louis, Susan was employed by the Special School District in St. Louis County to teach handicapped students. John then began his career as a lending officer with the Commerce Bank in downtown St. Louis.

In 1970 we made the decision to move from Colony Woods. I was getting more and more upset with the length of time it took me to get to work. Frequently the traffic delays, particularly in the winter or in rainy weather, resulted in it taking me more than an hour to get to or from work. Mary went along with my decision so, early in 1970, we began to look around for a house closer to downtown St. Louis. Quite unwisely, we placed our house on the market without any limits on occupancy so that, when it was sold, we had to move quickly on the purchase of a new home. Fortunately we liked a house in an area called York Hills, near the corner of Highway 40 and McKnight Road. We had sold our house for $64,000 and bought this one for $35,000, but it needed a lot of work. We lived in it for a little over two years, and during that time, spent another $35,000 on the house, finishing off the basement, putting on a deck, redoing the kitchen cabinets and taking down a wall to enable us to have a very large recreation room. It turned out to be a very beautiful home, and we were very happy with it. Since it was much closer to work, I was happier with the travel time. However, we realized after we had made the move, we had given up something very precious to us, the proximity to the people in and around Colony Woods. The new neighborhood had no interest in us.

During 1971 I almost went to New York to work with a man by the name of Ralph Creesman, the president of Lionel D. Edie & Company, an investment advisory firm with about $6 billion under management. Ralph had been with The Northern Trust Company, having started about a year after I did. We had played together on the bank's basketball team, so we had come to know each other very well. He wanted me because he was interested in retiring early and needed to bring someone in to take over for him. The offer aroused my interest, so with his encouragement, Mary went with me to New York to explore the housing situation. After much thought, we agreed I should accept his offer to go to New York and be a part of his organization as executive vice president, with the understanding I would become the president in a relatively short period of time. The salary was $100,000 with a nice bonus and 5,000 shares of Merrill Lynch stock that I would buy on a book value basis. The Merrill Lynch stock was available because they were in the process of buying (but not attempting to manage) Lionel D. Edie. I accepted on a Friday, but Mary and I spent the weekend at the Lake of the Ozarks feeling miserable about leaving the Midwest. When I got back to St. Louis on Sunday night, I called Ralph at home and told him I wanted to renege on my decision to come with him. He understood, and we stayed in St. Louis.

Business Life

I became the president of the St. Louis Society of Financial Analysts in the fall of 1968. Normally the presidency comes through a stairstep progression in which one is secretary, treasurer and then program chairman before becoming president. The society moved me ahead because it wanted me in charge in 1969, the year it was going to have the national conference of the Financial Analysts Federation. I enjoyed the challenge of being program chairman and president of the society and, most importantly, having the responsibility of organizing for the national conference. I was motivated entirely by the desire to have our society respected for its ability, and, by doing this, it undoubtedly became a factor in my becoming the chairman of the Financial Analysts Federation several years later. My first step in that direction was my election to the board of directors of the Financial Analysts Federation for the years 1972 and 1973. This honor was well publicized on both a local basis and nationally. It came to me as a result of my position at the St. Louis Union Trust Company, my presidency of the St. Louis Society of Financial Analysts, the publication of some articles I had written, and my participation in seminars and trust conferences that resulted in my becoming well known to my peers in the investment industry.

The Dale Carnegie course that I took in 1947 began to pay off, as I was frequently invited to speak before various civic clubs and other organizations in St. Louis. Also, the First National Bank had one large conference each year for its customers; my talk on the outlook for the stock market and interest rates was always one of the features. Most of the time, my speech topics were about the investment environment and outlook, but, at times, the audience was only interested in a discussion of economic developments.

Roland Behrens had set the precedent of taking a trip to Europe each year to make a survey of European economies. This was done for the benefit of the board of directors of the First National Bank and the St Louis Union whose member companies did a great deal of business in Europe and valued an unbiased report. I made the trip with him in 1965 and later by myself, until I asked Ed Anderson, my right-hand man, to accompany me in 1968. In 1966 the St. Louis Union published my report, entitled "1966 European Economic Report." We also published the report in 1968 when it was coauthored with Ed Anderson. The St. Louis Union also published a pamphlet I wrote in 1968, entitled "Performance Achievement for Pension and Profit Sharing Funds." In February 1967, I wrote an article for the *Missouri Business* magazine, entitled "The Outlook for Common Stocks." The *Trust and Estate* magazine asked for articles from me, so in January 1969, I wrote on "Common Stocks in Tax-Free Funds" and in March 1972 on "Investment Strategy."

William Kester, financial editor of the *St. Louis Post Dispatch*, and Ted Schafers, financial editor of the *St. Louis Globe Democrat*, both quoted me frequently in their articles on the stock and bond markets. In addition to my speeches at the First National Bank's annual conferences, which were the basis for newspaper comments, my other speeches frequently received coverage. The following is a list of most of my talks:

1. The Kiwanis Club of Downtown St. Louis, July 14, 1966, "The Common Market and You."
2. The Optimists Club in St. Louis, December 15, 1966, "The Stock Market."
3. The Institute of Internal Auditors, St. Louis, January 12, 1967, "The Economic Outlook for 1967."
4. The Trust Conference for Missouri Banks, Columbia, Missouri, March 20, 1968, "National Economic Crisis and Investments."
5. The Arkansas Bankers Association, Hot Springs, Arkansas, April 1968, "Investing in Current Market Conditions."
6. The Kiwanis Club of Downtown St. Louis, June 27, 1968, "Investing in Common Stocks Today."
7. The National Association of Investment Clubs, Chicago, Illinois, October 19, 1968, "An Investment Strategy for Today's Market."
8. A seminar on estate building, St. Louis University, October 30, 1968, "Investing an Estate: Sound Investment Policy."
9. The 37th Mid-Continent Trust Conference, Detroit, Michigan, December 6, 1968, "Common Stock Policies in Tax-Free Funds."
10. Pet Inc.'s annual management meeting, St. Louis, February 19, 1969, "Economic Overview."
11. Washington University Financial Investments Seminar, St. Louis, February 28, 1969, "Current Problems and Opportunities in Security Analysis."

12. Indiana State University Ninth Annual Investment Conference, Terra Haute, Indiana, March 13, 1969, "An Investment Strategy for Today's Market."

13. The Scottish Rite Club of St. Louis, December 18, 1969, "Investing in Common Stocks Today."

14. The St. Louis Club, August 20, 1970, "Timely Analysis in Today's Economy: Stocks, Bonds or Real Estate."

15. The Hannibal, Missouri, Rotary Club, September 21, 1970, "The Outlook for Common Stock Prices and Interest Rates."

16. The Scottish Rite Club of St. Louis, October 27, 1971, "European Reaction to President Nixon's Recent International Proposals."

17. The 45th Western Trust Conference, Denver, Colorado, September 25, 1971, "The Investment Outlook."

18. Saint Louis University Estate Building and Management Forum, October 17, 1971, "Fiduciary Investment Problems."

19. 40th Mid-Continent Trust Conference, Dallas, Texas, November 12, 1971, "Fiduciary Investment Problems."

20. California Bankers Association Conference on Trust Investments in San Francisco, December 2, 1971, "Investment Strategy."

21. The Financial Analysts Federation Conference, Cincinnati, Ohio, October 9, 1972, "What is the Real Function of the Analyst?"

The first time I was interviewed to be quoted in a national magazine was by the *Institutional Investor* in May 1971, when they quoted me in an article on, "What Top Trust Men are Doing." Prior to May 1, 1971, the commissions charged by stock brokers on trades were controlled but at exorbitant rates. The profits made by brokers on large trades (many thousands of shares in one execution) were ridiculous. For years all of us involved with big transactions did everything we could to obtain extra services from the brokers. Most of us were quoted in the article saying we could easily adjust to fewer services and were delighted with the lower costs. The lowest commission rates soon settled to around five cents per share.

In February 1973, the *Institutional Investor* magazine ran a lead article on "The Northern Trust Alumni Association." It was extremely flattering to eight of us and paid some well-deserved respect to Art O'Hara, our guiding investment genius.

One of the newspaper articles I value the most was an interview with Eugene Williams, our president, by Ted Schafers on October 6, 1972. I had prepared the material for Gene, and, in addition to a chart portraying our superior performance, Ted made this comment, "The Trust Company's performance would make many mutual funds managers green with envy. In each area, St. Louis Union's assets consistently have outperformed the Dow Jones Industrial Average since 1965."

At various times in the late 1960s and early 1970s, the senior management of the First National Bank in St. Louis and St. Louis Union Trust Company gave considerable thought to the advisability of consolidating the two organizations and eliminating the common stock ownership of the "Bank" that was held by the "Trust Company." This ownership was not meaningful from a management viewpoint since both corporations operated independently and cooperated in any endeavor where it was logical to work together.

For a variety of reasons, including the decision to acquire small banks throughout the state, a merger plan was consummated with a holding company, First Union Inc., created on July 1, 1969, which owned 100 percent of the common stock of each corporation. I was given the title and responsibilities of treasurer. The board of directors was small in number and had equal representation from the boards of the "Bank" and "Trust Company."

My primary responsibility as treasurer was to arrange for additional capital in the form of $15 million eight percent debentures maturing in eight years. This responsibility gave me the proper credentials for becoming a member of the Financial Executives Institute. I was eager to belong to this organization because it would bring me into close contact with the chief financial officers of most of the larger corporations in St. Louis, as well as some of the smaller and medium-sized companies. My membership became effective on July 19, 1972.

Leaving The St. Louis Union Trust Company

My decision to leave the St. Louis Union Trust Company was also a difficult one, for Mary and I had again planted our roots with the intention never to leave the company. However, for a variety of reasons, I was not happy. Because of the size and nature of our accounts, which included the endowment funds for big civic organizations, most of the corporate pension accounts in the St. Louis area as well as large personal trusts, I had gradually drifted into a client service mode in which most of my time was spent holding the hands of our customers. What I mean by hand-holding is that I was expected to attend all the customers' meetings, at which I would discuss the economic environment and the outlook for interest rates and the stock market. The portfolio manager I had assigned to the account would talk about the individual securities in the portfolio. Actually, either alone or with someone, this is what I had been doing ever since I started to manage personal trust accounts at The Northern Trust Company in 1949. By 1973 this part of my responsibilities was beginning to be boring and was not a challenge.

Still, that was not the most important reason for my unrest. Most important was that the salary policies at the St. Louis Union Trust Company made it difficult for me to attract the kind of people who could achieve superior investment results, particularly when I was spending more time away from deep involvement in the investment decision process. My concerns were accentuated when Ed Anderson decided to leave, not because of his salary but for personal reasons. When he left in 1970 and I was faced with the need for a replacement, I had no alternative but to go to the outside, and, in doing so, there were limitations on what I could pay for new talent. Fortunately, I was successful in attracting a very capable fellow, Jack Ellis, from United Denver Bank, who did a good job of filling Ed Anderson's shoes. However, I still felt constrained to employ other new people with only bachelor's degrees or people who had not been very successful from a financial viewpoint. The result was that I was beginning to worry about our ability to create above-average performance.

Finally, most important to me was the realization that I would not become president of the company. I had a good working relationship with Gene Williams and Dave Calhoun and knew they had great respect for me and for what I was doing. At first I believed that, with my years of experience in the trust business, I would become president if Gene Williams decided to relinquish that responsibility. In 1971 Dave Calhoun and Gene Williams made the decision to bring John Peters McCarthy, a lawyer, into the company as senior vice president. Peter was very capable, and it soon became apparent to me that Peter would become the one to succeed Gene. I added this to all the other things disturbing me and made the decision to be open-minded about other opportunities.

When I let it be known outside our company in late 1972 that I would make a move, opportunities developed that resulted in three attractive alternatives. One was to go to the Security Pacific Bank in Los Angeles as the chief investment officer. There were lots of good things about the situation, but I believed the bank management's attitude toward its trust department was too conservative and would adversely affect my ability to function effectively. Also, I did not want to move to the West Coast. Second, I very seriously considered taking a position with the International Telephone and Telegraph Company (ITT). I made several trips to New York to consider their situation and went through a whole battery of psychological tests given to people to see whether they can handle major responsibilities. My job would have been to supervise and establish investment policies for all of their investment operations on a worldwide basis. This included the Hamilton Group of Mutual Funds headquartered in Denver; the Hartford Fire Insurance Company located in Hartford, Connecticut; various mutual funds in England; and various insurance companies around the world. It was an interesting situation, and they were offering an annual salary of $125,000. I would have had to spend about a quarter of my time out of the country, an important negative, but I still seriously considered the ITT job. The discussion with them mutually broke down because of concern with some legal considerations having to do with their control of Hartford Fire Insurance Company. Specifically, it looked as if the parent company could not exercise investment control over Hartford. Without that, the job was not attractive.

The third opportunity was to join Waddell & Reed in Kansas City as executive vice president and chief investment officer. My decision to accept that offer was based on the following considerations:

1. My annual salary would increase from $60,000 to $95,000, with a large bonus potential.

2. Kansas City was beautiful, and I would not have to leave the Midwest or give up our home at the Lake of the Ozarks.

3. The parent company, Continental Investment Corporation, was located in Boston, and I would be reporting to Richard Roberts, an investment man whom I had known and respected in Chicago and who assured me that I would have control of all investment decisions.

4. As the manager of the company's United Group of Mutual Funds, I could achieve national recognition as a money manager.

5. I would be in a position to spend all my time making investment decisions and would no longer be spending several hours each day talking about investments with customers. I relished this aspect of the new job.

6. Waddell & Reed's investment results had been mediocre, so I would be given the opportunity to do something worthwhile for hundreds of thousands of small investors.

7. Because of the loss of my retirement benefits (I was 52), I would be provided with a supplemental pension equal to what I would have to give up at the St. Louis Union Trust Company.

8. I would be provided with a membership in a country club of my choice.

9. I would be in a growth environment where I would only be judged on the basis of my ability.

10. And, as was expected, Mary was perfectly willing once again to adjust to a new life and find new friends.

The plan was not to let the person I was replacing know of the decision until the Friday before I reported on Monday. I knew that, whether I or someone else took the position, nothing could help him. I also knew they were going to treat him very well from a financial viewpoint. Nevertheless, it was not a pleasant part of the move.

When I made the decision to move and announced it, Dave and Gene were very unhappy. Dave Calhoun asked me into his office and offered to pay me more money. Gene was courteous, as were the other officers, but I know they felt that I was letting them down. There were no farewell parties or gifts. Gene, Hugh Logan and Peter McCarthy did take me to lunch on my last day. After I left, they brought in one new person, gave parts of my responsibilities to Tom Henson and Harry Johnston, and created a triumvirate to manage the investment operation. Two of the senior people who had been with me left shortly after I departed: Jack Ellis, to join the Security Pacific Bank, and John Weil, to take over the management of his family's investments.

When we moved to Kansas City, we did not lose all our ties to St. Louis. In October 1968, I had joined the board of directors of Roosevelt Federal Savings and Loan Association, a $109 million institution headquartered in St. Louis. Two other local businessmen joined me as new members at the same time. They were Clarence M. Turley, Jr., and Brice R. Smith, Jr., both sons of men who had been members for many years. Walter Bolliger was the president and had assumed those responsibilities as successor to George Metcalfe, the founder. Metcalfe's son, James, was a member of the board. Walter Bolliger invited me to be a member as a result of our friendship that developed from our activities in the Kiwanis Club of Downtown St. Louis. The management of St. Louis Union Trust Company and the First National Bank in St. Louis did not object to my board membership, because the deposit base was very small in comparison with the First National.

For many years, my responsibilities as director were not very demanding. Roosevelt operated as a typical S & L with the most important decisions those related to the more substantial real estate loans. When I made the decision to move to Kansas City, I made continuation of my relationship with Roosevelt a part of my responsibilities at Waddell & Reed. At that time I was enjoying my friendships with the other board members and believed I was making a meaningful contribution to the responsibilities of the board.

CHAPTER 11

◆

Managing Mutual Fund Money

I started to work in Kansas City April 1, 1973, without any vacation or time off between the two jobs. I worked on Friday at the St. Louis Union Trust Company, drove over by myself on the weekend and, on Monday morning, started at Waddell & Reed. Once again I had potentially difficult personnel problems because my predecessor had been terminated without advance notice. However, as I learned later, neither he nor his staff at Waddell & Reed were surprised. The senior people in the investment division had used their telephones Friday to call their contacts on Wall Street and, as a result, already knew a great deal about me. Late the first day, I called a meeting of the staff to discuss my investment philosophy and give them the opportunity to get to know me. I made sure they knew I intended to be actively involved in the management of the funds but had no intention of making changes in the organization. I had been provided with background information on each person in the department and emphasized how impressed I was with the capability of the analysts and portfolio managers.

The company had made arrangements for me to stay in an apartment in the downtown area and paid for my commuting on weekends. Mary and I had made the decision not to live in an apartment and wanted to buy a house as quickly as possible. Mary came almost immediately, stayed at the Alameda Plaza Hotel and, in eleven days, went through the offerings of six different real estate agents. On the last day before she was temporarily going to give up the search, the opportunity came to buy the house at 8515 Cherokee Place. She called me at the office just before noon; we looked at the house for about an hour; and within another hour, our offer of $74,500, their asking price, was in the hands of the sellers. They accepted immediately. We had decided not to negotiate because we knew it was a good buy. It was about the same amount of money we had in the house in St. Louis, but it was not as good a house. It had a nicer lot but did not have a finished basement. We did that later at a cost of about $20,000. So, in effect, we ended up going into a more expensive house in a more expensive neighborhood, about a 25-minute drive and 10 miles from the office.

We moved into the house on June 15, 1973. Our next-door neighbors were Ockie and Gwyn Minnick; shortly after we moved in, they offered to sponsor us as members of Indian Hills Country Club. I was also interested in the Mission Hills Country Club, but there was an indication it would take some time to become members. Since we lived much closer to Indian Hills, the decision was an easy one, and we were accepted in the fall. Perhaps it was not as prestigious a club as Bellerive, but we sensed that Indian Hills was the kind of club in which it would be very easy to get to know people. We were not mistaken. We also retained a nonresident membership at Bellerive in the belief my trips to St. Louis to attend the board of directors meetings of Roosevelt Savings and Loan Association would provide us with opportunities to use the club.

My Money Management System

From April 1, 1973, to June 6, 1974, when I became president of the company, I was very busy introducing and implementing my approach toward managing money. And, as I had planned, I became

To my Relatives and Friends,

I hope you enjoy reading this record of my personal and business life. Perhaps the Epilogue will also be of value to you.

This is my gift to you, so please do not feel obligated to write or call me. The book was Mary's idea, and it was a very satisfying way to keep busy since her death in 1988.

With my best wishes,
Cal Korschot

deeply involved in decisions about the buying and selling of individual securities. To do this, I set up a structure in which all the managers provided investment recommendations to me prior to any implementation. Since the staff was very capable, I employed a flexible, yet disciplined, system. The portfolio managers could not be inhibited, but at the same time, I made sure all decisions were coordinated and consistent with our objectives. There are numerous facets to the money management approach I had developed over the years, so it was very gratifying for me to have the staff accept my beliefs and work very hard to implement them. First, however, I should comment on a very important investment timing concept they had in their hands but was not being utilized.

The Central Value Index

During the years from 1947 to 1973, I conducted various kinds of research to develop an approach toward making the most important decision one can make in managing money, namely, to buy and hold common stocks under all market conditions or to set up reserves at market peaks and reinvest near the bottoms of bear markets. In the 1940s and 1950s, much publicity was given to what were called "Formula Timing Plans." I had studied them at the University of Chicago and taught them at DePaul University. While at The Northern Trust Company, I personally took on the responsibility of heading up that kind of research. As I mentioned earlier, one of my studies was made for the Retirement System of the Federal Reserve Banks.

We never installed a system at either The Northern Trust Company or St. Louis Union Trust Company for several reasons. Most important was simply that the stock market from 1947 to 1972 was not very volatile and was in a strong upward trend that made timing the market hazardous. But the bear markets in the 1969–1970 period and, again starting in 1973, indicated to me that timing the market was once again relevant. Also, the ability to move quickly in all accounts at one time was vitally important. In a mutual fund organization, this could be done, whereas the diversity and number of accounts in a trust department made efficient implementation almost impossible.

Shortly after I arrived at Waddell & Reed, I became aware that Murray Sweet, an analyst who had retired and was working part-time, had developed a system that was close to the approach I had developed, but even better. My predecessor did not believe in Murray's system, but the staff was always interested in his thoughts. As soon as I understood his calculations, I felt as if we had the so-called "pot of gold" in our hands. Accordingly, as the bear market in 1973 gained momentum, we became increasingly aggressive in our use of reserves. In retrospect we should have been more aggressive. However, its implementation even on a modest scale helped our performance in the decline in 1973 and 1974, and, when the market bottomed out in December 1974, we were fully invested. From then until I retired in 1986, the "Central Value Index," the name of our system, was an integral part of our investment philosophy.

Selecting Individual Securities

While at the St. Louis Union Trust Company, I developed a system of evaluating the quality and growth characteristics of individual stocks. It was, and is, a logical approach toward putting together a portfolio of common stocks so that one can have a high degree of confidence in how individual stocks and the whole portfolio will perform. Each stock was evaluated on a quality basis (synonymous with risk) and placed in four categories graded either A, B, C or D. The A companies were less risky and more predictable. Those rated lower, such as C or D, were generally either cyclical companies or younger companies, with greater risk characteristics. Each stock was also rated in terms of the growth potential and placed in four categories ranging from 1 to 4; that is, from higher to lower growth potential. Accordingly, a stock rated D-1 was a volatile, high-risk, fast-growing company. An A-4 would be of high quality but slower in its growth potential. Strict criteria were used to establish these ratings. Our objective was to use the risk and growth characteristics of individual stocks as a way to structure a portfolio in accordance with its objectives. We could change the diversification of the portfolio as economic and business developments changed the outlook for different kinds of companies.

Evaluating The Performance Of Investment Analysts

I had also developed a system of measuring the performance of investment analysts but had not installed it in a rigid manner at the St. Louis Union Trust Company. Almost immediately I placed it in operation at Waddell & Reed, and with some minor modifications, it was well received by the staff. The system received national recognition by other investment organizations when it was published in the *Financial Analysts Journal* in August 1978.

The system is a complicated one because analysts operating in different industries face challenges that are dissimilar, and this must be taken into consideration. However, every analyst endeavors to select stocks for purchase or sale that will perform better than other stocks in the same industry as well as in the stock market generally. Accordingly, the system measures performance against both objectives. The performance figures for individual industries are available from the Standard and Poor's Corporation. Their 500-stock index is used by almost all investment organizations as the best performance measure of the stock market as a whole.

The time period over which an analyst should be measured is a vitally important factor. If a very short time frame is used, analysts would be required to make very short-term decisions that could not be consistent with the objectives of portfolio managers. Too long a time period would also not be very helpful to portfolio managers. Accordingly, we used approximately 12 months as a logical time frame in which to measure whether an analyst's recommendation was a good one.

Measuring the analyst also included comparing each one with the others in the organization in order to decide on the size of bonuses and salary increases. As the chief investment officer, this system made it very easy for me to be logical and fair-minded in evaluating the performance of analysts. They never complained about how they were being treated with salary increases and bonuses.

Measuring The Performance Of Fund Managers

Waddell & Reed had a system in place for measuring the performance of fund managers, but it was severely flawed. Accordingly, I devised a system that was well received. Specifically, each fund manager's performance was evaluated in four ways. One was how well each performed in comparison with the S&P 500-stock index. A second but even more important measurement was how well they performed against a universe of 11 or 12 other mutual funds managed by other organizations. These funds had to be comparable in size and with similar investment objectives. Each fund manager worked with me in developing the universe of other funds and, as a result, felt very comfortable with the fairness of how he or she was being judged. Both comparisons had time frames of one and three years, so that four sets of calculations were produced for each fund. The two time periods had the objective of making sure the fund manager never lost sight of the importance of both short-term and long-term results. Both salary changes and bonus payments depended upon the success of the portfolio managers. In effect they were in complete charge of their own destiny. During the 14 years the program was in place, not one portfolio manager objected to my conclusions. The maximum bonus was 50 percent of base salary; however, it was exceeded on a judgmental basis when a portfolio consistently ranked number one in its competition with the other portfolio managers in the universe of 11 or 12 other funds.

CHAPTER 12

◆

Taking Over As President Of Waddell & Reed

The problems of our parent company, Continental Investment Corporation (CIC), were largely associated with the tremendous amount of bank debt it had assumed when Waddell & Reed was acquired in 1968. CIC had paid $82 million for Waddell & Reed with bank loans from 16 banks around the country. Before I arrived, part of the debt had been refinanced with a convertible debenture issue that was very poorly conceived and ultimately became a problem for the company. CIC had to get rid of the issue and accomplished that early in 1974 by converting it into a straight debenture obligation. CIC desperately needed to refinance its bank debt, which was tied to the prime rate. As the prime rate was rising in 1974, the interest cost on the debt CIC owed to the banks was escalating rapidly.

Several other serious events, combined with the higher cost of the bank debt, forced CIC eventually to default on the bank debt. One was the severe collapse of the stock market in 1974 that reduced the earnings from Waddell & Reed. At the same time, high interest rates caused a collapse of CIC's earnings from one of the subsidiaries, a very large real estate investment trust. For a while early in 1974, I worked unsuccessfully with CIC's management on a private deal in which Prudential Insurance Company would have loaned CIC $20 million of longer-term debt; the proceeds would have been used to reduce the bank debt. The CIC and Waddell & Reed managements also considered whether Waddell & Reed's sales organization could sell a CIC long-term debenture obligation as a way of raising capital and retiring bank debt.

However, all attempts to consider a reduction in the bank debt were abandoned because of the uncertainty over the outcome of legal action that had been started in 1972 against CIC and Waddell & Reed's brokerage firm, Kansas City Securities Corporation. Several years before I joined Waddell & Reed, the managements of CIC, Waddell & Reed and Kansas City Securities Corporation had established a formula for allocating commission dollars (obtained by managing the mutual funds) to both the mutual funds and to Waddell & Reed. The Securities and Exchange Commission (SEC) sued the company on behalf of the shareholders of the mutual funds. In addition, a class action suit was filed on behalf of investors by Pomerantz, Levy, Haudek & Block, a law firm headed by Abraham L. Pomerantz. Their actions were based on their beliefs that all the commissions belonged to the mutual funds. With these legal actions hanging over the company in 1973 and early 1974, there was no way CIC could do any financing to get out from underneath the bank debt. The situation continued to deteriorate throughout the early part of 1974.

When I joined Waddell & Reed, I knew they were looking for a new president with a marketing background. In July 1973, John Kostmayer joined us as president of Waddell & Reed. John had been a group vice president of International Telephone and Telegraph Company and had come to Waddell & Reed in the belief he had enough money behind him to do whatever he needed to do. Consequently, he immediately began a program of bringing in people from the outside and, in a period of about six or seven months, brought in about eight people. He did not displace anyone internally, so we ended up with a larger organization with lots of salary costs at a time when Waddell &

Reed's earnings were beginning to deteriorate as the stock market declined. When I had first thought of joining Waddell & Reed, the assets under management were about $2.7 billion. When I did join on March 31, 1973, the amount was close to $2.3 billion. By the low point of the market in September 1974, our assets only amounted to $1.3 billion. This meant a sharp decline in Waddell & Reed's earnings, because earnings of a mutual fund company are tied to its fees and the fees are based on the market value of the assets in the mutual funds.

I received a telephone call from Dick Roberts, executive vice president of CIC, early in June asking me if I would meet with him; Sam Marinella, CIC president; and Julius (Reb) Jensen III, the number two man in CIC, in Chicago on June 4, 1974. I did not know what was going to happen, so I went with some apprehension. When I met with them, Sam Marinella told me they were on their way to Kansas City to ask John to resign. They emphasized cost cutting and asked me if I believed costs could be reduced. I had been observing our expenditures and told them much could be done. No dollar amounts were mentioned. He then asked me to accept the presidency of Waddell & Reed. I was also told that Steve Beckman, a part of the management team at CIC, would become president of Waddell & Reed's life insurance subsidiary, United Investors Life Insurance Company. This was very acceptable to me because the special nature of the insurance business was certainly an area where I had no expertise.

I made the decision to become president for a variety of reasons, despite never having planned on the responsibility. I had no reservations about my ability to handle the job and knew they needed my capabilities. Financially, there was not much change. My salary increased from $95,000 to $110,000; I was given a stock option for 5,000 shares of CIC common stock at $2.25 per share; and the promise of bonuses and an improvement in salary when the financial position of the company improved sufficiently. Kostmayer had an annual salary of $100,000 with a guaranty of another $50,000 as an annual bonus, which I later learned he had been willing to eliminate in his efforts to cut costs at Waddell & Reed.

When we arrived at the office the next morning, Marinella, Jensen and Roberts went in John's office and were there for several hours. Later I was told John would not resign voluntarily, so they discharged him. When John was terminated, Jack Enright, who was John's number two man and president of our life insurance subsidiary, United Investors Life Insurance Company, was also terminated. He had just moved to Kansas City a couple of months earlier. I stayed in my office, and later that day, Bob Strader, who was executive vice president in charge of our marketing department, and Richard Mitchell, who was executive vice president as well as our chief financial and operating officer, came to my office to discuss what had happened. Richard Mitchell immediately said very emphatically that he thought he should have had the job. I felt badly for him but could only express the hope that we could work together. There was no question in my mind about Bob Strader cooperating with me, but Richard Mitchell's plans and feelings were unclear.

I also had a conversation that day with Ed Delaney, the general counsel of Waddell & Reed, who had been brought in by John Kostmayer. Ed made a very specific point of saying how unhappy he was with Kostmayer's departure. It was apparent I was starting off with a very bad personal relationship with our general counsel, even though I had not been involved in any way with what had happened.

The Presidency Of The United Group Of Mutual Funds

It is my understanding that John Kostmayer was interested and willing to remain on the board of the United Group of Mutual Funds. I knew the board of directors had respected him and, for that reason, might want him to stay on the board as president of the United Group. Arrangements were made for the board of directors to meet with John the day before their next board meeting to discuss his situation. I do not know what transpired at that meeting, but, at the board meeting the next morning, John resigned as president of the United Group of Mutual Funds. Needless for me to say, I was highly honored when I was asked to become a member of the board and the president of the United Group.

During the first few weeks with my new responsibilities as president of Waddell & Reed, it became obvious to me that Ed Delaney's personality and my personality could not blend together in the kind of relationship the president of a corporation should have with his general counsel. It was also apparent to me that Ed was concerned about, and unhappy with, how we were getting along. I expressed my concerns about our incompatibility to the board of directors of the United Group of Mutual Funds, so they met privately with Ed and advised me that they agreed our personalities did conflict with each other. Subsequently, Ed resigned, returned to Washington D.C. and joined a prestigious law firm where he continued to specialize in the mutual fund industry. Ed was, and I believe still is, a highly regarded and capable mutual fund lawyer.

Cutting Costs

It had been easy for me to say I could cut costs, but doing it was difficult. Our management team (myself, Steve Beckman, Richard Mitchell, Bob Strader, Wayne Miller and Robert Heckler) approached it from the top down. We had to maintain morale and ease the fears that existed at all levels of employees in every department. So we acted quickly and, during the last two weeks in July, terminated the men whom John had employed. Another development was the resignation of William Reasoner, the man who had been president when I joined the company. When John Kostmayer had joined the company, Bill had assumed the position of vice chairman of the board of Waddell & Reed. Bill Reasoner was very much aware of our need to control expenses and believed it was logical for him to resign. Another departure was Sherman Jones, a very capable man, who was responsible for executing all securities transactions and had established our securities trading company, Kansas City Securities Corporation. Sherm was not surprised when I approached him, and we parted as good friends. He recognized that, under my money management system, there would be a greatly reduced level of trading activity and a corresponding decline in the need for his expertise. There were just a few people in operations, the computer programming area, marketing and accounting whose services appeared redundant. By the end of July our salary costs had been reduced by about $1.5 million. We paid generous termination fees by giving people from one month to even six months of pay depending on the circumstances. It was an unpleasant experience, but we fulfilled our responsibilities and placed the company in a position to operate in a very lean, yet still capable, manner.

Working With The SEC

A good relationship with the Securities and Exchange Commission (SEC) in the early months of my presidency was a vitally important challenge. I was called to Washington within a month after I became president to meet with the SEC to prove that we had enough capital to continue in business. Their concerns were created when, on June 30, 1974, CIC, in its attempt to stay solvent, had drawn virtually all of Waddell & Reed's cash to Boston. Dick Mitchell believed we were still fulfilling our minimum capital requirements, but our position was questionable. So Dick Mitchell, Bob Hechler (Dick's assistant), Rod McWhinney (our assistant general counsel) and I from Waddell & Reed, and Mitchell Valicenti, our legal counsel in New York, met with the SEC. When we walked into the meeting, there must have been 30 people from the SEC sitting around the room. They obviously thought Waddell & Reed, one of the biggest of the mutual funds complexes, was on the verge of collapse. We went into a lengthy discussion of our capital position and the reasons why Waddell & Reed was operating profitably. Since we had a net cash inflow, we knew our capital position could improve in a relatively short period of time if we did not send more money to CIC. So, what started out as a meeting with involvement by almost every department of the SEC ended about three hours later, with just a handful of SEC people present as we worked out the final terms of an agreement.

Sid Mendelson was the SEC person responsible for monitoring the mutual fund industry. He and I developed a good personal relationship as a result of that meeting. I promised him two things: one, that we would send no money to CIC, our parent company, without the approval of the United Group board of directors; and two, I would keep him informed of any changes in the personnel of Waddell & Reed. This was important because any attempt to reduce personnel could impact our ability to manage the shareholders' money for which we were responsible. He also wanted to be informed if other organizations attempted to raid us for people and talent to the detriment of the shareholders. I assured him we would keep in close touch with him and that I would make a similar commitment to the board of directors of the United Group. We also agreed to report to him on a weekly basis about our net capital position. So, we came through our meeting with flying colors and were off and running. We were able to continue to operate Waddell & Reed on a satisfactory and profitable basis.

The other important conflict we had with the SEC was how to settle the lawsuit filed against Kansas City Securities Corporation because of the SEC's unhappiness with the allocation of commission income between Waddell & Reed and the mutual funds in the United Group. Accordingly, we had a second very important meeting in Washington, D.C., with the SEC. I was ready for the meeting because, by that time, I had become familiar with the Kansas City Securities Corporation operation and the basis of the lawsuit. My method of managing money was such that the trading activity in the portfolios was not as great as it had been prior to my arrival. This meant we were not generating as many commission dollars and were not earning very much money from Kansas City Securities Corporation. While the meeting was going on, the thought occurred to me that all we needed to do was to tell the SEC we would close down Kansas City Securities Corporation. I whispered to Mitchell Valicenti, "Let's close it down; that's what they want." Val made the suggestion, and they agreed immediately. We also agreed to pay a penalty charge of one million dollars. With the SEC happy, it was easy to settle the civil suit by Pomerantz. We settled out of court with him by agreeing to pay $500,000 to our shareholders. That was the end of another important series of events in my taking over the management responsibilities at Waddell & Reed.

During this time, Sam Marinella and Reb Jensen were deeply

involved with the banks and were trying hard to avoid a CIC bankruptcy. This led them to give Dick Roberts the responsibility of being the chairman of the board of directors of Waddell & Reed. Dick Roberts in turn delegated to me the responsibility for all of the operations at Waddell & Reed. We had things under control.

♦

CHAPTER 13

Managing Waddell & Reed

We had several serious management problems as a result of CIC's financial difficulties. When I took over the presidency, we were in the midst of closing down an offering by our marketing organization of a real estate limited partnership. One of the responsibilities one has in selling any kind of an investment product is to make sure the buyers are fully informed about everything that could have an impact on the success of the investment. This meant complete disclosure of all the developments in connection with the insolvency of CIC. We instructed our salespeople to contact all the investors who had purchased partnerships and offer to refund their money. A fairly substantial amount of the money went back to the potential investors, but enough was retained to make the offering viable. Handling a challenge like this was serious because we needed to keep the confidence of the salespeople who were losing commission income. My approach was a conference call with all the regional vice presidents (RVP) in which we went over the CIC situation, told them exactly what was happening and had them work through their division managers to accomplish the task while retaining everyone's confidence in Waddell & Reed.

Also, immediately after I took over the presidency, our national sales manager, Bob Strader, and I called all 13 RVPs into the office. Bob and I, along with Steve Beckman, the president of our insurance subsidiary, explained what had happened, why it had happened and where we stood. We said that Waddell & Reed itself was in a strong financial position and it was only the parent company that was in difficulty. We also emphasized that the board of directors of the United Group had complete confidence in us and asked the RVPs to convey this information to all the people reporting to them. They said they would, and a high proportion of our sales force stayed with us throughout this very difficult period. It proved to be a very loyal group of RVPs and division managers. Bob Strader performed in a very superior manner as he had one-on-one discussions with the people he supervised. Later, in several situations, Bob proved his management skills as he interfaced with all the management people in our sales force.

During this period, I worked closely with Steve Beckman. As I said earlier, Steve Beckman was made president of United Investors Life Insurance Company on the same day I became president of Waddell & Reed. Steve's knowledge of the insurance industry was superb for, prior to joining CIC in Boston, he had worked with a management consulting firm with the assignment of advising insurance companies, particularly those that were experiencing some difficulties. It was soon apparent that combining my investment knowledge and ability to manage the operation with Steve's insurance management capability worked very well. Steve and I developed a good working relationship that carried us through a very difficult period.

Adverse Publicity

The *Kansas City Star* and *Kansas City Times* made life very difficult because of our parent company's financial problems. Since the Commerce Bank in Kansas City was one of CIC's lenders, the newspapers reported any company news, usually in an adverse manner. I developed close personal relationships with the financial writers, but that did not help very much, particularly in the earlier years of my presidency. Since CIC would report its earnings every quarter, this information was almost always the subject of a news article. One of the worst articles, and a difficult one to handle, appeared when we closed down Kansas City Securities Corporation and CIC had to write off about $17 million of losses. It was written as if there had been a great financial loss to Waddell & Reed when, in fact, we were operating profitably. The telephone calls we received from shareholders, combined with the challenge of pacifying those shareholders who came into the office to see us, were problems we could handle, but they were stressful and unpleasant to experience. During that period, I developed some strong feelings about the way newspapers are run and the unfair way in which articles can be slanted. I quickly learned that the people who write the headlines are different people than those who write the article itself. The article may not be badly done, but often a misleading headline will result in adverse publicity since very few people read the entire article.

Another difficult bout with the media happened when The Charter Corporation in Jacksonville, Florida, made some overtures to acquire CIC. In the publicity associated with this action, a statement was made by the Charter people implying Waddell & Reed itself was on the verge of bankruptcy. To counteract the publicity in our local newspapers, I took advantage of an opportunity to be interviewed on television for the evening news. I was also interviewed at a local radio station and made the unequivocal statement that Waddell & Reed was not in financial difficulty. It was a pleasure to say this in such a positive way, for it was important to maintain the confidence of our shareholders and employees.

One of the key supporting factors was the confidence the board of directors of the United Group had in me, the management at CIC, the people at Waddell & Reed and in the kind of job we were doing. It was very important for them to have such confidence, because it was up to them to protect the shareholders of the United Group. Keeping them closely informed and giving them a high level of confidence in what we were doing was crucial. The independent members of the Board in 1974 were Dodds Buchanan, Associate Dean, School of Business at the University of Colorado; Jay B. Dillingham, President,

The Kansas City Stock Yards Company; Glendon E. Johnson, President, American National Insurance Company; John A. Kroh, Sr.; Frederick Vogel III, President, Univest Corporation; Doyle Patterson, Vice President, The Vendo Company; and E.P. (Ted) Williams.

If the board had lost confidence in the ability of Waddell & Reed to manage the money or if they thought that CIC and its problems were going to be too difficult to overcome, they could have made the decision to place the management contract with some other mutual fund organization. They also could have decided to "internalize," like the Vanguard Group under Jack Bogel did in Philadelphia during the 1970s. In our case, that would have meant they would take the management of the United Group away from CIC and retain whatever people they needed to set up a separate management organization. CIC would then have lost all of the management fee income derived from its management of the United Group and, as a result, would have been out of business. We had no desire to let this happen, and we did not let it happen. The end result was the survival of both CIC and Waddell & Reed.

We were also fortunate that our insurance company's products were in great demand and began to provide more than 50 percent of the commission income earned by our salespeople. Despite the reduction in sales of mutual funds (which also happened to all other companies in the mutual fund industry), our profitability increased, and we were gradually able to introduce new mutual funds as well as to update and introduce competitive insurance policies. We were a supplier of term life insurance products at a time when it was logical for most whole life insurance polices to be canceled and replaced with term insurance and investments such as mutual funds.

Important Decisions

A most important management decision was my establishment of a management council that was comprised of about 40 of our key management people. Periodically (usually once a month), I would call them together and update them on CIC's efforts to work out its financial problems. During the five years I was president, I supported CIC and always endeavored to put them in the best possible light by never letting our people forget that CIC's difficulties were not all of their own making. By doing this, I was successful in making sure the officers and employees of Waddell & Reed did not lose confidence in the management of CIC. At the same time, our salespeople effectively diverted unwarranted criticism or concern about Waddell & Reed to CIC.

Although our employee turnover rate was not large, some unforeseen changes in our senior management group required a great deal of my attention during the five years of my presidency. The first change was the resignation of our chief operating and chief financial officer, Richard Mitchell, at the end of December 1974, when he became the chief financial officer at Rich's Department Store in Atlanta, Georgia. He recommended giving Wayne Miller his responsibilities of chief operating officer and chief financial officer, and I agreed with him. Wayne did not have a background in finance but was a well-rounded, capable individual, who did a very satisfactory job as chief financial officer by delegating his responsibilities in that area to those working under him who had strong accounting backgrounds. The personnel manager reported to Wayne, and with his help, we were very effective in controlling our costs in ways that did not interfere with our performance.

Despite these successes, Sam Marinella persuaded me that the job of chief financial officer should go to Tom Nave, a former employee of CIC who had been the president of CIC's Texas-based real estate development subsidiary. Tom was terminated from that responsibility when CIC closed down the subsidiary after it went bankrupt. His background included being a chief financial officer, so I had no counter argument to Sam's request to take on Tom. Accordingly, I agreed to hire him but, ironically, Tom was not with us for much more than a month before he resigned. During the time he had interviewed with Sam and me, he was also discussing a job opportunity with Dayton-Hudson Department Stores. Obviously, the CFO responsibility with a large retailer was a better opportunity. That left me with the fairly difficult situation of what to do about a chief financial officer. Robert Hechler had worked with Dick Mitchell and Wayne

Miller and was qualified, so I made the decision to give the responsibility to Hechler, while Wayne Miller continued as chief operating officer. That seemed to work out pretty well; however, Hechler became disenchanted with the problems we were having and the length of time it was taking for CIC to work out of its difficulties. In the meantime, Richard Mitchell had left Rich's and gone to Zale's Jewelry Company in Dallas, Texas. He needed a chief financial officer and successfully enticed Hechler to go with him. That left me in a difficult situation again.

Sam Marinella helped me solve the problem of Robert Hechler's departure by making available Robert Hood, who was the controller of CIC and one of the very few people still left on the staff in Boston. CIC had cut the staff from about 62 people to 12. Bob Hood built a house in Kansas City and moved his family here, but I knew he had some reservations about coming because he had loved sailing his yacht on the Atlantic. After just a few months had passed, Bob Hechler became disenchanted with the situation in Dallas and let me know he was looking for a job in Kansas City. I talked to Bob Hood and, as a result, we offered Hechler the job of working under Bob Hood as the assistant chief financial officer, a position he quickly accepted. In the fall of 1977, Wayne Miller resigned. Bob Hood then assumed the additional responsibilities of chief operating officer. A few months after Wayne's departure, Bob Hood left us to go to Itel Corporation in San Francisco where he could also have his sailboat on the Pacific Ocean. I immediately made Bob Hechler chief financial officer and chief operating officer. In 1996 Bob continues as the principal financial officer, and since April 26, 1993 he has been the Chief Executive Officer of Waddell & Reed Inc.

Our Marketing Organization

Robert Strader, executive vice president and head of our marketing department, was a very capable and likable person, with the extremely difficult job of keeping his RVPs, division managers and about 3,000 salespeople happy and highly motivated when bad publicity could not be ignored. We managed to hold them together, but it was with great difficulty. With the passage of time, some of our sales managers left, so that Bob Strader, Steve Beckman and I were continually wrestling with the problem of how to keep achieving good sales production. More important than these departures was the language in every prospectus that disclosed the status of CIC's financial difficulties. In almost every sales presentation, the first 10 or 15 minutes had to be devoted to explaining why investors did not need to be concerned. Most of the time, our salespeople were successful, but it was very discouraging. Unfortunately there was no indication when CIC would work out of its problems.

Steve, Bob and I had many discussions and conducted numerous studies as to how our marketing department should be structured. We were particularly concerned with the role of the RVPs and the cost of maintaining their offices. We considered whether they should be brought into the home office, whether they really did the job they were supposed to do, and whether we had any other viable alternatives. The result was the decision to keep the RVP system because it was better than any other approach to managing a sales organization such as ours at that time.

One of Bob Strader's RVPs was Art (A.L.) Williams. Art had joined us in 1973 as the RVP in charge of the southeast region, headquartered in Atlanta, Georgia. He brought with him three people who had worked with him in a Denver-based financial planning company. Art, like all of us at Waddell & Reed, believed very much in term insurance and shared our conviction that every conceivable effort should be made to make people aware of how they could improve their financial situation and, at the same time, protect their family with a much larger amount of insurance.

Most insurance policies that had been sold since the 1930s were "whole" life policies, meaning that a significant part of the premium paid by the owner was to be invested by the insurance company with a gradual increase in the cash value of the policy. Unfortunately for the policy holder, all the policies provided a very low interest rate for the increase in cash values. With interest rates moving to very high levels in the 1970s (caused by the high rate of inflation), it was extremely difficult to justify continuing to hold a "whole" life policy. Thus, it was logical to cash in a policy, buy term (pure) insurance and reinvest the remainder of the premium in some investment vehicle such as a mutual fund. It was easy to prove that the amount of insurance coverage could be increased to much higher levels and that the increase in the value of a mutual fund would be much higher than the increase in the cash value of the policy. Waddell & Reed was at the forefront of this movement to educate policy holders, because our salespeople had no restrictions or limitations on being completely forthright in their sales efforts. The sales organizations of most of the insurance companies in the United States faced the need to try to keep business on the books, while still making sales of various types of insurance policies. There were always some insurance policies that should not be disturbed, so one of our procedures was to have the home office in Kansas City give final approval of a change.

At the first meeting of the RVPs after I became president, Art came to us and said we should have a deposit term policy in order to compete in the insurance world. Steve Beckman was completely knowledgeable on the product, but since there was a cash value in any such product (none of our term insurance products had any cash value), he had some legitimate concerns about our salespeople coming to the conclusion that we were abandoning our pure approach to the term insurance concept. Nevertheless, Steve came up with something that satisfied the three objectives of (1) making money for us, (2) making money for the sales force and (3) treating individuals who bought that insurance fairly. Art sold it very effectively in his region. It also sold with increasing volume in other parts of the country as the RVPs were convinced that the product was a very good one and appealed to a good proportion of the people being contacted.

Art also developed what he called a "fast start" program for recruiting new salespeople. The program was designed to help them sell term insurance, and it was effective. The other RVPs, not unexpectedly, accepted this fast start concept with varying degrees of enthusiasm and success. The division managers and district managers who brought in the new salespeople participated in, and got a meaningful part of, the commission dollars. Unfortunately — and predictably — the insurance sales made by these new people were to friends and relatives. As a result, many of these salespeople did not stay with us very long. Art's sales efforts were aggressive, which once in awhile resulted in the scrutiny one would expect from some of the insurance regulatory authorities in the states in his region. None of this kept Steve and me from giving some consideration to promoting Art to the position of national sales manager.

Very early in 1977, Art made the decision to leave the company. After he told us of his decision, Bob Strader and I, along with Jim Williams (manager of our marketing offices around the country), went to Atlanta for a few days to talk to his division managers. We tried to persuade them to stay with us by saying that, in the long run, they would be more pleased with us. However, Art Williams was probably one of the most effective insurance salespeople our country has ever seen, and nothing could stop them from staying with him. A few of our people from other regions went with him, too, and in a few years, the A.L. Williams Company became the largest insurance sales organization in the United States. Art's departure left a void in the southeastern part of the country, but only for a few months, as we continued to pursue our policy of building a marketing organization where emphasis was placed on having both term insurance and mutual funds as the cornerstones of our approach to financial planning. We felt very strongly about making sure our new salespeople were well trained and licensed as quickly as possible to sell both insurance and mutual fund products.

Soon after Art's departure, Bob Strader resigned, and we brought William Morgan, the RVP responsible for most of our sales on the West Coast, to the home office as executive vice president in charge of marketing. In a breakfast meeting earlier with Bill Morgan in Houston, Texas, he had indicated his interest in coming to Kansas City by asking me who would have my job some time in the future. I had told him there had been no commitment to a successor, so I was confident he would join us if the opportunity was presented.

Bill was in a position to join us, fortunately, just a few days before we were going to Nassau on March 4, 1977, to recognize about 100 of our top salespeople. As soon as the ship left Miami for Nassau,

I announced Bill Morgan's promotion and, as anticipated, it was well received. On the trip, Sam Marinella announced he was going to be more deeply involved in Waddell & Reed. We had the understanding Bill would report directly to him, so when we returned home, I distributed a memorandum clarifying Bill's responsibilities and announcing that Sam would be the chief executive officer and I would continue as president and chief operating officer.

During the next two and one half years, I continued to manage our home office people by delegating much of the responsibility to Bob Hechler and Rod McWhinney, our general counsel. This, along with not being directly involved in our marketing activities, enabled me to begin to devote more time to our money management responsibilities. At the same time, Sam Marinella and his management group in Boston did, as he had said on the Nassau trip, begin to spend a great deal more time with us in Kansas City. In effect, their involvement was so great that it gradually became apparent that most final decisions concerning our financial and legal affairs were being made in Boston. Accordingly, late in October 1979, when Sam asked me to begin devoting all of my time and efforts to managing the investment operation, I accepted immediately with great enthusiasm and anticipation as I looked forward to being fully involved with what I loved best in the business world. Nothing was more important to me than the investment performance of all the assets we had under management. It was also easy for me to see ahead and know I would be much happier if I did not have to be involved with business matters where I could not make the final decisions. My title became vice chairman of Waddell & Reed Inc. with Bill Morgan as president, The board of directors of the United Group was pleased that I welcomed this change. The management of our investment operation had always been completely my responsibility, and now I was in a position where I could immerse myself in every phase of our management of several billion dollars of investments in a very wide variety of investment products. On January 1, 1980, Larry Lady, a Regional Vice President in Omaha, Nebraska joined us in the home office as our National Sales Manager.

Managing The Investment Operation

From my first day as president of the company, I had to decide how to handle the investment responsibilities. I divorced myself completely from decisions about individual securities but retained the responsibility for decisions about personnel, portfolio strategies and investment policies. I was able to delegate most of my investment responsibilities because we had a great many capable people in the investment management division.

All the fund managers still reported to me individually. Nevertheless, the only way I could handle the responsibility was to operate with a minimum of involvement. That was a key decision. From then on, the approach I followed of delegating responsibility worked out quite satisfactorily. Accordingly, I was comfortable with the decision to continue supervising the investment operation and Research Management Associates (RMA), our investment advisory company, while I was also president of Waddell & Reed.

It was important to me and the board of directors of our mutual funds to make sure the investment people were compensated on a competitive basis and our employee turnover remained at a low level. As we approached the end of 1974, it was apparent that some of our analysts and portfolio managers had earned bonuses; however, from a management perspective, it was obvious that bonus payments to investment people, at a time when no one else was receiving them, would not create good will throughout the organization. To solve this problem, I set up a program of deferring the payment of every bonus until our company's earnings during a six-month period exceeded the earnings of a previous six- month period. This kept the investment people happy and did not disturb the rest of the organization. The bonus payments were made at the end of 1975. Since the loyalty of the investment people to me and Waddell & Reed has been so impressive, some comments about most of the more senior people are mandatory.

During the five and one half years I was president and was limiting my involvement with our investment operation, two investment men, Jerry Boettcher and David McLaughlin, were especially helpful. Jerry was the head of the investment research department and manager of the United Science Fund. Dave was vice chairman of the investment policy committee and manager of the portfolio of the United Income Fund, our largest fund investing in common stocks. Unfortunately for us, Jerry had to leave in May 1979 to take over his family's business in western Kansas. Since the research of our analysts was so important, I assigned the responsibility of managing the department to Dave. That decision resulted in our losing him because he did not want to give up managing money. Fortunately, I gave the responsibility of managing the United Income Fund to Russell Thompson. He had been an investment analyst on equity securities as well as manager of the United Continental Income Fund (a balanced fund) and the United Bond Fund. Russ has now managed the United Income Fund for 16 years and is recognized as one of the best managers of common stocks in the mutual fund industry.

Two of the more senior members of the staff were Larry Neal and Lowell Benson. Larry was head of our investment research before Jerry took over, then manager of the United Accumulative Fund until I gave him the responsibility for our lower-quality, high- yielding bond fund (United High Income) when it was established on July 12, 1979. Lowell Benson was very knowledgeable on both stocks and bonds and handled various accounts at different times. Most important to me was his management of the United Municipal Bond Fund that came into existence in 1976. Prior to that, federal tax laws precluded the use of mutual funds as a vehicle for passing the interest earned from tax-exempt bonds through to investors. I was the only one with experience in managing this type of money, and we could not afford to bring in someone from the outside. Lowell educated himself in this type of investment vehicle and performed impressively.

Two other men present when I arrived who have been very important to Waddell & Reed were Fred Mitchell and Henry (Hank) Herrmann. Both were investment analysts who gradually moved into portfolio management. Fred managed various kinds of portfolios, with United Retirement Shares (a balanced fund designed for employee benefit money) being a very important responsibility for him from June 30, 1976, to December 31, 1986. Fred also became executive vice president and general manager of RMA in 1979. As an analyst, Hank had specialized in common stocks in technologically-oriented industries. Since the United Vanguard Fund was a growth fund, the technology area was important to the fund. Hank took over management of the United Vanguard Fund on January 1, 1978. He also managed the United Science Fund for a few years after Jerry Boettcher's departure. However, the United Vanguard Fund was his primary responsibility. By the time I retired at the end of 1986, he had achieved the best performance of all our fund managers and ranked near the top of that part of the mutual fund industry specializing in growth stocks. In 1983 it became apparent that our salespeople could effectively use a mutual fund that concentrated its attention on small companies that could grow more quickly than large companies. We named it United New Concepts, and Hank also managed it from its inception on June 22, 1983, until I retired at the end of 1986.

In the early 1980s, we also decided that a mutual fund that concentrated on investments outside the United States could be helpful in financial planning for our shareholders. We could have established a new fund, but instead we decided to convert the United Continental Growth Fund to the United International Growth Fund. Our sales force was not utilizing the fund very often since we had several other common stock funds with growth as the objective. We did not have anyone with us who had experience in international investments, so we had to bring in someone from the outside. Fortunately, my successor as chairman of the Financial Analysts Federation, Marion Van Dyke, had a portfolio manager (Shreekant Panday) working for her in Montreal on international investments in the Bell Canada pension fund, and he wanted to come to the United States. He accepted my offer, and after overcoming numerous obstacles to admittance to the United States, he commenced managing the fund on January 1, 1982. Shreek had been born in India but lived in many countries as his father represented India with various political responsibilities around the world. His background, education, experience and ability enabled us to achieve very good investment performance and resulted in our being recognized as an organization that could manage an international portfolio even though we were located in the center of our country.

Very shortly after I joined Waddell & Reed, Antonio Intagliata, an investment analyst I had hired at the St. Louis Union Trust Company called and asked if he could follow me to Kansas City. He was a specialist in insurance stocks and had received his master's degree from Washington University in St. Louis. Tony had come to the United States from Sicily after he received his bachelor's degree in Italy. He immediately accepted my offer, and although he did not have major responsibilities during his first few years, I welcomed his presence as a very close personal friend. Initially he was accepted with reservations by the staff, but quite soon they recognized how he could contribute to our success. On January 1, 1979, I gave him the responsibility of managing the United Continental Income Fund (a balanced fund), and when Larry Neal gave up the responsibility of the United Accumulative Fund to manage the United High Income Fund on July 12, 1979, Tony assumed that responsibility and is continuing to manage the United Accumulative Fund in 1996.

As my summary of how our funds have been managed indicates, we seldom had to employ investment people from the outside. So when John Holliday came to me in May 1978, I was not absolutely sure as to where he would could best be utilized. There was no question, however, as to the great contribution he could make. John was vice president and director of investments at Kansas City Life Insurance Company, where he had the responsibility for $800 million of tax-exempt bonds. Initially, he assumed the responsibility of developing a service for some large local corporations to manage their short-term cash reserves. He was successful with this as well as doing the planning necessary for creating a new no-load money market fund. This new fund, United Cash Management, was introduced to our sales organization on August 23, 1979; John was its manager. In September 1974, we had introduced a money market fund (one of the first in the country) named United Daily Dividend Fund. The RVPs insisted on having a sales charge of 4.5 percent. I was appalled at this attitude, but we had no alternative but to go along with their wishes. Very few sales could be made, and on September 30, 1976, we closed it down. Eventually it became obvious to our sales force and our marketing management that we needed a no-load fund, and United Cash Management was the result.

Since this new fund had no sales charge, its value to our sales-people was in financial planning and the short-term investment of savings, which could later be put to work on a more permanent basis. As a money market fund, it could only invest in securities that would mature in less than one year and did not fluctuate in price. The commercial paper of corporations and U.S. Treasury bills were its two primary types of investments. The fund grew rapidly as individuals and smaller companies began to place their savings and reserves with the numerous money market funds introduced by the mutual fund industry. Since checks could be written against the funds, much of the money came from banks and other savings institutions. In the early 1980s, the banking industry was doing everything it could to thwart this development. Bills restricting the use of money market funds one way or another were introduced in the legislature of almost every state. None of these proposals were successful, and because of this investment vehicle, investors became much more familiar with mutual funds. The growth of our industry was directly related to the development of money market funds.

The growth of our United Municipal Bond Fund had been quite rapid, so on June 30, 1980, about two years after he had joined us, I gave John Holliday the responsibility of managing the fund. Later a lower-quality, tax-exempt bond fund was introduced to our sales force with John overseeing the investments. At the end of 1995, John managed about $1.5 billion of tax-exempt money and has achieved results that identify him nationally as one of the most capable managers of tax-exempt mutual funds in the country. John was also responsible for our employment of Robert Alley in the early 1980s. Bob was a capable manager of taxable fixed income investments and on September 30, 1984, commenced managing the United Bond Fund.

Periodically, the RVPs in our sales force would ask us to consider having a fund that invested in gold and/or gold bullion. Since I believed this type of investment was only attractive as a hedge against inflation, I was reluctant to make such a vehicle available to them. However, after considerable thought, we came up with a concept that made good sense. Specifically, we designed the fund with the objective of permitting virtually 100 percent of the assets to be in government securities when gold was not attractive. One of our senior analysts, Jack Olsen, an oil industry specialist but very interested in gold stocks, asked to be assigned to this fund, which then came into existence on September 3, 1985. When our marketing department and salespeople asked me how I felt about the fund, I never responded favorably. At the same time, I accepted the fact that many investors are believers in gold, and for this reason, it is logical to have a well-managed fund of this type available to them.

Other outstanding people who were with me and are with Waddell & Reed in 1995 are: Abel Garcia, manager of the United Science and Technology Fund; Dick Poettgen, manager of the United Cash Management Fund; Louise Rieke, manager of over $1 billion of lower-quality, higher-yielding corporate bonds; Gene Sturgeon, our head trader; and Jim Wineland, now the manager of the United Vanguard Fund. David Upshaw, our portfolio strategist, and Dorothy Ochsner, our economist, both retired in 1995.

I could devote a great deal of space to discussing my secretary, Margie Hein, and her skills, but perhaps it suffices to say that she was more of an executive assistant than a secretary. Her talents as a secretary could never be questioned, and with the wide variety of responsibilities I assumed, her ability to communicate and interface with every type of personal contact I had, both inside and outside the company, helped me in every conceivable way to do whatever job had to be done.

The Development Of RMA

About one year before I joined Waddell & Reed, the company had established an investment advisory firm named Research Management Associates (RMA). When they were talking to me about coming to Waddell & Reed, I was told one of the first decisions I would make would be either to continue to build up RMA or abandon the whole effort. With my background of investing pension fund money and with my belief this would be an attractive source of business in the years ahead, it was easy for me to decide to attempt to build RMA into a meaningful investment advisory firm. A key factor in giving me such a high level of confidence in the future of RMA was the presence of Robert Marchesi and Sam DeKinder. Bob Marchesi had been with Waddell & Reed as an investment analyst, and just prior to my arrival, he had assumed the responsibility of managing the investment portfolios, as well as the administration and marketing of this fledgling company. To assist Bob in promoting the business, Sam DeKinder, a division manager in Portland, Oregon, had been brought into the home office. Bob had a natural affinity for marketing, and with Sam's experience, they were a powerful duo. Bob and Sam immediately seized upon my background and were very innovative in getting our capabilities recognized in our geographical area in 1973 and the early months of 1974.

In the last half of 1974, they found that developing RMA when CIC was in financial trouble was almost impossible. Nevertheless, I was shocked when Bob and Sam told me at the end of 1974 they were leaving RMA to develop a pension consulting business. All I could do was wish them the very best. Today, the company they formed, DeMarche Associates, is recognized as one of the largest and best pension consulting companies in the country.

Fortunately we had a very capable marketing executive, John Watts, working with our mutual fund sales force who was willing to assume Bob and Sam's responsibilities. John had a natural talent for both the administration and marketing of an investment advisory firm. The result was that, against great odds, we continued to be successful in adding new accounts. Early in 1979, John decided to leave us for another very attractive situation, so at that time I gave the responsibility of managing and developing RMA to Fred Mitchell. Fred was given the title of executive vice president, and I continued my responsibilities as president. The decision to give the management of RMA to Fred proved to be a good one. New accounts were acquired, and our investment results were good, We changed the name to Waddell & Reed Asset Management Company in 1985, and when I retired at the end of 1986, we had about $1.5 billion under our management. The buildup of this company was one of the important accomplishments during my career, even though I devoted less than 10 percent of my time to its management.

CHAPTER 14

♦

Communicating During Time Of Adversity

Earlier I discussed some of the actions I took to keep key people in the company fully informed of developments related to the financial problems of our parent company, particularly at the time I became president. In a financial service institution, I believed that virtually nothing was more important for the morale of the company than communications. Accordingly I utilized every avenue available to me. Most important was the written word, and several approaches were available. They included the *World*, a publication for our salespeople; the *Image*, the home office publication; special memoranda from me; and two investment-oriented publications, *Ask IMD* (the IMD meaning investment management division) and *Money Managers Memo*. These were supplemented by cassette tapes designed to motivate and educate our salespeople. At the same time, my semiannual letters to our half-million shareholders in 17 mutual funds were valuable messages for our salespeople.

Waddell & Reed has distributed the *World* with regularity

from almost the inception of the company. This publication serves a vitally important need to communicate all kinds of information efficiently to the sales force from the home office. Heavy emphasis was always placed on graphic information along with the written word. When I joined Waddell & Reed, we put together an article in a question and answer format, which had the objective of familiarizing the entire organization with my background and investment philosophy. It was published in May 1973 and coincided with the speech I gave to the sales force at their convention in Kansas City in May just six weeks after I joined the company. That speech was one of the highlights of my investment career because it was well received, as exemplified by a heart warming standing ovation from nearly 1,000 people.

Commencing in March 1976, about nine months after I became president, I conceived the idea of writing an article every month for the *World* with the headline "President's Corner." We changed the format of the publication in May 1978, and we changed the title of my monthly article to "President's Page." My last article was in the September 1979 issue when my responsibilities were changed to vice chairman of the board of Waddell & Reed, Inc. I always gave a great deal of thought to the subject matter for the month, for this was an effective way for me to communicate with the home office as well as the sales force. For example, many times I used it as a way of presenting the investment performance of the funds. We were doing an outstanding job of managing the money turned over to us, and the staff and sales force needed those insights.

When I took over the presidency on June 6, 1974, I knew contact with our field sales force was vital if we were to survive. So on July 3, we prepared a cassette tape with the title "A View From the President" and sent it to all the division officers with the request for a meeting where all salespeople could hear what I had to say. Then on July 5, we distributed a four-page memo on the state of the company with copies available for every person in our sales force and our home office. I was convinced forthrightness, openness and honesty with our people were mandatory. That memo concluded by telling them we would be eliminating what we believed were unnecessary costs.

My second memo was written on August 7, the third on September 10 and my final one on October 22. By that time, we had settled down so that I could rely upon normal methods of communicating through our regional vice presidents.

Just as important as communicating with the sales force was the urgency of effectively keeping 430 home office employees well informed. So on August 2, 1974, I sent a memo to all home office employees explaining why I had terminated so many senior management people during the last two weeks in July.

Two other memos seemed to complete the need for that type of direct contact with employees. One was just before Thanksgiving; the final one on April 7, 1975, called attention to the introduction of our first money market mutual fund. By that time, most of my efforts were focused on the positive things we were doing to help our company grow.

Not long after I joined the company, I became aware of the need to provide our sales force with answers to the investment questions they were being asked by our shareholders on a day-to-day basis. As a result, we introduced two methods of assisting them in their sales efforts.

One, called a "Money Manager's Memo," was first written in the summer of 1973. These memos were used to discuss or explain important subjects. Examples were: the investment performance of the funds; investment policies; the 1973 energy crisis; the economic outlook; and potential inflation. Eleven of these were written before they were discontinued in 1975.

The *Ask IMD* program of written communication with our salespeople commenced in a formal way on July 2, 1973. The sales force submitted investment questions to me, and from those, answers were provided for the whole sales force whenever the subject matter was of sufficient general interest. In other instances, the answers were provided by telephone or a personal reply. The program of sending *Ask IMD* memos to the field was discontinued on February 10, 1983. Before it ended, I personally wrote 66 memos, with dozens more written by the senior portfolio managers working with me. During 1976 and 1977, Richard Halverson (manager of the United Vanguard fund) prepared most of the replies, because my workload as president necessitated the delegation of duties; he was an effective writer. Most memos were one or two pages in length and sometimes included charts and tables.

Since our salespeople were in their automobiles much of the time, cassette tapes provided an excellent means of transmitting information to them from the home office. The speech I made at the national convention in Kansas City just after I joined the company in 1973 was the first tape sent to them on investments. Some others were as follows:

On August 29, 1973, I spoke to 600 of our shareholders in Kansas City on the "Markets and the Economy" and then distributed the tape to our sales force. During the next eight years, we prepared 14 tapes. The subject matter was always in one of three categories: the mutual funds, the investment environment or the future of the company.

In regard to the investment environment, I usually was reacting to some significant investment situation. On February 6, 1974, when we were in the midst of a sharp decline in common stocks, it was necessary for me to encourage our people to keep their eyes focused on the longer-term outlook. Other tapes of a similar nature were made in November 1974 (the bottom of the bear market), in June 1975 (when the stock market was rising sharply), in July 1978 (when I gave it the title "Now is the time to invest") and again in May and November 1981 (when I repeated my optimism).

Three of the tapes were on the mutual funds and the people managing them. Our largest fund, United Income, was the subject in June 1974. The introduction of the United Municipal Bond Fund in November 1976 was such an important innovation in the industry that it also deserved special attention. Finally in May 1980, I talked about our investment people and how we were achieving superior investment results.

Following my cassette tape in July 1974 on "A View from the President," which was of vital importance to the morale of the salespeople, we prepared two tapes in 1975 with the titles "Where We've Been and Where We're Going" and "Looking Ahead with You and Waddell & Reed." We were also encouraging our salespeople to help us develop our investment advisory business, so in August 1974, I spoke on "The Expanding Role of Research Management Associates."

During the period from 1981 until I retired at the end of 1986, my contacts with the sales force continued unabated. However, we no longer prepared tapes at the home office so my interface with them was through speeches at shareholder meetings or at sales conferences. We also had a steady stream of salespeople touring the offices, and presentations to them were customary.

CHAPTER 15

◆

From Bankruptcy
To Torchmark

In the early stages of Continental Investment Corporation's (CIC) financial difficulties, the management under Sam Marinella worked diligently with its creditors to achieve a financial restructuring without declaring bankruptcy under the protection of Chapter 10 of the U.S. Bankruptcy Act. The Commerce Bank in Kansas City was the leading lender in the banking group and was not very cooperative.

Shortly after I became president in 1974, Richard Mitchell, our chief financial officer, spent a great deal of time with the lending officers of the Commerce Bank educating them about the nature of our business. He persuaded them that their banking relationship with us would not be affected by the problems they had with CIC. After the lending officers felt comfortable, a meeting was arranged with James Kemper, the bank president, to allay his fears. Dick and I were accompanied to the meeting by Wayne Miller and Bob Hechler. Mr. Kemper was not receptive to our beliefs and said he believed an announcement of bankruptcy by CIC could result in a loss of over $1 million by Commerce, the transfer agent for several of our mutual funds. After the meeting; we moved quickly to transfer the banking relationship to a competitor in Kansas City. I have a very high regard for James Kemper because he has been, and is, an extremely capable banker. In our situation, which was complicated, we simply could not satisfy his concerns.

Specifically, the banking group had made the loan of $57 million to CIC with the Commerce Bank's participation being $2.5 million. In February 1975, CIC was able to delay bankruptcy by making a $2.8 million payment and deferring all other payments until June. This money came from the sale of some of CIC's subsidiaries. In the meantime, in 1974, Waddell & Reed operated at a profit of $2.2 million after taxes. About this time, our insurance subsidiary, United Investors Life Insurance Company, received word that it had won a number one ranking in two categories among the nation's 125 largest life insurance firms: $58,124 was the size of our average policy written in 1973; and $37,142 was the average size of all our policies that were in force. The sale of term life insurance was increasingly vital for our survival.

Unpleasant Financial Publicity

Our annual stockholder meeting in April 1975 was difficult and stressful. Reb Jensen, as chairman of the board of directors of the United Group, and I, as president, had to handle the disruption created by one stockholder. This man had a small investment in one of our mutual funds and wanted the entire board to be replaced by a board of his choosing and Waddell & Reed terminated as the manager of the funds. He was unsuccessful and had no support from other stockholders. The *Kansas City Star* publicized the details of the meeting.

On May 30, 1975, the *Money Manager* magazine headlined its editorial with this article, "Waddell & Reed holds on to its own earnings as fate of troubled CIC parent is decided." This kind of publicity, which was reproduced in detail by the *Kansas City Times* on July 2, 1975, was very helpful in reassuring our salespeople and the shareholders of our mutual funds.

On June 19, 1976, the *Kansas City Times*, under the headline, "Waddell & Reed Parent Firm Faces Chapter 10," wrote at length on CIC's efforts to avoid bankruptcy by having the banks and debenture holders accept its plan of reorganization. Naturally the headline and article created some concerns around the country, but by that time, our sales force and managers were confident of Waddell & Reed's sound financial position and handled shareholder questions without too much difficulty.

Early in 1977, I was approached by the *Forbes* magazine with a request for an interview focused on Waddell & Reed and CIC's financial difficulties. After discussing the advisability of such an interview with Sam Marinella, I agreed, and the interview took place in my office in Kansas City. As we suspected, one of their objectives was to focus on Monte and Niel Wallace, two brothers who owned the controlling interest in CIC. The article was headlined "Survival Game," and under my picture were the words, "Holding the fort at Waddell & Reed." The article was accurate and complimentary to me personally as well as Waddell & Reed. The Wallace brothers had declined to be interviewed, and under their picture were the words, "Very Private." This was very true, and during all of the time I was president, I had no meaningful contact with them.

Despite CIC's difficulties, we also received some very good publicity from a regional magazine, *Outlook*, in its August/September 1977 issue. Under our company's name were the words "Responding to the Ever Changing Needs of its Clients" with a picture of myself at my desk accompanied by five senior officers.

CIC Is Declared Bankrupt

Throughout 1977, the CIC management group, with court approval, worked diligently to have their reorganization plan approved by the banks, debenture holders, SEC staff and CIC board of directors. They were successful; however, the Wallace brothers, who had not participated in the planning, did not support the plan. The court, at the request of the SEC, then placed CIC in Chapter 10 of the Bankruptcy Act. The April 8, 1978, article in the *Kansas City Times* had the headline "Waddell & Reed Parent Bankrupt."

On May 8, 1978, I assumed the extracurricular job as chairman of the Financial Analysts Federation (FAF), a position that added to my burdens but placed me in the national scene of the investment world. With hindsight, the years 1974 through 1977 were the most stressful I experienced in my business career. I did not slow down in 1978 and 1979, but the pressures were of a different kind and much easier to handle. I continued to work long hours, made numerous trips, wrote several articles for publication, spoke at numerous meetings, participated in all of our important investment decisions, and interfaced with many individuals throughout the country as I conducted the affairs of the FAF. By delegating many responsibilities to those working with me at Waddell & Reed, I did not find it very difficult to carry out my duties as the chief operating officer of the company.

Out Of Bankruptcy

The trustee appointed by the court to handle CIC's bankruptcy was Paul Lazzaro. He made one or two trips to Kansas City in 1979 and 1980 and relied on the management of CIC to guide his thinking. The development of a reorganization plan was the assignment of the CIC management in Boston.

The "Circle of Champions" meeting for our top salespeople was held the last week of March 1981 at the Hilton Hawaiian Village on the island of Oahu in Hawaii. During that meeting, we received a telephone call from the trustee advising us he had received an offer from Liberty National Insurance Company in Birmingham, Alabama, to purchase CIC for $166 million. Included in this offer would be payment in full for all debt owed by CIC, plus the accrued interest.

During the period from June 1974 to April 1981, Waddell & Reed, with its subsidiary, United Investors Life Insurance Company, had become increasingly profitable, so it was apparent to me that something like this could happen. Several times different corporations approached us to discuss acquiring CIC, but they were always looking for a bargain. Accordingly, it was easy to turn them away.

An interesting aspect of this seven-year period was the price action of the debentures of CIC. I was told by the management of CIC that one large holder of about $4 million of this issue sold its entire investment for around $40,000. I do not recall when this happened, but this meant they almost gave it away. Not much time passed after I became president before it began to look to me as if there was a good possibility that the debentures would eventually be paid in full. Naturally, I could not personally benefit from the opportunity to purchase the debentures, because I possessed inside information relative to our financial strength.

The purchase of CIC was consummated on October 27, 1981, and we became the subsidiary of a newly formed company, Liberty Financial Services Company, which was owned by Liberty National in Birmingham. This then began our relationship with Frank P. Samford, Jr., who was their chairman, and Ronald Richey, the president. All the management of CIC remained in place. Those of us in Kansas City believed there would be no change in Boston, because the primary value of the Boston group was their entrepreneurial capabilities, and none of us questioned their ability to generate new ideas for the Liberty organization. At the same time, we wondered whether Samford and Richey had a good understanding of the cost of maintaining the group in Boston.

Torchmark

With the acquisition of Waddell & Reed, it was apparent the name "Liberty National Life Insurance" did not accurately reflect the type of company with which we were associated. The management of Liberty wanted to convey the impression it was no longer just an insurance company, and the name "Liberty" was too widely used to be distinctive. After thorough research, on July 1, 1982, the name was changed to "Torchmark Corporation."

From the outset Frank Samford, Jr., and Ron Richey wanted to have a personal relationship with the officers in Kansas City. One of my meaningful contacts with them was when they made the decision to employ a chief investment officer to be located in Birmingham. Sam Marinella had tried to convince them they needed a chief financial officer, but he was unsuccessful. They narrowed their search to three individuals and asked me for my recommendation. I recommended, and subsequently they employed, Herbert Evert, a good personal friend who had worked at The Northern Trust Company while I was there and for several years after I had resigned and left Chicago. Over the years, we had been in rather frequent contact with each other; his wife, Charlene, and my wife were good friends. Herb Evert joined Torchmark on July 1, 1984, and from then on, I reported to him rather than to Boston. Herb's confidence in me was such that our working relationship could not have been better. However, it did mean my contacts with Samford and Richey were not extensive.

In the meantime, I continued to receive national recognition resulting from my chairmanship of the Investment Company Institute and the investment performance of the United Group of Mutual Funds. This culminated in my invitation to appear on Wall Street Week on August 31, 1984. My performance was satisfactory, greatly appreciated by our sales force and complimented by my peers, company associates, friends and relatives. Afterward, the management of Torchmark under Frank Samford's leadership held a dinner for me in Birmingham at the time of one of their board meetings to present me with a mocked-up trophy that resembled an academy award. Hank Herrmann, manager of our United Vanguard Fund, had also received national publicity on the excellent performance of his fund and was similarly honored.

Shortly after Herb Evert was employed, we learned Frank Samford, Jr., a man whom we had come to regard very highly, was suffering from bone cancer. He exhausted every medical resource available, including highly regarded doctors in Canada and in France, but it was to no avail. Frank Samford died in December 1986, a great executive, a fine person in every respect and a great one for us to work with. I attended his funeral in Birmingham.

Torchmark And Boston Separate

As Frank Samford's health deteriorated and Ron Richey became more deeply involved with the Boston operation, friction between Ron and Sam was obvious to the management in Kansas City. We suspected that Sam wanted to be completely responsible for Waddell & Reed, but Ron would not accept that kind of a working relationship. It was apparent to us that the situation might not continue. Around the beginning of 1985, Richey worked out a separation arrangement with the entire Boston group, which we were led to believe was a very generous one.

Dinner meetings of the board of directors of the United Group and the management of Waddell & Reed were always held the night before the board meeting. So on February 12, 1985, Reb and Sam attended and spoke at length about their years of involvement with the board, how much it had meant to them and also what they believed they had contributed to the success of Waddell & Reed in its management of the mutual funds. After Sam and Reb had spoken, one of the directors asked us all to stand up and sing "Blest Be the Tie that Binds." Sam and Reb had always been highly regarded by the directors, so the feeling of empathy towards them was genuine.

At the beginning of the board meeting on the 13th, Reb announced his resignation as chairman, thanked the board for their support and left the meeting. The board then asked me to become chairman. Twelve years had passed since my employment at Waddell & Reed had been negotiated with Sam, Reb and Dick Roberts. My working relationship with Sam had not been perfect, but it was quite satisfactory. The most important indication of my loyalty was the fact I had stayed with him and Waddell & Reed for the five years, from 1974 through 1979, when I was at the peak of my earning power and received no bonuses or increases in compensation. Sam's explanation during those years was that he did not believe my salary should be as large or larger than his. I believed that Sam, sometime in the future, would compensate me fully for the sacrifice I had made. Quite frequently and before many diverse audiences, Sam emphasized that Waddell & Reed would not have survived the 1974-1979 period if I had not been the president. My business and personal relationships with Reb Jensen and Dick Roberts were excellent in every respect. We have continued to keep in touch with each other, and I value their friendship.

TMK United, Inc.

1985 was another good year for Waddell & Reed and United Investors Life Insurance Company. The management group in Birmingham was now working very closely with us in Kansas City, with the result that we became more familiar with their people, polices and thoughts in regard to the future. We also were in a position to convey directly our aspirations and objectives. From these contacts, the idea emerged of creating a name for our complex and selling some of the shares to the public. This culminated in the decision to form TMK United, Inc. and sell 15 percent of our stock to the public. Our primary motivation was the possibility that the shares of the smaller company, operating primarily in the mutual fund industry, might trade at a higher price-earnings ratio than Torchmark. If it did, it could be an attractive approach toward buying other companies. Most of the work developing a prospectus was done in Birmingham. However, we were deeply involved with decisions about the offering price, our dividend policy and a description of our business operations. The prospectus revealed our salaries, and for the first time, it became public knowledge that I was the highest paid person in the organization. My compensation in 1985 was $395,000. The salaries of the next four highest paid executives ranged between $229,000 and $300,000. Obviously we were being paid quite well for what we were doing. It was interesting to observe that the publication of this information did not attract the attention of our local media. In the media environment of the late 1980s, salaries of executives often became hot stories.

The public offering of the common stock of TMK United, Inc. was very successful. Between April 17 and April 20, 1986, we cooperated with our underwriter in making presentations to investment analysts in Kansas City, New York, Boston, Chicago and Los Angeles. Richey would give a general overview of Torchmark; Morgan discussed our sales organization; Beckman presented the history, success and growth potential of our insurance operation; and I presented the record of our management of the investment of the assets in our mutual funds. Ron's introduction of me at these meetings was most complimentary.

He knew the audience respected the fact that I had been chairman of the Financial Analysts Federation and the Investment Company Institute.

Following the completion of the offering, Richey invited Morgan, Beckman and me to Birmingham for a special dinner with the board of directors of Torchmark, at which time we were presented with facsimiles of Hollywood Oscars with the words "TMK UNITED RAIN-DANCE," in recognition of our nationwide barnstorming tour for the company. It was a fun way to celebrate this phase of TMK United's corporate life.

My Presentation To Investors

A keepsake that I value is the booklet we had prepared for our meeting with analysts. In it, among other things, we highlighted the investment performance of the mutual funds, the stability of the investment organization and the growth of our investment advisory subsidiary, Waddell & Reed Asset Management Company. On March 31, 1986, the company had more than $1.6 billion under management.

To emphasize the performance of the mutual funds, which had a total of $4.9 billion under management on March 31, 1986, I showed a comparison of each of the seven common stock funds with the Standard & Poor's 500-stock index during the nine-and-a-quarter years from January 1976 to the end of March 1986. The index was up 250 percent while six of the seven funds had appreciation ranging from 261 percent to 557 percent. One fund, a balanced fund that was burdened with varying amounts of bonds during the period, was up 224 percent. There was no questioning the success of our investment management.

To illustrate the experience and stability of my 10 portfolio managers, a table set forth their years of experience and years with Waddell & Reed. I was then, and am still, proud of them. The only justification I have for taking some of the credit for our success was my ability to identify portfolio management capabilities, establish and implement an investment philosophy, and delegate responsibility when it was advisable to do so.

The Presidency Of Waddell & Reed Investment Management Company

On July 17, 1985, the investment management division of Waddell & Reed became a separate corporation named Waddell & Reed Investment Management Company, and I was named president. From the day I had joined Waddell & Reed in 1973, I had always reported to someone in a parent company, not to anyone in Waddell & Reed. Sam and Reb had always agreed with me that the division should become a separate corporation, but, it was not until I discussed it with Herb Evert that action was taken. A secondary reason, which I believed would benefit my successor, would be the elevation of the stature and importance of the investment responsibilities at Waddell & Reed. Realistically, the separation of the two parts properly reflected the autonomy of each of the operations.

CHAPTER 16

◆

The FAF And ICI

Two of the important honors I received during my investment career were the chairmanships of the Financial Analysts Federation (FAF) in 1978–1979 and the Investment Company Institute (ICI) in 1980–1982. In both instances, the invitation to assume those responsibilities came as a complete surprise.

The Financial Analysts Federation (FAF)

I became a member of the Financial Analysts Society of Chicago, Illinois, a few years before I left Chicago in 1964. I had been attending the annual meetings of the FAF and the normal weekly meetings of the Chicago Society but had not been offered any positions of responsibility. The FAF commenced its program of chartering financial analysts in 1964, and because I had 17 years of experience as an investment analyst and portfolio manager, I was only required to take two rather than three of the tests that are given annually. I was the 532nd analyst to receive the charter, which I earned in 1965, as I mentioned earlier. My year as the president of the St. Louis Society and participation in numerous conferences as a panelist in various programs brought me into contact with my peers all over the United States and the FAF headquarters staff. These developments culminated in my being sponsored by the St. Louis Society for membership on the board of directors of the FAF in 1972. From then on, I was caught up in all facets of the FAF, and trips to New York City were routine requirements. At that time, there were approximately 10,000 financial analysts who were members of 40 different societies in the FAF.

Not long after I joined the board, the New York Society of Financial Analysts, under the presidency of Peter J. DeAngelis, took various actions to separate the New York organization (whose membership amounted to about one-third of the total membership of the FAF) from the national organization. On December 1, 1973, Peter wrote a letter to the FAF board in which he stated the New York Society's reasons for wishing to establish professional status for its members at the state level. I wrote to him on February 5, 1974, and outlined reasons for uniform national regulation. In March 1974, the New York Society voted overwhelmingly against state regulation. The vote was 4,740 against and only 464 for state regulation. The FAF then proceeded to develop a program of self-regulation, which unfortunately was not immediately approved by the New York Society. During this period, I was also a member of the Investment Analysis Standards Board, which had the responsibility for developing a self-regulation program. On September 20, 1974, I wrote to the new president of the New York Society, Arthur Carlson, to express our disappointment and ask them for cooperation. Art Carlson provided excellent leadership for the New York Society; however, a dissident group continued to pursue state regulation. On February 9, 1976, a bill was introduced in the New York state legislature that would have resulted in licensing analysts in New York. I had written on February 3 to the Commissioner of Education for the state of New York and, in my two-page letter, discussed at length the reasons why it would be bad legislation. My letter as well as other letters from board members were too late to stop introduction of the bill, but they did make him realize that licensing by each state was an illogical and unworkable approach to a profession that was national in scope. In my letter, I stressed that action by the

New York state legislature would be a disservice to the whole country. On April 26, 1976, *Barron's*, the national business and financial weekly, reviewed the conflict in detail under the headline "NYSSA vs. FAF." Fortunately, the majority of the members of the New York Society under new leadership voted against state regulation. My participation in this conflict and its resolution may have been a factor in my selection as vice chairman of the FAF on June 30, 1977, and chairman one year later.

It was with great pleasure that I, as chairman of the FAF, and four members of the FAF staff had breakfast on October 28, 1978, with nine members of the New York Society as we embarked on a program of moving forward with national self-regulation. I was deeply involved in attempting to resolve this conflict, but its successful resolution was due to the efforts of many people in the FAF as well as the New York Society.

Chairmanship Of The FAF

As vice chairman of the FAF, I worked closely with Solon Patterson, who was chairman. This meant numerous trips to New York as we planned seminars around the country, moved ahead with self-regulation and prepared for board meetings. Our conference at Bal Harbour, Florida, in the spring of 1978 was the occasion for my taking the office of chairman. I also participated in the program by acting as a workshop leader for a panel discussion on "Structuring a Portfolio." The *Miami Herald* interviewed me for an article with my photo, which ran under the headline "Control of Inflation is Necessary for a Strong Market, Analyst Says." The *US News and World Report* also interviewed me for an article on "What Big Investors See Ahead in the Stock Market." This was the beginning of a year characterized by monthly trips to New York and visits to several of the financial analyst societies around the country. Much of my time devoted to the FAF was spent in staff meetings in New York where we gave a great deal of thought to our seminars and conferences as well as longer-term plans for the FAF.

I was in Lafayette, Indiana, on August 14, 1978, for the

Korschot family reunion and was interviewed by the *Lafayette Journal & Courier*. The article was quite lengthy, with the headline "Stocks Good Buy Now, Says Fund President." At that time, the Dow Jones Industrial Average was at 800.

On September 21 and 22, 1978, I was in Chicago for an FAF seminar at the Palmer House on "Security Analysis: What is Happening." At this seminar, I was also the moderator of a session entitled "Evaluating the Research Product." Two of the members of the panel were men who had worked for me: Jack Ellis in St. Louis and Ernie Frohboese in Kansas City. At the meeting, I was privileged to give an award to Marshall Ketchum, the professor at the University of Chicago who had started me on my investment career. The award to Marshall was for his contributions to the FAF over many years. He developed and managed the FAF seminars that were held annually in Rockford, Illinois, and were a vital part of the FAF program of education for investment analysts.

In October 1978, Mary and I took a 10-day combination vacation and business trip to Europe with the primary objective of representing the United States FAF at the annual conference of the European Society of Financial Analysts.

The sessions were all interpreted or spoken in English, so the meeting was rewarding from a professional viewpoint. The highlight of the conference for me occurred at the closing banquet. A part of the program was a demonstration of crossbow archery by two teams, one from Holland and the other from Belgium. After they concluded their contest, I was invited to compete along with the chairman of the Financial Analysts Society of Japan to see who could hit a target set up on the stage. The Japanese chairman did not wish to try, so a younger man from Japan shot for him and missed the entire target. I had never shot a crossbow, but since it was like a rifle, I had no difficulty and, with luck, hit the bull's-eye. The members from both teams were astonished and gave me a plate that is a reminder of a very pleasant event in my life.

On that trip, Mary and I visited Winterswijk, the town in Holland where my great-grandfather had lived before coming to the

United States. There were about 20 relatives assembled at the farmhouse to give us a most friendly welcome and visit.

In the month of March each year, the *Financial World* magazine recognizes the top 10 chief executive officers in the United States. A banquet is held in New York City, and that month's issue is devoted to articles about those who were chosen. Each year the chairman of the FAF is one of the three judges. I was assisted by Dr. D.C. Caroll, dean of the Wharton School of Business, and Dr. David B. Hertz of McKinsey and Company, the largest management consulting company in the country. We were assisted by 50 senior security analysts who first selected 63 managers and then narrowed the list to the top 10. The three of us then selected the top chief executive officer, who for 1978 was T. Wilson of the Boeing Company. The dinner was held on March 15, 1979, at the Waldorf Astoria, and Ronald Reagan (the year before he became President of the United States) was the principal speaker. I had the privilege of introducing the top 10 finalists and Mr. Wilson. Ronald Reagan autographed my program, but he was not particularly sociable with us.

Later in March, Mary and I were in San Diego to recognize and honor Waddell & Reed's top salespeople. That month I also spoke at a seminar sponsored by the Kansas City Society of Financial Analysts. On April 28, we attended the 25th anniversary party of the Glen Ellyn Kiwanis Club, and on May 4, I spoke at a conference of the St. Louis Association of Financial Planners on the subject "Common Stocks as an Inflation Hedge in the Next Five Years." The *St. Louis Globe Democrat* publicized the speech with the headline "Forecast calls for the stock market to double." The DJIA was at 833 at that time, and I was right on the direction. However, it took until February 14, 1986, a period of almost seven years, for the DJIA to double and reach 1666. In that speech I also emphasized that the stock market was on the bargain counter and that we were fully invested.

My final official responsibility as chairman of the FAF was our annual conference in San Francisco, May 13–16, 1979. I had many duties to perform, among them introducing our principal speaker, Paul Erdman, who had written a fascinating book titled *The Crash of 1979*.

Mary was an integral and vital part of this conference because of her visibility and involvement with all the functions, particularly those pertaining to the women present.

At the end of my term in office, it was a privilege to write an article for the *FAF Newsletter* summarizing activities during the year. Accordingly, I wrote in a positive way on the following subjects: our financial position; progress in self-regulation; the decision to establish a newsletter; improving readability of the *Financial Analysts Journal*; the success of 15 seminars, symposia and conferences; two new societies during the year to bring the total to 51; committee activities at a high level; involvement with the federal government in several ways, particularly a cut in capital gains taxes; establishing speaker bureaus in societies; and moving our headquarters in New York.

The full-time president of the FAF during all my years of deep involvement was Theodore Lilley. In my opinion, he performed in an outstanding manner and was invaluable to me as chairman. His was a most difficult responsibility because the FAF(with so many societies) meant he had to interface with hundreds of individuals in a great variety of situations. Unfortunately, a few years after my term of office, he resigned. At that time, I was so deeply involved with the Investment Company Institute that I could not find the time to be active in the FAF. Following his resignation, the FAF went through a period of struggling with different approaches to management until, finally, the FAF and the Institute of Chartered Financial Analysts (ICFA) merged in 1989. I had attempted, along with others, to begin the merger process in the late 1970s and early 1980s, but the resistance to change was too great at that time. As a result, we concluded it would be necessary for the Chartered Financial Analysts (CFA) program to move ahead until there would be so many CFAs as members of the various societies in the FAF that merger attempts could not be stifled.

Over the years, my association and friendship with many investment men and women added tremendously to how much Mary and I both enjoyed the investment business. Elsewhere in this book, I have mentioned in some detail those who worked with me at The Northern Trust Company, the St. Louis Trust Company and Waddell &

Reed. But there were many people in other financial organizations deeply involved in the FAF and Institute of Chartered Financial Analysts (ICFA) who, as a result (along with their spouses), became an important part of our lives. The two- and three-day seminars and conferences created opportunities for both of us to develop lifelong friendships, many of which are part of my life today.

One couple who is in the forefront of my mind as I reminisce is William (Bill) S. Gray, III, and his wife, Gloria. Bill was the chief investment officer at the Harris Trust and Savings Bank in Chicago and a graduate of the University of Chicago, so we had much in common, including an enjoyment of golf courses around the country. Bill preceded me by three years as chairman of the FAF in 1975-1976. He was also the person who invited me to join the investment committee of the American Red Cross as I approached retirement in 1986.

Eugene (Gene) Vaughan, Jr., has been an important part of my life. Gene was chairman of the FAF in 1973-1974, and when the FAF and the ICFA joined together as the Association for Investment Management and Research (AIMR) in 1990, Gene was the first chairman. One of Gene's partners in his company is Walter S. McConnell, also a past president of the FAF (1976-1977). Walt and I worked together on many assignments.

The investment careers of two more men, Richard (Dick) Burridge and C. Roderick (Rory) O'Neil, whose years at The Northern overlapped mine, have kept us close to each other. Dick was treasurer of the University of Chicago and now has his own investment advisory company, The Burridge Group, Inc. Rory and I had numerous opportunities over the years to work together, but his presidency of the ICFA at the same time I was chairman of the FAF could not have created a more conducive environment for cooperation between the two organizations. We did our best to make major progress in 1979 toward melding the two organizations into one, but as I have mentioned before, it was not accomplished until 1989. Dick, Rory and I share (along with Frank Hausmann, Dean Coleman and Herb Evert (all of whom I mentioned earlier) the memory of working in the investment environment created by Art O'Hara at The Northern Trust Company.

Chairmanship Of The Investment Company Institute (ICI)

I was actively involved with the Investment Company
Institute (ICI) during the last half of the 1970s and while I was chairman of the FAF. I had become a member of the board of governors of
the ICI as the result of the resignation of John Kostmayer as president
of the United Group of Mutual Funds in June 1974. While I was
attending the board of governors meeting in Hawaii in January 1980,
David Silver, president of the ICI, accompanied by the chairman of the
nominating committee, asked me to become chairman for the fiscal
year beginning October 1. Although the offer was totally unexpected, I
did not hesitate to accept the responsibility. My term of office was for
one year, and they invited me to continue for a second year. This part
of my life did not end until October 1982. I firmly believe honors and
responsibilities such as these come as the result of just doing the best
you can at whatever task is set for you.

The board of governors of the ICI meets three times a year.
They have a January meeting, usually in a resort setting like Hawaii,
Palm Springs or a Caribbean island. The May meeting of the board of
governors is always at the time of the general membership meeting in
Washington, D.C. The third meeting is held near the end of September.
I was a member of the executive committee during most of the 1970s
and until I retired from the board of governors on January 1, 1989, a
date that coincided with my resignation from the board of the United
Group of Mutual Funds. The executive committee met almost monthly in Washington because this committee of about six members had to
work very closely with the management of the ICI. The combination of
the rapid growth of the industry, the need to work with the Securities
and Exchange Commission, and — most important — the need to work
with Congress to thwart the attempts of the banking industry to get
into our business resulted in unbelievable activity.

One reason my term in office demanded a great deal of my
time was the success we were enjoying with money market funds. Our
industry began to introduce them in the middle 1970s, but explosive
growth came in the late 1970s. By 1982 the amount under management was over $200 billion industrywide, and we were in difficult legal

and political battles in Congress, as well as every state, because the banking industry did everything it could to stop the flow of money into money market funds. Their high quality, complete liquidity, check-writing capability and higher income made it easy for money market funds to take money away from banks and savings institutions. This investment vehicle made millions of people aware of mutual funds for the first time, and by the end of 1995, the mutual fund industry managed over $2.8 trillion of various kinds of investments with over $750 billion of the total in money market funds. Money market funds also enabled the mutual fund industry to promote itself more aggressively to investors because the privilege of moving money from one fund to another could be done at virtually no cost. Not only could such exchanges be made between stock and bond funds, but exchanges could also be out of those funds into the safe, liquid haven of money market funds whenever the investor wanted that kind of security.

Three other developments affecting the success of the mutual fund industry were the creation of tax-exempt bond funds, high-yielding corporate bond funds and the passage of legislation making individual retirement accounts (IRAs) extremely attractive. Prior to the legislation permitting tax-exempt income to be passed through a fund to investors, the only way tax-exempt bonds could be acquired was on an individual basis. This was a difficult problem for the average investor, so the development of tax-exempt mutual funds was well received. My experience in managing tax-exempt portfolios made it possible for Waddell & Reed to be in the forefront in introducing this type of fund. Our fund commenced operation on November 5, 1976.

The high-yielding corporate bond funds became very popular in the late 1970s, and Waddell & Reed introduced the United High Income Fund on July 9, 1979. This type of fund was very popular because of the high level of income the fund made available to investors. Their acceptance by investors accelerated in the early and the middle 1980s because price fluctuations were no greater than higher-quality bond funds. Unfortunately, these funds became known as "junk" bond funds. This was, to some extent, a misnomer, particularly in the earlier years when most of the investments were in young, fast-growing companies. Later much of the activity was in leveraged buyouts, which are extremely risky and were one cause of the price collapse of lower-quality issues in the late 1980s and early 1990s.

The third development, individual retirement accounts (IRAs), was beneficial to all kinds of savings and investment organizations, to the investors themselves and, most importantly, to our country because they created investment capital. The passage of favorable legislation encouraging everyone to consider their usage coincided with my chairmanship of the ICI. Accordingly, during my two years in office, I toured the country on behalf of our industry on two occasions to be interviewed on television, radio and by the newspapers. This was an enjoyable and productive responsibility because almost every household in the country needed to be aware of the value of an IRA. This tax-deferral approach to building a nest egg for retirement made dependence on the social security program less important.

Two ICI Committee Assignments

In the fall of 1980, just before I became chairman, our industry was advised by the Financial Accounting Standards Board (FASB) that their staff believed the effects of inflation should be reflected in the prices of the shares of mutual funds. They were proposing a new regulation, identified as FASB 33. They saw a relationship between requiring corporations to reflect inflation in their accounting statements and requiring the prices of the shares of mutual funds to reflect inflation. To us it was obvious this was a completely illogical concept, but, since the FASB was serious and we knew it would be disastrous for our industry, we did not take it lightly.

Since I was the only person on the executive committee who had an investment background, David Silver asked me to take the job of being chairman of the committee to meet with FASB to present our position. We attacked their belief with two approaches. One was that the regulation was inappropriate because of the differences between the functions of financial statements of operating businesses and mutual funds. The second was that it was unnecessary because the various securities that comprise the value of mutual fund shares are priced daily in the marketplace and continuously reflect economic, social and political changes. Our meeting was on May 20, 1981. I was accompanied by Mathew Fink, general counsel of the ICI, one other member of the staff of the ICI and five representatives of the industry. We were well prepared with charts and written materials, and we were successful. It was a vitally important victory for our industry.

If FASB 33 had been put into effect, it would have placed us at a disadvantage relative to other types of investments, such as savings accounts, because only our product was being adjusted downward in price for inflation. I believe the strength of my personal convictions was very helpful in having the FASB overrule its staff and agree with us. My main contention was that investments should be judged not only on how well they do against inflation, but also how well they do against the Standard and Poor's 500-stock index, how they do against other investments, how they do against bond indexes and so on. If the FASB staff had prevailed, it would have forced the mutual fund industry to accept inflation as the standard of measurement of the performance of all kinds of mutual funds. No matter whether they were money market funds, common stock funds or bond funds, all would be judged only on how well they did against inflation. This was all wrong, and we prevailed.

The second committee assignment I accepted that was of major importance to the industry was the chairmanship of a special committee created for the purpose of determining how the income (yield) from non-money market income mutual funds should be calculated and advertised. The need for this study arose because of the manner in which some mutual fund companies were promoting the sale of their funds, particularly the lower-quality, high-yielding bond funds. The staff of the ICI and the executive committee of the board of governors had been observing the kinds of advertisements being used. Furthermore, the SEC had identified those firms where the inference could be made that the misleading nature of their advertisements as well as the statements in their prospectuses, annual reports and marketing literature were not good for the industry. However, for most of the industry, honest differences of opinion existed about how to measure and advertise the yields on income funds. The urgent need for consistency also became apparent to the industry as the SEC threatened to establish rules and guidelines if nothing was done by the industry to police itself. The first meeting of my committee was on October 24, 1985, at the offices of the ICI in Washington, D.C. The membership of the committee was large, with approximately 50 people representing almost all of the larger mutual fund organizations. Frequently more than one person from an organization participated as it soon became evident we needed knowledgeable people in the areas of accounting, law, marketing and investments. With such a large and diverse group speaking on behalf of organizations in which the subject was of crucial importance to the success of their companies, we were confronted with a monumental challenge of identifying the issues and resolving them so that a unified conclusion could be presented to the SEC. Mathew Fink and several other members of the ICI staff became deeply involved with me as we prepared material for the consideration of the committee and met separately in attempts to focus on solutions to our assignment.

After numerous meetings of the committee and even more meetings with the staff of the ICI, we submitted our proposals to the SEC on March 11, 1986, in a nine-page letter supported by research data to substantiate our position. We were able to devise a single formula for calculating yields and presented that concept along with our recommendations as to how disclosures should be made in advertising and other communications with investors. We knew the SEC had in mind an approach different from ours; nevertheless we submitted what we knew was the best approach. During 1986 we had numerous meetings with the SEC, and some mutual fund organizations supplemented our report with their specific insights. The SEC submitted its proposed rules to the industry on September 17, 1986. On December 22, 1986, we responded with a 33-page letter emphasizing the flaws in much of what the SEC planned to place in effect. During 1987 additional meetings of the committee were necessary as a result of ongoing discussions of the staff of the ICI with the SEC. Finally a mutually acceptable agreement was reached, and the SEC released a 92-page report on February 2, 1988, on the guidelines to be followed by the industry. It had been a frustrating challenge, but we had solved a monumental problem for the industry. Unfortunately it had taken 27 months to reach a conclusion, and by that time, interest rates had declined so much the industry was no longer as interested in aggressively promoting low-quality, fixed-income funds. The problem was history, and some investors may have made their investments on misleading premises; nevertheless the standards are in place and will be invaluable in the future.

The ICI Organization

My comments on my involvement with the ICI would not be complete if I did not emphasize the outstanding quality of the organization. Much of the credit belongs to the leadership that, during the years when I was on the board, was on the shoulders of David Silver, Mathew Fink and Richard Pogue, executive vice president. Dave had been the general counsel prior to becoming president, and when Dave retired in 1991, Matt assumed his responsibilities as president. This meant that now, as in the past, the senior person had a legal background. This structure has been of tremendous value to the mutual fund industry, because the industry is regulated by the SEC and the growth and success of the industry have been based on the confidence of investors in those who have had the responsibility of management of their money. A very important aspect of the responsibilities of this leadership has also been the ICI's relationship with various congressional committees, which are instrumental in regulating our industry as well as those with whom we compete. Since there are thousands of mutual fund management companies, one of the great achievements of the leadership of the ICI has been the ability to work, in an unbelievably effective manner, in leading the industry to decisions, where the ICI could speak as one voice for the industry. Much of the credit for this goes to the power that the board of governors has delegated to the executive committee. Membership on the executive committee rotates among the board members and always includes significant representation from the larger mutual fund complexes. This is a wise policy, because those leading the organizations have always had the years of experience in the industry, which enables them to guide the ICI staff whenever their knowledge is important. As in any organization, changes in personnel occur with the passage of time, but in the ICI, Richard Pogue has remained as executive vice president, where everything works so well that it is just taken for granted. Dick Pogue has been a vitally important part of the team. I hesitate to mention the names of some key people I respect and had the pleasure of working with because, quite unintentionally, I may omit one. Nevertheless, Al Johnson, Don O'Conner, Catherine Heron, Reg Green, Tom Simmons, Ann Swanson, Erick Kanter and Julie Doerr quickly come to mind as those with whom I had a great amount of contact.

With Henry Bodwell at my home in St. Louis, November 15, 1964. He was my portfolio mentor at the Northern Trust Company.

Art O'Hara, my common stock investment mentor at the Northern Trust Company.

With senior officers at the St. Louis Union Trust Company in 1969.
(From left to right) Benjamin C. Korschot, Hugh Logan, Leroy Ozment,
Fred Shepherd, John Peters McCarthy and Hord W. Hardin.

*A dinner of some directors of the United Group of mutual funds to recog-
nize Chauncey Waddell, founder of Waddell & Reed. March 1976.
(From left to right) Julius Jensen, III, Chairman of United Funds;
Mitchell J. Valicenti, Director; Gerald L. Gilbert, Executive Secretary of
United Funds; Cornelius Roach, Former President of Waddell & Reed;
Benjamin C. Korschot, President of Waddell & Reed and United Funds;
Chauncey L. Waddell, Founder of Waddell & Reed, Inc.; Sabino
Marinella, President and CEO of CIC; and Jay B. Dillingham, Director
of United Funds.*

*With members of our investment Policy company in December 1976, at
Waddell & Reed, Inc. (From left to right) Russ Thompson, Fred Mitchell,
Lowell Benson, Larry Neal, Ben Korschot, Dave McLaughlin, Dick
Halverson and Jerry Boettcher.*

Waddell & Reed corporate management, August 1977. (From left to right) Rodney O. McWhinney, Chief Legal Officer; William T. Morgan, Executive Vice President of Marketing; Wayne Miller, Executive Vice President of Corporate Development; Benjamin C. Korschot, President (seated); Robert Hood, Executive Vice President and Chief Financial Officer; and Stephen Beckman, President, United Investors Life Insurance Company.

With Bill Morgan and Steve Beckman (in the car) at the beginning of one of our periodic sales campaigns of our marketing department. August 1977.

Board of Directors of Financial Analysts Federation, 1978-1979. (Back row, from left to right) H. Kent Adkins, Dennis R. Bouwer, Solon P. Patterson, William Goodman III, James L. Woods, John S. Chalsty, Erwin H. WIll, Michael M. Ryan, David G. Sutliffe, Daniel J. Forrestal III and C. Roderick O'Neil. (Front row, left to right) Dave H. Williams, Theodore R. Lilley, Benjamin C. Korschot and Marion VanDyke.

Congratulating Professor Marshal Ketchum, of the University of Chicago, on behalf of the Financial Analyst Federation for his organization and management of an annual seminar held at Rockford, Illinois, for investment analysts. September 22, 1978.

Board of Directors of Roosevelt Bank, 1981. (Back row, from left to right) Sheldon K. Stock, William E. Pettit, Hiram S. Liggett Jr., James W. Metcalfe, Alvin D. Vitt. (Front row, left to right) Robert M. Clayton II, Raymond T. Gusnard, Walter U. Bolliger, Benjamin C. Korschot and Clarence M. Turley Jr..

David Silver, Presdient of Investment Company Institute, congratulates George Bissell, the new chairman, as I look on as former chairman. October 1982.

With Louis Rukeyser on "Wall Street Week." August 31, 1984.

United Fund Board of Directors, August, 1986. (Seated, from left to right) Jay B. Dillingham, John A. Kroh, Benjamin C. Korschot, WIlliam T. Morgan and Wallace F. Bennett. (Standing, from left to right) Glendon E. Johnson, Gerald Gilbert, Doyle Patterson, Herbert P. Evert, Henry L. Bellmon, Frederick Vogel III, Dodds I. Buchanan and Leslie S. Wright.

CHAPTER 17

◆

Speaking – Writing

O ne of my regrets when I left St. Louis and the trust business was that I had to resign from my responsibilities of teaching trust investments to bankers who participated in the Southwestern Graduate School of Banking's program at Southern Methodist University in Dallas, Texas. Ever since I had taken over this responsibility from Art O'Hara, I had enjoyed the two weeks each summer and the year-round monitoring of case studies by the students. I enjoyed teaching, as well as the opportunity to work very closely with Norman Wiggins, who had the responsibility for teaching the administrative and legal obligations. It was a delightful and stimulating experience. Norman knew trust laws and regulations as well as anyone in the country. His wife, Millie, was always with him, so she and Mary became good friends. Norman is now the president of Campbell University in Buies Creek, North Carolina, and has led this Baptist institution superbly. We have kept in touch with each other, and I have been a guest speaker for him. For several years, and even after my retirement, he invited me to become involved with their business school, but the distance to North Carolina was an obstacle I could not overcome.

Teaching has always been a source of enjoyment for me, so, as I became more involved with opportunities to speak and talk to a variety of audiences, it was obvious that these were really teaching opportunities. Whether a person is sensitive to this or not, anyone who is selling something, whether it is a product or a concept, is in effect being a teacher. At Waddell & Reed, we were always endeavoring to employ school teachers and athletic coaches, because selling financial services is essentially a teaching function.

For a variety of reasons, a major part of my activities involved communicating with the news media (newspapers, magazines, radio talk shows and television interviews), our sales force, our shareholders, money managers, financial planners and various organizations interested in financial matters. These activities did not develop because I sought them. Instead they were a natural adjunct to my responsibilities at Waddell & Reed, the Financial Analysts Federation and the Investment Company Institute. Since Waddell & Reed was a financial planning organization with more than 3,000 financial planners in over 100 offices, as well as manager of investments for several hundred thousand shareholders, the obligation to speak and write was enormous. Our parent company, CIC, was having financial problems; money market funds were initially controversial; and IRAs were introduced at a time when I was chairman of the ICI — all of these proved to be reasons for my receiving the attention of various media. During my nearly 14 years at Waddell & Reed, I was interviewed more than 200 times by about 30 magazines and more than 50 newspapers, spoke on 12 radio talk shows, and appeared on 10 television stations. Also our division managers and regional vice presidents were continually organizing meetings of our shareholders where I was the principal speaker.

Newspapers, Magazines, Radio And Television

When I was interviewed or quoted in a newspaper or magazine, the subject matter was almost always one or more of the following: our company, our mutual funds, money market funds, IRAs, the mutual fund industry, the economic environment, or the investment outlook. The financial editor of the *Kansas City Times*, Ben G. Schifman, and his associate, Janet Meyer, gave us a great deal of attention. It seemed to me that they never missed an opportunity to publicize CIC's financial problems. But we were pleased when they wrote about the performance and growth of our mutual funds every quarter after I gave them the figures with my comments. My opinion about the outlook for the stock and bond markets and investments generally was the basis for numerous articles in the *Times* and *Star*. Also when I was promoted or recognized in some way, they treated my achievement in a very flattering way. The *St. Louis Post-Dispatch* and *Globe-Democrat* always covered my promotions and frequently publicized my stock market forecasts long after my departure from St. Louis. My two hometown newspapers, *The Journal & Courier and the Leader*, also covered my promotions, and, when I was in Lafayette, the *Journal & Courier* usually interviewed me and wrote about my outlook for the stock market.

My two years as chairman of the board of governors of the Investment Company Institute (ICI) gave me a great deal of visibility around the country. During this period, I visited Miami, Fort Lauderdale, Tampa, Atlanta, Houston, Dallas, Fort Worth, Tucson, Sacramento, Oakland, San Francisco, San Jose and San Mateo, California. I was interviewed by one or two newspapers in each town and frequently participated in radio talk shows and television programs. All the arrangements for my travel program were made by Reginald D. Green, vice president of public information for the ICI, who accompanied me to every interview. His ability to make the arrangements and knowledge of how to interface with the media were superb. He and I were in complete agreement that the focus from our viewpoint was IRAs and why the mutual fund industry was an attractive way to invest the money in an IRA. On all the television programs, the interviewer stayed with that subject. But, on the radio talk shows and in the newspapers, my responsibilities at Waddell & Reed came to the forefront, so much of the conversation centered on the outlook for the economy, interest rates, common stocks, bonds and mutual funds in general. The staff of the ICI and the board of governors were delighted with the acceptance of my tours and the excellent publicity the industry received. The mutual fund industry continues to be an attractive approach to investing IRA money. The investment objectives of an individual, whether income or growth or some combination, can easily be satisfied. Investors can calculate the value of their assets every business day and switch easily from one kind of fund to another whenever it is logical to do so.

It is important for me to emphasize that preparing for all of this activity was easy to fit into my schedule of responsibilities. The reason is that I was talking about matters that I had to be on top of simply because they were part of the investment world.

The decline in the stock market throughout 1973 and 1974 was persistent and devastating in terms of the loss of money and confidence in the future of our country. However, all the financial statistics available to us said, as we approached the end of the third quarter, "this is not the time to lose your courage. It is the time to buy." During the four months from September 1974 to the end of the year, I was interviewed or spoke five times in various places around the country where I expressed my convictions in a way that I had never done before or since. Most of the time one must talk about the longer trend of the stock market in order not to mislead people. But 1974 was different, and here are some excerpts from my interviews:

Omaha, Nebraska, to a Regional Sales Convention, September 12, 1974

"Now is the Time" (backed up with numerous charts).

Money Magazine, September 1974

"I think you have one of the great opportunities that people, at least in the 50 years or so that I have been around, have ever had."

Register-Guard , Eugene, Oregon, October 24, 1974

"The stock market is bottoming out now because we are about six months away from a turnaround in business."

The Oregonian, Portland, Oregon, October 25, 1974

"You can take the stock page from a paper, put it on a wall, throw a dart at it and about any stock it hits will go up."

The Wall Street Journal, "Abreast of the Market," November 11, 1974

"By any fundamental measure, whether it's price-earnings ratios or price-to-book value relationships, the stock market continues to be undervalued, and this is the second greatest investment opportunity I've ever seen in my lifetime. The first was in the 1947-1949 period when a depression was feared."

The stock market's bottom in 1974 was either in September or December, depending upon whether the DJIA or S&P 500 is considered to be more important. The low area for the DJIA was just above 550 in both months. It moved to the 1000 level in 1976 and then drifted down to the 800–900 level in the late 1970s. On October 11, 1979, before the National Association of Investment Clubs in Chicago, I made a prediction that the DJIA would rise from 850 to around 1350 in five years. It came close to doing that for, in 1983, the index traded at the 1300 level. It moved lower in 1984 and traded for a few months below 1100. We established some reserves at Waddell & Reed, and during the summer, I traveled to New York to be interviewed on CNBC, at which time I gave some reasons why we were not fully invested. Early in August, we reversed our policy, and when I was interviewed on August 20 by the *Investors Business Daily* newspaper and the market had risen above the 1200 level, I said the rally would carry the DJIA to well above the 1300 level. On August 21, I was in Great Falls, Idaho, where in an interview with the *Great Falls Tribune* I said the Dow Jones Industrial Average could easily be above 3000 by the end of the decade. The headline was "Investor says Dow could break 3000." I based my confidence on what Paul Volcker, chairman of the Federal Reserve Board, was accomplishing. He had tightened the money supply so that interest rates had gone high enough to break the back of the inflationary psychology that had produced around 18 percent inflation annually. Inflation was now declining; interest rates had been lowered; and a healthy business environment was developing. I also said that, if interest rates did not go lower than they were in 1983, I would be surprised if the DJIA was above 1600 by the end of the decade. Such a forecast is easily made because common stocks automatically sell at lower price-earnings ratios as interest rates rise. Conversely, very low interest rates can produce very high price-earnings ratios. Lower interest rates also mean a healthier business environment and higher corporate earnings as the basis for optimism about the future.

When I was interviewed as a market timer on "Wall Street Week" on August 31, 1984, by Louis Rukeyser, he noted that we had been holding large reserves but had become bullish. In this discussion, I explained our "Central Value Index" and what had persuaded us to change our position. In an interview for our "W&R World" in October 1984, I said that, in the immediate future, our "Central Value Index" indicated the DJIA should not go below 1000 nor above the 1300 level. I also said, "The outlook for common stocks after this period of consolidation is excellent, and after some slowdown in the economy in 1985, it will be positioned for expansion at a very satisfactory rate for several more years, and investors should take advantage of this opportunity."

On February 17, 1985, the *New York Times*, in an article with the heading "How Likely is a Market Correction," made some accurate comments under the following heading: "A Big Bear Joins the Bulls." The writer went on to say that, for the last half of 1984, Wall Street pointed to Kansas City's Waddell & Reed as one of the most bearish investors around. They then quoted me saying, "We felt interest rates were at relatively high levels and the stock market could not move up strongly." And finally, after mentioning we had placed $400 million into stocks, they finished the article with my statements, "We are now fully invested," and "We were convinced the bear market would not develop because of the inflation numbers and the change in Fed policy."

From the 1300 level of the DJIA in early 1985, the stock market rose steadily to 2709 on August 21, 1987. This had been an unbelievably great move where, in less than three years, common stock prices had doubled. Then it had a traumatic decline in just a few weeks to a low of 1738 on October 19. This decline was caused by technical factors, such as "program trading" and "portfolio insurance," not by fundamental factors such as economic activity, interest rates, corporate earnings, inflation and price–earnings ratios. For these reasons, I did not foresee the collapse. Since I had retired, my only concern was my personal investments where I had no difficulty in making the decision to remain fully invested in common stocks. I maintained that position throughout 1995 and 1996, and benefited immensely by having so much confidence in the outlook for common stocks and identifying the attractiveness of technological developments. I continue to be optimistic about the longer-term outlook for common stocks, but one should never forget that many developments have the potential for undermining the confidence of investors. The market will always be volatile, and some declines shake the confidence of a vast majority of investors. This is when it is mandatory for investors to remain focused on the longer-term upward trend of the market.

Before leaving this subject, I reiterate the dangers in making specific forecasts of the trend of the market despite my willingness in late 1974, 1979 and 1985 to make specific forecasts. Market technicians and editors of stock market newsletters make a living doing this, and they seldom agree with each other. It is educational and interesting reading but, for most individuals, it is wise to let the professional institutional investors attempt to do it if they wish. In my opinion, their full-time dedication to managing money will usually result in rectifying their mistakes in judgment before too much damage is done. That certainly is what happened to us in 1985.

Being interviewed by various magazines and newspapers was a pleasure for me for several reasons. One was that the people in our sales organization found it to be helpful in their marketing of financial planning. Also, it was an ego trip for me and, in a sense, a fulfillment of my personal goals. On a continuing basis, the "Abreast of the Market" columnists from the *Wall Street Journal* interviewed me 10 times between July 16, 1973, and February 13, 1978. Other interviews were: three by the *New York Times*, five by *U.S. News & World Report* and two by *Business Week*. The invitation to appear on "Wall Street Week" was unusual because, most of the time, they relied upon investment people on the East Coast. But by far the most important articles to me were one by the *New York Times* on October 7, 1980, two in the *Kansas City Star* on October 7, 1980, and December 7, 1986, and the one I discussed earlier in this book that was in *Forbes* on February 1, 1977, with the heading "Survival Game."

The *New York Times* article resulted from my becoming chairman of the ICI. The headline was "Talking Business with Korschot of Investment Company Institute." Most of the questions dealt with mutual funds, but the subheading was "Stocks Viewed as a Hedge." The article in the *Kansas City Star* on the same date was headlined, "Path Changed for Head of Investment Company Institute." The subheading was "Korschot's Dream Shifts from Coaching to Mutual Funds." The article accurately described how I had changed my plans after World War II. The article on December 7, 1986, in regard to my retirement was headed: "Korschot Nursed Funds to Growth." One of the statements was this, "Korschot, who joined Waddell & Reed in 1973, is credited by colleagues and outsiders with helping to guide the company through some troubled times." It was a lengthy and accurate article that mentioned, among many other things, that we had grown from eight funds to 16 funds and from $2.7 billion in assets to more than $7 billion in assets. Steve Rosen, the reporter on both of the *Kansas City Star* articles, interviewed my associates about my investment philosophy that they described as flexible and with which I agreed. Today, for example, the common stocks I own include value situations, as well as those that are simply growing their sales and earnings at very high rates. As I have said elsewhere in this book, I also believe in concentrations, but only when they are based on knowledge and the ability to stay on top of an investment.

Shareholders And Salespeople

Since I enjoyed talking about investment matters, most of our division managers and regional vice presidents arranged for me to visit them whenever I could. They usually wanted about a month's notice of my coming, so that they could arrange a meeting place, send out the invitations and contact the local newspapers. The attendance at most of the meetings ranged between 50 and 100 people. On one trip to California, the attendance reached about 1,500 people in San Jose and 400 in Sacramento. On another to Cupertino, California, about 1,000 were present. We had four meetings in various parts of Kansas City with around 600 in attendance at each meeting. In every city, I visited our company office and talked informally with all our people. This enabled me to answer any questions they had about what was going on in Kansas City. By employing charts or slides from which I could develop my thoughts, it was very easy for me to make the presentation. Some of my charts would defend my conclusions in regard to the outlook for the economy, interest rates and inflation. Others would illustrate whether bonds and stocks were attractive or unattractive. Discussing the investment performance of our funds at times created questions from the audience that revealed their displeasure. This was very true in the middle and late 1970s, when yields on fixed-income securities were very attractive and the performance of common stocks was unimpressive. Frequently I would meet with unhappy shareholders after the meeting and suggest changes from one fund to another when it was appropriate. Most of the time, the investors, for various reasons, had invested in the wrong fund. I thoroughly enjoyed shareholder meetings. My records indicate I visited 16 states and handled 34 meetings of this type. Six of the meetings were in Kansas and six in California. We had always had good sales leadership in Kansas so it was a great place for us to do business. In general, we were much stronger west of the Mississippi River than in the east. Florida, Georgia and upper New York state were exceptions.

Over the years, Waddell & Reed, like many sales organizations, honored its best producers by treating them and their spouses to several days at some very nice resort-type locations. The mornings of these meetings were devoted to business and, after lunch, leisure activities, either organized or personal, were sometimes available. My talk to the group was always an important one and always very well received. Standing ovations were normal (and very pleasing to one's ego). My speech format was only slightly different than what I would say to shareholders. One exception was that I usually spent more time discussing the fund managers along with the results they were achieving. In total, I spoke to just our sales people at 22 meetings in 12 states as well as in Switzerland, Mexico and Quebec. Our most popular places were Florida, where we had five meetings, and Arizona, where we had three. At most meetings, which we called the "Circle of Champions," we honored about 100 salespeople along with their spouses. In 1986, my last year, the format was changed to six sectional meetings and one meeting called "Silver Crest," which was a somewhat smaller group that met in Montreaux, Switzerland. Mary and I always studied the names and faces so that we could relate to every person present. Mary's health prevented her from going to four of the six sectional meetings.

Speaking To The Public

The demands upon my time made it impossible for me to accept all the invitations I received to speak in public. Nevertheless I made as many speeches as I could reasonably schedule. The speeches I did make were as follows:

1. The 23rd Annual Convention of the National Association of Investment Clubs, St. Louis, Missouri, October 19, 1973, "Portfolio Strategy in a Controlled Economy."
2. The Rotary Club, Liberty, Missouri, October 26, 1973, "Outlook for the Stock Market."
3. The Financial Executives Institute, Kansas City, Missouri, May 13, 1974, "Financial Strategy in the Current Economic Environment."
4. A Public Employees Conference, New Orleans, Louisiana, November 20, 1974, "Investment Policy for Pension Funds."
5. The Kiwanis Club, St. Louis, Missouri, August 21, 1975, "The Outlook for Common Stocks in Our Free Enterprise Society."
6. The General Membership Meeting of the Investment Company Institute, Washington, D.C., May 19, 1976, "How

Investment Policy Is Set, Executed and Controlled."

7. A Mutual Funds and Investment Management Conference, Albuquerque, New Mexico, March 23, 1977, "ERISA, The Employee Retirement Security Act."

8. The Country Club United Methodist Church Business Meeting, Kansas City, Missouri, August 21, 1977, "Why Corporations Should Be Allowed to Operate Profitably."

9. The Kansas City Chamber of Commerce Year-End Business Outlook, October 28, 1977, "Private Financing in 1978."

10. The FAF Annual Conference, Bal Harbour, Florida, May 9, 1978, "Structuring a Portfolio."

11. The Kansas City Society of Financial Analysts, May 10, 1978, "Plans for the FAF for the New Year by the New Chairman."

12. The St. John's United Methodist Church, Kansas City, Missouri, October 26, 1978, "Inflation and How to Handle It."

13. The Financial Executives Institute — Kansas City Chapter, February 12, 1979, "Outlook for the Securities Markets."

14. A Professional Financial Management Seminar of University of Missouri, University of Kansas and Kansas City Society of Financial Analysts, April 10, 1979, "Current Issues Affecting Investments."

15. The St. Louis Association of Financial Planners 1979 Conference, May 4, 1979, "Common Stocks as an Inflation Hedge in the Next Five Years."

16. The National Association of Investment Clubs 29th Annual Convention, Chicago, Illinois, October 11, 1979, "Taking the Pulse of the Next Five Years."

17. A Kansas City Chamber of Commerce Business Outlook Breakfast Meeting, October 26, 1979, "Introductions and Closing Remarks."

18. The Financial Executives Institute, Kansas City, Missouri, December 8, 1980, "The Securities Markets in 1981."

19. The International Association of Financial Planners, Kansas City, Missouri, May 18, 1981, "Money Market Funds: Past, Present, Future."

20. The Investment Company Institute General Membership Meeting, Chairman's Report, May 28, 1981, "The Annual Report to the Fund Industry."

21. The Investment Company Institute General Membership Meeting, Chairman's Report, May 20, 1982, "The State of the Fund Industry."

22. The St. John's United Methodist Church Business Meeting, Kansas City, Missouri, May 4, 1983, "Economy, Inflation, Interest Rates, Stock and Bond Markets."

23. The South Kansas City Chamber of Commerce, July 19, 1984, "Interest Rates and the Stock Market."

24. The Kansas City Chapter of American Marketing Association, December 11, 1984, "Outlook for the Stock Market."

My last public speech was before the members of the Kansas City chapter of the Financial Executives Institute on April 21, 1986. I had spoken before them three times, in 1974, 1979 and 1980, about the outlook for the securities markets. But this time it was a special honor because it was our "Education" night, when we recognized the top student in accounting in each of the 13 colleges and universities in our geographical area. The students were accompanied by the heads of the accounting departments. The subject was my career, with the objective being to give the students guidance in the various ways their careers could develop. Jim Judd, the managing partner of Peat, Marwick, Mitchell & Company in Kansas City, also spoke on the same subject.

Published Articles

The first article I wrote after joining Waddell & Reed was written in collaboration with John Watts, the vice president who worked with me in the development of Research Management Associates, our investment advisory company. In 1974 Congress passed new legislation for employee benefit plans called "The Employee Retirement

Income Security Act of 1974," which was soon identified as ERISA. It was immediately apparent to me that mutual funds met every requirement the new law placed upon those who managed the investment of the assets in employee benefit plans. Features or requirements, such as adherence to the prudent man rule, exercise of fiduciary responsibility, diversification of assets, performance measurement, fiscal soundness, flexibility and so forth, were all available in mutual funds. My article "ERISA: A Blueprint for Mutual Funds" was published in the August 1975 issue of the *Forum*, a monthly publication of the ICI. Since then there has been a steady upward trend in the dollar assets of employee benefit funds invested in mutual funds. It was an uphill battle for the mutual fund industry because many money managers still believed that, as soon as one had enough money in a portfolio to be attractive for money managers, one should have one's own individual securities. This attitude ignores the advantage of having very capable mutual fund managers who pay attention to their portfolios every day. Unless an individually managed portfolio is very large, it is usually reviewed by the manager only periodically and, in most instances, just four times a year.

My second publication was an article entitled "Prudent Investing — Before and After ERISA," which was published in the July/August 1977 issue of the *Financial Analysts Journal*. The article compared the change from the pre-ERISA era of 1945 to 1974 with the first three post-ERISA years (1974, 1975 and 1976). In writing this article, I was drawing upon my firsthand knowledge of everything significant from an investment viewpoint that had occurred between 1945 and 1977.

About the same time I was writing on prudent investing, I wrote an article with the title "Capitalism and the Stock Market" for the September 1977 issue of our company publication, *Investment/Economic Perspectives*. The Investment Company Institute reprinted the article in the October 1977 issue of the *Forum*. I wrote the article to emphasize the importance of equity capital and corporate earnings in creating a growing economy and reducing the rate of inflation. This was a period in which the stock market was in the doldrums and very much maligned as an investment vehicle. In the article, I stressed that the alternative to private investment was public investment that could only be done with deficit financing and ultimately higher, rather than lower, inflation. The financial editor of the *Kansas City Star* read the article before it was published and, after interviewing me and discussing my rationale, published my thinking in the Sunday issue of the paper on August 14, 1977.

My next article was published in the July/August 1978 issue of the *Financial Analysts Journal* under the title "Quantitative Evaluation of Investment Research Analysts." I explained this system of evaluating the abilities of investment analysts in Chapter 11, when I discussed my system of managing money at Waddell & Reed. The article was well received, and, in subsequent years, the concept was utilized in numerous other investment research organizations that are on the "Buy" side of the business, namely, mutual funds, insurance companies, investment counseling firms and the trust departments of banks.

To my knowledge there are no "Sell" side investment research organizations willing to publicize a quantitative approach to evaluating their analysts. Accordingly one of the difficulties we had in deciding how to evaluate the capabilities of "Sell" side analysts was the absence of a track record of their decisions. Our analysts had to depend on their recollections and qualitative factors such as personal attention. Usually three, four or more of our analysts and portfolio managers would have enough contact with the institutional salesperson representing the "Sell" side firm to make a fairly sound decision. These decisions were the basis for attempting to allocate our commission dollars in some logical way to all of the brokerage firms that were of service to us. Of course, we also had to consider their ability to execute all kinds of orders at competitive commission rates. In judging the performance of "Sell" side analysts, we also were sensitive to their objectivity (underwriting relationships, for example) and such things as how they handled bad decisions in the past. The managements of these organizations had to have their own "in-house" methods of evaluating their analysts, but making that information available to "Buy" side organizations could lead to misleading information that might be unfair to their analysts. They sent their recommendations to many kinds of "Buy" side organizations that all have different needs. For this reason, it is easy to understand why, as sales organizations, they could not provide us with their evaluation of their own analysts. As in so many situations, the old saying about the "buyer beware" holds true for evaluating "Sell" side analysts.

Near the end of 1978, I attended a planning conference as chairman of the FAF. With me were Solon Patterson, the chairman in 1977–1978; Dennis R. Bouwer, president of the Los Angeles Society; and Theodore Lilley, president of the FAF. We met for two days in Washington as an ad hoc committee to study the long-range planning for the FAF. We summarized our conclusions in an article that was published in the January/February issue of the *Financial Analysts Journal*. I wrote the concluding section on "The FAF"s Current Planning Activities." In that report, I emphasized our current efforts to establish a continuing education program. I also stressed our belief that analysts must embrace the diversity of our business and we should continue to broaden the definition of an analyst. Other matters I discussed were the importance of our self-regulation program and the need to improve our ongoing relations with the government and the public at large.

After almost eight years of experience in the management of investments in mutual funds, it occurred to me that I should set forth the reasons why mutual funds do a better job of managing other people's money than banks. It seemed to me I was in a unique position to write such an article because I also had 26 years of experience in the trust operations of two banks. In my article, which was entitled "Why Mutual Funds Outperform Banks" and published in the January 1981 issue of the *Forum*, I discussed 10 distinct advantages of mutual funds. One example is the freedom to implement decisions quickly. The banking industry immediately became aware of the article, and in the March 6, 1981, issue of *American Banker*, in a section called "required reading," they published the article in its entirety with only a few editorial comments. The article may have been beneficial to professional money managers in the banking industry, because they were able to use my arguments as a reason for making constructive changes in their own organizations.

During the spring of 1981, the public relations vice president at the ICI advised me that Delta Airlines was soliciting an article that would be published in *Sky*, Delta's in-flight magazine. Since this was a great opportunity for publicity, the staff of the ICI, with some guidance from me, wrote the article. It was entitled "The Maturation of Mutual Funds" and appeared in the May 1981 issue of *Sky*. In this article, we stressed how the industry had changed from primarily a manager of common stock funds to one which made available an extremely wide variety of funds to the public. Thus it was capable of providing investment management skills for almost every need. The superior investment performance of many different types of common stock funds was also highlighted with interesting charts. The article was reprinted in the July 1981 issue of the *Forum*.

In the fall of 1981, the *Kansas City Times* asked me to write an article for the newspaper on the importance to investors of having the privilege of exchanging one type of fund for another within a "family" of funds, at either no cost or possibly a slight charge. My article was printed on September 21, 1981, under the title "More Investors Cash In on Chance to Use Fund Exchange Privileges." This led me to write a longer and more statistical article on the subject, which was published in our company publication, *Investment/Economic Perspectives*, in November 1981, and also in the *Forum* that same month under the title "The Exchange Privilege Is for All Investors." There is no question that this privilege enables an investor in mutual funds to become very professional in switching from one type of fund to another as economic conditions change or as the needs of the investor change with the passage of time. This feature is a big selling point for the mutual fund industry, but it has been abused by some investment advisory organizations that seized it as a way to develop a new business, namely, advising investors on how and when to switch from one fund to another. Switching in and out of specialty funds, such as those concentrating in one industry or one country, has considerable merit as a portfolio management technique, but it is not easy to be successful and achieve superior investment results. Mutual fund investors must be aware of the risks and cost.

My second term of office as chairman of the ICI ended on September 30, 1982. It was customary for the chairman to speak at the annual general membership meeting in May on the subject "The State of the Fund Industry." My speech, published in the *Forum* and *Investment Dealers Digest* in July 1982, was a fairly lengthy discussion of the progress of the industry with emphasis on challenges for the future such as further progress in persuading institutions to invest in mutual funds.

I wrote my last article in May 1984, when the *Kansas City Business Journal* asked me to prepare a piece for them on investing in mutual funds. Accordingly, I presented them with a paper from which they wrote an article entitled "Mutual Funds Come in Many Shapes and Sizes." Only minor modifications were made in what I had written, and the title was descriptive of its contents.

One of the ongoing pleasures in my nearly 14 years at Waddell & Reed was writing the cover letters for our semiannual and annual reports to shareholders. It was a responsibility I considered vitally important to me as well as to all our shareholders. The letters were usually two to four pages in length and attempted to answer any questions a shareholder might have. In total, with letters twice a year and between seven and sixteen funds, the number of letters came to 188. There were no ghost writers involved, so everything that was said came from me, although they were cosigned by Julius Jensen, III, when he was chairman and by William Morgan when I was chairman and he was president. Today the SEC is mandating the inclusion of certain kinds of data, but when I was responsible, my judgment was what mattered. I always started the letter with a statistical analysis of our results in comparison with appropriate indexes and benchmarks. This logically led to an explanation of why and how we had either underperformed or outperformed our competition. I then discussed the economic environment, the trend of interest rates, the rate of inflation, and the outlook for common stock and bond prices. I usually avoided talking about specific sales and purchases but never hesitated to emphasize the size of our reserves and plans for future transactions if it was appropriate. With our sales representatives trained as financial planners and having personal contact with our shareholders, they quite naturally received some telephone calls and answered the questions that might have been created by my comments. Having our own salespeople was also of great value to us, because our redemption rate, or liquidation of investments, was always about one-half of that experienced by the average mutual fund complex.

I would like to conclude this chapter by mentioning a very personal matter that was of great importance to me. I have attempted to be thoughtful in my prayers to God, and, I believe, He guided me in the great variety of challenges I have had in my professional life. The one prayer I always made was to ask for guidance in whatever I might say as I spoke before so many diverse audiences. My prayer simply asked that I would never mislead anyone by my comments in a way that might result in something being done with their savings and investments that could be harmful to their family. Obviously, I have no way of knowing whether I always helped people make the right decision. I do know that the reactions of my audiences gave me the feeling that my presence had made a fairly large number of people more comfortable with what they had done, and might do, with their investments in the future.

CHAPTER 18

◆

Retirement

In August 1986, Jon W. Rotenstreich became president of Torchmark and TMK United. Jon had been a director of Torchmark since 1983 and prior to that had been treasurer of IBM Corporation.

Herb Evert had the responsibility of being the go-between for Jon and me as we began to make plans for my retirement. Two men in the investment operation were logical candidates for the position of chief investment officer. They were Fred Mitchell, president of Waddell & Reed Asset Management Company (WRAMCO), the investment advisory subsidiary; and Henry Herrmann, chairman of our common stock policy committee and manager of United Vanguard Fund and a number of large pension accounts.

Hank Herrmann was nationally recognized as an outstanding money manager. His record of managing the United Vanguard Fund was quite superior to most managers of mutual funds that had comparable objectives and assumed similar risks. His results were also significantly better than the market averages such as the Dow Jones Industrial Average and Standard & Poor's 500- stock index. For the nine and a quarter years ending on March 31, 1986, his fund had appreciated 557 percent while the S&P index was up 250 percent. This time period is relevant because it was an important factor in my thinking as to how to use his talents after my retirement. Most important to me was his ability to manage money and my belief that, to be one of the best money managers in the country, you could not be distracted by administrative and other extracurricular responsibilities of the type I had assumed over the years. On June 10, 1985, I prepared for Herb Evert a lengthy memorandum listing and discussing my responsibilities in 12 different areas, as follows:

Task	% of Time	Decision Time as % of Total
Fund Management and Training	10	4
Portfolio Strategy and Statistical Support	15	4
Investment Research	5	2
Marketing Department and Stockholders	20	0
Legal Department	5	0
Operations, Treasurer and Personnel Department	15	0
Director of the United Funds	5	0
Waddell & Reed Asset Management Company	5	1
Torchmark	5	1
Investment Company Institute	10	0
Roosevelt Federal Savings & Loan Association	4	0
Civic Responsibilities	1	0
	100%	12%

My objective in preparing this table was to indicate to Herb and Jon the nature of the demands upon a person with my responsibilities. The 12 percent of my time devoted to investment decisions was a very meaningful number. In essence, there was a need for the chief investment officer to fulfill a great many obligations. The person following me would not need to be involved in some of the responsibilities of a non-investment nature that I had assumed, but the job would always require an abundance of general management capabilities.

As a candidate for the top spot, Fred Mitchell's strength was as a sound and knowledgeable money manager, a proven administrator of an investment operation, and an excellent speaker and communicator. He also handled himself well in marketing our investment counseling business. The above table indicated to me that the combined strengths of the two men could produce excellent results. Herb Evert and I had numerous discussions of what should be done, and about a year before I retired, he concurred with my belief that Fred and Hank should share my responsibilities. To put it simply, I had great confidence in Hank Herrmann's ability to manage money and wished to keep him free of my numerous, miscellaneous responsibilities.

Jon Rotenstreich, as president of TMK United, drew upon his experiences and insights and concluded that, since Herb Evert was chief investment officer at Torchmark and most of the assets under management were in Kansas City, Herb should go to Kansas City and handle his responsibilities from there. Fred then decided to resign and implement his long-standing desire to establish his own investment advisory firm. Waddell & Reed provided him with a good retirement package, and when this was combined with the value of his options to purchase common stock of Torchmark, he was able to accomplish his personal objectives. Herb Evert then became president of both Waddell & Reed Investment Management Company and Waddell & Reed Asset Management Company. This was effective on January 14 and was well publicized. However, during the next two months, Herb decided that staying at Waddell & Reed did not appeal to him. Accordingly, on March 15, he resigned, and Hank Herrmann took over all the investment responsibilities and the presidency of Waddell & Reed Asset Management Company. I had not anticipated these developments but, having worked with Hank Herrmann for 13 years, I knew he could exercise all of his responsibilities in a superior manner.

Herb Evert had the responsibility of preparing my retirement parties. The first was a dinner that coincided with a meeting of the board of the United Group of Mutual Funds. All the senior officers of Waddell & Reed were invited, along with the members of the board of directors. Fred Mitchell made the presentation speech, and I acknowledged with relatively few comments. Fred's speech was a lengthy one in which he enumerated my achievements. The invitation to this dinner on December 2 was very complimentary and came from Ron and Jon. I was also presented a silver plate that listed all of the responsibilities I had assumed from April 1, 1973, at Waddell & Reed Inc., Waddell & Reed Investment Management Company and Waddell & Reed Asset Management Company.

Two weeks later, all the employees were invited to an after-lunch party in my honor. Mary attended; Bill Morgan presented me with a watch; and Fred Mitchell presented me with a painting.

This was an opportunity for me to make some comments about Mary that were taped and that I treasure. What I did was talk about how and why Mary had been such an important part of my life. Some of my thoughts were planned, but other were extemporaneous. It turned out to be humorous as Mary reacted to my comments.

My Resignation From The Board Of
The United Group Of Mutual Funds

I was very fearful of how I would handle retirement, consequently my staying on the board of the United Group of Mutual Funds became vitally important to me. Although it was a mandatory policy at Torchmark to retire at 65 years of age, I had remained for an additional nine months with full support from Ron. However, he did not feel comfortable with my remaining on the board of the United Group of Mutual Funds after I retired from my management responsibilities. My reasoning for remaining was that I could become an independent director in two years and, as a member of the executive committee of the Investment Company Institute, I would be in a position where Waddell & Reed would continue to have great visibility at the national level of the mutual fund industry. Just before I retired at the end of the year, Ron called to say he agreed with my staying on the board in 1987.

To become an independent director before January 1, 1989, I

sold all my investments in Torchmark and United Investors Management Company (the new name given to TMK United, Inc. in April 1988). However, late in the fall of 1988, Bill Morgan asked me to meet with him. At the meeting, he said Ron, Jon and he believed I should resign from the board at the end of the year. Their reason was that they believed my presence on the board was interfering with the ability of Hank Herrmann and the portfolio managers to function freely. I was disappointed in this description of my position, because during the two years I had remained on the board following my retirement, I had purposely endeavored to present a low profile when the investment people were present. Nevertheless, I could relate to these concerns and immediately complied with their request. As Bill and I ended our conversation, he went on to say Ron would like for me to be an outside director of United Investors Management Co. I declined but sincerely appreciated the invitation.

At my last board meeting before the end of 1988, I was presented with a silver cup thanking me for my 14 years as president and chairman of the board of directors of the United Group of Mutual Funds. In the January 1989 meeting of the board of governors of the Investment Company Institute, they thanked me for my 14 years as a member of the board. They also presented me with the copy of a resolution recognizing my contributions to the industry as chairman of the board from September 1980 to October 1982.

My comments about retirement from the board of directors of the United Group of Mutual Funds would not be complete if I did not emphasize the importance to Kansas City of Jay Dillingham and Doyle Patterson. They are two local business men who have contributed their time and excellent judgment in fulfilling responsibilities as independent directors for the shareholders of all the United Group. Those years when our parent company was bankrupt, placed them, as well as all the directors, in a situation that was very unique if not unparalleled in the history of the mutual fund industry. The decisions they made at that time, as well as in other situations, were difficult and, in my judgment, always right. They also never lost sight of one of our objectives, namely, keeping Waddell & Reed in Kansas City.

Professional Recognition

Being recognized by *Marquis Who's Who Inc.* had never been one of my goals in life, so I was pleasantly surprised when I was included in the 1974 edition of *Who's Who in the Middle West.* I assumed that their decision was related to my becoming part of Waddell & Reed, Inc. However, 1974 was also the year I became a member of the board of trustees of the College for Financial Planning, an organization with headquarters in Denver, Colorado, which had developed the professional designation for financial planners known as a "Certified Financial Planner"(CFP). To obtain this certificate, participants had to pass five very difficult tests of their knowledge of taxes, insurance, mutual funds and estate planning. The CFP designation has become very important to financial planners. I left the board of trustees in 1977, and Steve Beckman took my place.

In 1979 I was included in *Who's Who in Finance and Industry.* This was after I had become chairman of the FAF. Then in 1982, after I became chairman of the ICI, I was added to *Who's Who in America.* I have no insights into whether my involvement with the FAF and ICI were factors in my selection, but from my viewpoint, they were positions with significant responsibilities. In 1991, four years after I had retired from management responsibilities, I was invited to be a part of *Who's Who in the World.*

I certainly appreciate being included in these publications but most important to me has been the respect of those with whom I worked on a day-to-day basis and those whose financial affairs have been helped by my involvement with their money.

CHAPTER 19

Roosevelt Financial Group, Inc.

As I said at the end of Chapter 10 when I was commenting on my move to Waddell & Reed in Kansas City, the demands upon my time by Roosevelt had been minimal from 1968 through 1973. This situation did not change meaningfully until the late 1970s.

In 1977, Walter Bolliger, the president of Roosevelt, came to me with the question of whether Raymond T. Gusnard, a member of the board who had become a director shortly before I joined the board in 1968, would be an attractive person to bring into the management of Roosevelt. Walter's plan was to bring Ray in as executive vice president preparatory to succeeding Walter as president. I was asked this question because I had been in a position to observe how Ray had performed as the chief financial officer of Edison Bros. Stores, Inc. My answer was an affirmative one. Ray also talked to me at length about the position, and I encouraged him to make the move. In July 1979, Walter recommended, and the board approved, Ray as president and chief operating officer. Walter continued as chairman and chief executive officer, and I became vice chairman of the board. The *St. Louis Post-Dispatch* published our pictures in a feature article. My duties as vice chairman were not demanding until Walter approached 65 years of age in 1982 and decided to resign from his responsibilities. We had hoped Walter would stay on the board as chairman, but he preferred to be free to pursue other opportunities available to him. Ray then became chairman and chief executive officer while I remained vice chairman.

Walter Bolliger's contributions to the success of Roosevelt were outstanding. For example, our assets under management at the end of 1982 were approximately $800 million, about eight times as large as when I joined the board 14 years earlier. More importantly, we accomplished this growth while maintaining a high level of quality in all aspects of the company's business. Late in the 1970s, Walter guided the board's thinking toward his conception of a new headquarters building to be located in a suburb, rather than in the downtown area. The building located in Chesterfield, Missouri, about 20 miles from downtown St. Louis was completed on October 15, 1982. In the St. Louis area and on a regional basis, Walter was recognized as a very capable executive. He also had the foresight to understand the importance of Roosevelt becoming a public company so that it would have access to the capital necessary for growth in the future.

Higher-Yielding Low-Quality Bonds

On August 20, 1982, as the savings and loan industry was experiencing high losses from escalating short-term interest rates (the prime rate charged by banks was in excess of 21 percent), Congress passed legislation authorizing S & Ls to invest 10 percent of their assets in corporate bonds as an alternative to commercial loans of the type made by commercial banks. It was obvious to me, the management and all of our board that the greater risk to us would be nonmarketable commercial loans. One reason for this conclusion was the probability that most of the loans available to us would be those that had been turned down by the banks. But there were some other reasons why investment in corporate bonds seemed quite logical. Any time a corporation goes to the marketplace with an offering of corporate bonds, a tremendous amount of financial information (all audited) is made available to the investing public. The Securities and Exchange Commission is the regulatory agency that supervises this requirement. Once the issue has been sold, the corporation is also obligated to provide updated financial information on both a quarterly and annual basis. Most important, then, is the liquidity in the marketplace that enables the investor to liquidate (sell) the investment immediately. The commercial loans made by banks are not very liquid, so when a company's financial position weakens, the bank can do very little to prevent a loss. This is why banks are required to establish reserves against their probable losses.

During 1983, Ray Gusnard and I had several discussions as to the advisability of purchasing higher-yielding, low-quality bonds. After three of my investment analysts and portfolio managers attended a conference in California in April 1984 that was attended by a large number of S & L representatives, I wrote to Ray to mention this. It certainly looked to my people as if S & Ls would begin to acquire higher-yielding corporate bonds. He followed that up by visiting me in Kansas City, and on July 27, 1984, Ray recommended to the board a program of investing in low-quality bonds.

In 1979, as I discussed earlier, I had assumed the responsibility at Waddell & Reed of introducing a new bond fund to invest in higher-yielding, lower-quality bonds. We had the people to do the research and manage the portfolio, so the fund grew rapidly with very satisfactory results. During the summer of 1984, Roosevelt surveyed three alternative managers of low-quality bonds and, after comparing them with W & R's qualifications and fees, made the decision to recommend W & R as the portfolio manager. The board approved this recommendation, and as expected, I refrained from voting on such a matter.

Commencing in 1984 and continuing through 1988, the investment results achieved with low-quality bonds were outstanding. In 1988, for example, the total return for the year was 17.5 percent. However, on August 9, 1989, Congress (because of concerns about the investments of S & Ls in low-quality bonds) passed legislation, the Financial Institutions Reform, Recovery, and Enforcement Act

(FIRREA), which mandated the liquidation of all low-quality bonds within the next five years. One development that alarmed the regulators was the practice in some state-regulated S & Ls of investing more than 25 percent of assets in this type of security. Roosevelt's position was never more than 7 percent of assets under management. By this decision, the regulators placed the public accounting profession in such a position that it had no alternative but to require S & Ls to price the bonds at their market values instead of at their original cost. The S & Ls were then placed in a situation in which the organizations knew the federal regulators would require some discounting of whatever market values were applicable. The result was that Congress had created an environment for a selling debacle. Billions of dollars worth of bonds were then for sale, and there were few buyers. Regardless of the quality of a bond, its price began to decline, which in turn began to impact the prices of the mutual funds that invested in low-quality bonds. Accordingly, the fund managers stopped buying and were forced to sell holdings to provide cash for liquidations that they were anticipating. This sad situation was then exacerbated by widespread publicity about low-quality bonds of the type brought to market in leveraged buyouts (LBO's). In the middle 1980s and through 1988, Drexel Burnham & Co. had taken the lead in providing this kind of speculative financing. This financing was much riskier than the financing of young, growing companies that had characterized the early years of the development of the low-quality bond market.

I found it difficult to believe Congress would make such a poor decision. Fortunately, the management at Roosevelt had already begun to liquidate its portfolio. At the beginning of 1989, the portfolio amounted to $168.7 million, or 6.6 percent of assets. As of June 30, the portfolio amounted to $132.5 million; and on September 30, the investment was $88.8 million, or 3.3 percent of assets. On September 30, 1989, we advised our shareholders we would liquidate the portfolio, and by December 31, 1989, our portfolio dropped to $36.1 million. The remaining bonds were then liquidated in the first quarter of 1990.

Prior to the passage of FIRREA, most S & Ls in bankruptcy had run into financial difficulty as, because of fraud or very poor judgment, they had invested in the type of commercial loans Roosevelt had avoided. After the legislation, those S & Ls holding large positions in low-quality bonds could not avoid the same fate as the S & Ls that had made poor-quality loans. Thus the taxpayers of the United States are paying a penalty that could have been lessened had there been a more thoughtful approach by Congress to regulating high-yield investments. The insurance industry, with its big investments in nonmarketable and lower-quality bonds, could have been confronted with a similar fate, but Congress took no action. Accordingly, insurance companies are still permitted to hold bond investments at cost values rather than market values.

Smith Breeden Associates, Inc.

During 1983, 1984 and 1985, my location in Kansas City presented me the opportunity to observe, through newspaper articles and magazines, the progress of an S & L called Franklin Savings Association, located near Kansas City in Ottawa, Kansas. The principal owner of Franklin, Ernest Fleischer, took the S & L from under $100 million of assets in 1980 to approximately $10 billion in 1988. His strategy was a program of purchasing deposits, investing primarily in marketable mortgage pools and hedging both the assets and liabilities from changes in interest rates. Doug Breeden and Greg Smith, partners in Smith Breeden Associates, were employed to advise Franklin in a sophisticated approach to hedging techniques using futures, interest rate swaps and other disciplines. In addition to reading about the company, I had a very productive face-to-face meeting and lunch with Wayne Angell, one of Franklin's directors, at which he explained their strategy to me. This information was interesting to me, so in 1984 and 1985, I urged Ray Gusnard to lead Roosevelt in the same direction. This culminated in Ray bringing some of his staff to Kansas City to pursue aggressively the possibility of employing Smith Breeden to advise Roosevelt. The cost of more than a half-million dollars annually for their services seemed very worthwhile, so the board approved management's recommendation. Stanley Bradshaw, who had joined Roosevelt in 1985 with an excellent background in the industry, had the credentials necessary for supervising the investment agreement with Smith Breeden that commenced May 13, 1986. Under Stan's leadership, the program was successful, and he was given the title of executive vice president and chief operating officer on October 21, 1988.

Management Changes

After Roosevelt had completed its sale of low-quality bonds during the first quarter of 1990, everything seemed to be working smoothly. On March 2, we had brought Charles Stout into the management team as senior vice president and manager of the real estate and retail banking group. As the board discussed this addition with Ray, it was understood Chuck could be considered along with Stan as successor to Ray, who was three years from retirement. Chuck had management experiences in both banks and savings and loan associations. However, in August, Ray made the decision to resign and become the chief executive officer of a large S & L in Florida.

The resignation of Ray Gusnard from Roosevelt was one of the saddest experiences of my business career. We had worked together as non-management board members from 1968 to 1977 when he became the number two man to Walter Bolliger. I had been instrumental in his having that opportunity and encouraged him to make that decision. I worked closely with him as we were successfully investing in low-quality bonds. He had the courage and foresight to employ Smith Breeden in 1986 to advise and work with us on our hedging program. He seized the opportunity to have us become a public company in January 1987. He had the good judgment to employ Stan Bradshaw and worked closely with him from 1986 to 1990. Numerous, highly important management decisions were made in those years as Roosevelt grew in size and profitability. As vice chairman, chairman of the compensation committee, and a member of other committees, my contacts with Ray Gusnard were frequent and very satisfactory. Ray did a marvelous job of taking Roosevelt through perilous times for the savings and loan industry. He is a great executive and a fine person I regard as a good friend. After Ray made his decision, the board then directed its attention to the chairmanship of the board and the organization of the management team.

Since I was vice chairman, I could have assumed the responsibility of chairman; however, I was somewhat concerned about my health and I was only seven months away from mandatory retirement on March 22, 1991. Accordingly it was much more logical for Clarence Turley, Jr., to assume the responsibility. We had come to the board together in 1968. Instead of giving the responsibility of managing the company to one man, the board temporarily established an office of the president with three coequals: Bradshaw, Loyd Garrison, the chief financial officer, and Stout. About six months later, on March 8, 1991, we made Stan Bradshaw president and chief executive officer and abandoned the office of the president. Most important to the boards decision was Stan Bradshaw's excellent execution of all his responsibilities. We also made him a member of the board of directors on August 30, 1991.

Roosevelt — A Public Corporation

Roosevelt became a public company on January 29, 1987, when we sold 5.4 million shares to the public at $9 per share. Each of the directors was allocated an option to purchase 10,000 shares at the offering price.

During this very important era in the development of the company, the Roosevelt board and management made a number of pivotal decisions to establish a good relationship with our shareholders. One decision we made when we became a public company was to pay dividends of .80 cents per share annually, even when we faced the need to build our capital base. Our policy was a reflection of our conviction that a liberal dividend policy would attract investors and facilitate additional equity financing in later years. Another important decision was to buy back about 10 percent of the shares that were outstanding, even though we knew we would face the need in the future to add to our equity base. At that time, the stock was selling at a very low price relative to its book value, and by purchasing the stock, we were automatically increasing our earnings on a per share basis. These decisions, in addition to the various policy and management decisions I have already discussed, were crucial to Roosevelt's financial stature. We had become one of the strongest savings and loan corporations in the country.

April 24, 1992

Following my retirement on my 70th birthday on March 22, 1991, the board asked me to continue as an advisory board member with no change in my participation in the responsibilities of the executive committee. The board believed the executive committee should meet twice monthly, as we stayed in close contact with the management group. This need seemed apparent in view of the numerous changes following Ray Gusnard's departure on August 24, 1990. During 1991, the meetings of the board, the executive committee and the compensation committee necessitated my making 19 trips to St. Louis. As my 71st birthday approached on March 22, 1992, I decided it was time for me to retire from my advisory board responsibilities. Roosevelt was in a strong financial position; the management group had been stabilized; and I believed there was no longer a need for my services.

The annual meeting of the shareholders and monthly meeting of the board of directors on April 24 marked the end of my 24 years of involvement with Roosevelt Financial Group, Inc. The common stock traded at $13.25 on February 28, so I added 500 shares to those I owned. When I was recognized at the luncheon meeting following the shareholder meeting, I used the opportunity to respond by emphasizing what I believed Roosevelt should strive to achieve in the growth of its earning power in the next 10 years. As I spoke, there was no doubt in my mind about the bright future of this very fine company.

On May 18, 1994, the common stock was split three shares for each share held, (the cost of my options became $3 per share), and the new shares traded at $18.25 per share. On June 30, 1994, the consummation of a merger with Farm and Home Financial Corporation was completed, bringing the total assets under management to over $8 billion and total deposits to over $5 billion. This made Roosevelt the third largest banking institution in Missouri when measured by assets under management. During the last half of 1994, the shares traded as low as $12.75 but ended the year at $15 per share. The DJIA moved to the 5200 level late in 1995 and closed the year at 5117 with Roosevelt at 19 3/8. Near the end of 1996: Roosevelt agreed to merge with Mercantile Bancorporation at $22 per share.

CHAPTER 20

◆

Insights Into Our
Personal Lives

As I mentioned earlier, Mary and I were pleased at our success in finding a house that appealed to us so quickly after I commenced working at Waddell & Reed on April 1, 1973. Its similarity to the two ranch-style homes we owned in St. Louis made our decision an easy one, yet it was not quite our dream home. Accordingly, at various times, we looked at houses in other areas just to see if we would find something with more amenities. Also, to make the house more satisfactory, we decided to finish off the basement. So, in addition to 2,400 square feet of living space on the first floor, we had a similar amount of space in the lower level. The basement was finished off very nicely with a bar, a lounge area, ping-pong area, pool room and another bathroom. Although it was satisfactory, we still wanted something more convenient for entertainment purposes on the first floor. So after living there for four years, we hired an architect to draw plans to enlarge the family room and were pleased with the ideas presented to us. Mary and I worked during the Christmas holidays in 1977 to refinish the cabinets in the kitchen, but the change in the family room was never accomplished.

About a year before we made the decision to move to Lakewood, we came very close to buying a house at Whispering Hills, a development in Kansas west of Interstate 35 on 87th Street. The developer had built a home for his family on top of a hill overlooking the entire development, but after only building a few hundred homes, the development went into bankruptcy. When the developer went bankrupt, he removed the hi-fi system (which had large speakers in every room), the swimming pool equipment, the sprinkler system, light fixtures, appliances and power draperies from his home. We estimated it would cost $25,000 for repairs. Apparently because of the damage, the bank was finding it very difficult to sell the home. It had five furnaces, five air conditioners, six bedrooms, six baths, and many very nice features, except it was not laid out very well. It also had a tennis court and three or four acres of land. An intriguing aspect of the house was a very special feature, namely, the supply of gas to the house was free in perpetuity. We liked what we saw enough to negotiate the purchase of the house for $180,000, but with the provision we would check with Cities Service Gas Company to be sure of the perpetuity clause. I immediately sent a lawyer to Tulsa, Oklahoma, to verify the validity of the gas clause. He found a slight loophole in the contract that, conceivably, could be used by Cities Service to void the perpetuity clause. When we combined this information with Mary's growing dislike of the prospect of living in the house, we came to the conclusion it was not for us. A few years later, we learned the house had sold for $500,000. Nevertheless, we had no regrets because of the isolation of the house and what it would have been like for Mary to be there by herself during all of my travels.

The Move To Lakewood

We had always wanted to live either on a lake or a golf course. Lakewood, a development by Farm and Home Financial Corporation east of Kansas City in Lee's Summit, Missouri offered us the opportunity to do exactly that. We liked the idea of living on a lake because we had thoroughly enjoyed our house at the Lake of the Ozarks. With the children out of college, we were not using the house at the Lake of the Ozarks, so it seemed logical to buy a house on a lake in the Kansas City area and sell the house at the Lake of the Ozarks. It would make better use of our money and eliminate the problem of maintaining the Lake of the Ozarks property. We had established contact with a real estate agent in the Lakewood area who kept enticing us with ideas, but after all the work we had done on our kitchen at our current home, we were reasonably content. But one cold Saturday morning the realtor called us about a house that had been sold and was back on the market. It sounded like the kind of house we wanted, and as soon as we walked into the house, we knew it was for us. That afternoon we made an offer to buy it for $175,000; the asking price was $188,000. We came up $1,000 to satisfy the seller and consummated the purchase on February 15, 1978. One of the reasons we made the decision quickly was that the location on the lake was perfect and the layout was almost identical to a house that had appealed to us on Lake Quivera. So in June, 101 Hackberry in Lee's Summit became our new home, and we were back in Missouri. Our house in Leawood sold for $150,000.

One other decision we made in connection with the move to Lakewood was to maintain membership in St. John's United Methodist Church. We liked the church and were influenced by our decision to maintain our membership with Indian Hills Country Club, which is located near the church. Since we enjoyed golfing with other couples on Sunday afternoons, we thought it would work out quite well if we kept the membership in St. John's, went to church on Sunday mornings, played golf in the afternoon and stayed for dinner afterwards. If we didn't play golf right after church, we would eat Sunday brunch at the club, play golf later in the afternoon and then go home. Over the years, that became our favorite Sunday routine.

We purchased a membership in Lakewood Oaks Golf Club because it was inexpensive and only about a five-minute drive from our new home. Mary played golf with the women at both clubs, and I would play either 9 or 18 holes with Mary at Lakewood after work during the weekdays and on Saturday afternoons. We retained our membership at Bellerive Country Club in St. Louis as a justifiable business expense because of my membership on the board of directors of Roosevelt Federal Savings and Loan Association. We also always had in mind the possibility of eventually retiring to the St. Louis area if John and his family lived there.

Our Lake Of The Ozarks Home

After we made the move to Lakewood in 1978, we made the decision to sell the house at the Lake of the Ozarks for $110,000. We had it on the market for about nine months but took it off the market when it was apparent we were in a buyer's market. At that time, we decided we could justify holding the house as a source of rental income, with John and ourselves taking turns to make the trip to the lake as people moved in and out on the week ends. John rented the house to people living in St. Louis, and we rented it to people we knew in Kansas City, primarily people who worked for me at Waddell & Reed. Unfortunately, because John became so involved with studying for the banker's school at Rutgers, it was difficult for him to get to the lake. So, during the summer of 1980, we ended up making numerous trips to take care of the place as people went in and out. Since it made some sense from an economic viewpoint, we decided to rent it out again in the summer of 1981. Again we found ourselves in a situation in which John was not available. That summer we made 12 one-day trips to the lake just for cleaning and maintenance. Even though it was successful from a financial viewpoint, it was discouraging to have people damaging the property and creating extra work for us. We also decided the lake at Lakewood was no substitute for our enjoyment of the Lake of the Ozarks, so we stopped renting out the house.

To make the house at the Lake of the Ozarks more enjoyable, we bought a pontoon boat in order to have a roof as protection from the sun. We thought this would make it possible for us to be out in the boat for a long time, anchor in some cove, swim off the boat and have a picnic lunch. We were right, and the pontoon boat became a very pleasant way to enjoy the Lake of the Ozarks. We also commenced making physical changes to modernize the house and add special features to the property to make it more comfortable. Prior to 1982, we had done many things, such as reinforcing the rock wall along our 240 feet of lake frontage, adding a 10 x 40-foot deck, and buying a new boat dock and a new Sea Ray speedboat in 1970. Storm windows, carpeting, a new roof, a large black-topped parking area, a new furnace and central air conditioning made the place appealing. In 1983, we modernized the kitchen completely, which, not unexpectedly, increased Mary's enjoyment of the house. In 1984, we bought a new pontoon boat and a new speedboat.

Following my retirement on December 31, 1986, we spent most of the winter and the spring at the lake, with contractors completely remodeling the lower level, vaulting the living room ceiling, remodeling the upstairs bathroom, installing ceiling fans and repairing the deck. The most important decision, from my viewpoint, was to find a place to build a basketball court. This we accomplished that spring, and when people ask how to find our place when coming by water, we just say to look for the lake house with half of a basketball court along the shore.

Our Social Life

The various business and extra professional responsibilities I assumed in Kansas City dictated a lifestyle that both Mary and I thoroughly enjoyed. Until John and Susan moved to Kansas City in 1984, Mary and I were seldom in contact with the children and grandchildren except by telephone. As the chief investment officer of a large investment organization, I had to spend some of my evening and weekend hours studying investment material. Mary cooperated fully and happily so that, other than golfing, church activities and attending the basketball games of the Kansas City Kings, our lives in Kansas City were quite reclusive. If I had been married to a woman who wanted an active social life, entertaining and being entertained by our friends, business associates, golfing partners and others with whom we had some kind of contact, I could never have done the kinds of things I have written about in this book. Mary was an avid reader and quite content with occupying herself in that way, while I read investment research reports, prepared speeches, wrote articles for publication and did a great amount of traveling. We were fortunate to have the opportunity for Mary to accompany me on many of my trips. In almost every situation, we were able to play a few games of golf, quite frequently at some of the most attractive and challenging golf courses on the U.S. mainland and in Hawaii. We even worked in seven days of golf in Scotland with 13 other couples from Indian Hills Country Club.

Mary developed many close personal relationships with the women golfers at Indian Hills, so her summers were filled with pleasant days and luncheons. She also was a volunteer worker for the Research Medical Center. My numerous trips to visit with our sales offices around the country and speak before shareholder meetings arranged by division managers and regional vice presidents also provided Mary an outlet for her natural outgoing approach to associating with people. Although we felt the stress associated with my responsibilities, our lives during all my working years could not have been more peaceful, harmonious and satisfying.

Mary, John and I were taken by surprise when Lynne arrived in Greencastle, Indiana, for John's graduation in May 1973. We had kept her informed of our plans, but she had not mentioned leaving Austin, Texas. Unexpectedly , some friends of hers were driving to the East Coast, and they were able to drop her off the night before the ceremony. She and John had always had a good relationship, and she thought it would mean a lot to him. When she arrived, she was accompanied by her part coyote dog, Ono. Lynne had gotten her as a puppy for companionship while she was hitchhiking up the West Coast. During the summer of 1973 following John's graduation, Lynne lived with him at our house at the Lake of the Ozarks. While at the lake, Ono gave birth to a litter of puppies, and we could not resist the temptation to select one to bring to Lee's Summit, since by then all our children were out of college and we were alone. We named her Bulldozer because she was the most aggressive dog in the litter when they were feeding.

Bulldozer was tan-colored, lean like a Greyhound and about the same size. She was smart, obedient and could run very fast. Her hair was short, and she shed a lot, so, we kept her outside when the weather permitted. When Bulldozer was in the house, she liked to follow Mary around and sit beside her, which at times exasperated Mary, but not to a point where she objected to having a dog. During the years we had Bulldozer, I was more faithful about walking and running than I had ever been before. She was truly a good companion for both of us and came close to meaning as much to me as Spot, the dog who was my pet when we lived on Northwestern Avenue in West Lafayette, Indiana.

When we moved to Lakewood, the area in front of the house toward the lake was fenced in, but Bulldozer could jump over it when she wanted to roam the neighborhood. Most of the time, she was content to stay at our home and guard our property. In Leawood our back yard was enclosed in a very high fence, so this change was something she liked. One day late in the spring of 1982 (Bulldozer was about nine years old) when she was outside the fence, she did not come running home when I called her. After searching the neighborhood that day and the next morning, we contacted all of the animal shelters within about 10 miles of our home. Every day for the next few days, we drove all around Lakewood, but to no avail. The weekend was approaching, so, with the remote possibility she had gone to the Lake of the Ozarks, we drove the 150 miles with Mary looking out one side of the car and me the other. We did the same thing on the return trip. About three weeks later when we were away on a business trip, one of our neighbors, a medical doctor, found her body washed up on the shore of the lake. When we returned, he told us that, since there were no wounds on her body, she must have died of a heart attack caused by jumping into the ice cold water. Ice was still on the lake, but the area close to shore had melted, so his explanation seemed plausible. One of her ways to cool off after running was to jump in the lake at almost full speed. All of our family felt badly about the loss of a really great pet.

Beaver Lake, Arkansas

The parents of Virginia Davis, our good friend from Glen Ellyn, Illinois, were retired and lived near Eureka Springs and Beaver

Lake in the northwest portion of Arkansas. A real estate broker, Jim Overton, in Eureka Springs was short of cash and desperately anxious to buy two parcels of land on the lake. One 200-acre piece was priced at about $88,000, and the other, with three miles of shoreline, was around $130,000. On a trip to visit Virginia's parents, she and Rolly, her husband, became very enthusiastic about the formation of a partnership with Jim Overton as a general partner and Rolly and me as limited partners. Although we could borrow almost all the money needed to buy the property, the stock market was depressed; for this reason, I told Rolly I would feel more comfortable about the advisability of the venture if we added other partners. He agreed, and with this objective, he invited Jim Overton to attend a meeting in Glen Ellyn, Illinois, with some of our friends. Rolly had prepared a number of slides, and when the meeting was concluded, eight of us became limited partners on April 4, 1970. My investment was only $3,750, and with that I was entitled to buy one or more lots having that value. After visiting the property, we selected two waterfront lots.

Our general partner, Jim Overton, employed an expert on earth-moving equipment to accompany him as they rode on horses to notch out the trees to cut down for building more than eight miles of roads. Electricity was brought into both properties, and water wells were also drilled. Sales were made, and the property began to produce profits. In 1972 we were concerned about our financial statements, so I employed two partners of Arthur Andersen & Co. to audit the books in Arkansas. After having been in Arkansas with Jim Overton and his accountant for two days, they advised me to forget having an audit conducted if we were satisfied with the profitability of our venture. The decision was easily made, and the unorthodox accounting accepted because we were delighted with Jim Overton's performance. We completed the project in 1996 and dissolved our partnership. The appreciation in value on our investment over the 26 year period was about 30 percent a year.

Over the years we traveled to Arkansas frequently and, beginning in the late '70s, twice a year. Rolly and Virginia had retired to Arkansas, and when Jim Overton's health deteriorated, Rolly became general partner. We enjoyed visiting the area and being with our friends, the Davises. However, Mary had no desire to live in the area because it was so isolated from those things important to her. She was also fearful of the time it would take to get medical assistance in emergency situations.

Our Personal Finances

As I mentioned in Chapter 9, our investments when we arrived in St. Louis in 1964 had a value of about $24,000. Quite naturally we hoped to begin to make greater progress with my higher salary, yet with Barbara in college we knew saving money would continue to be a challenge. I was also confronted with the difficulty of executing sales and purchases only when no one could question my motive for doing so. This was because my position as chief investment officer required me always to approve the decisions of all my money managers in buying or selling common stocks in the accounts for which they were responsible. This meant my trading activity was severely hampered. In effect, I was committed to hold any stock I owned until all our customers had been reviewed and action taken by the money managers if it was appropriate for the account. On the opposite side, when we purchased a stock, I could not buy for myself until I was sure I would not benefit personally from the effect of our company's buying power on the price action of the stock. Although this limitation on my trading activity had been a problem for me at St. Louis Union Trust Company, when I joined Waddell & Reed it became even more serious because the greater activity in the portfolios made it almost impossible for me to defend any trades I would have liked to make. Nevertheless, I was still able to make steady progress in building our portfolio.

By December 1968, our common stocks had a value of about $335,000, but I had borrowed $115,000, which meant the net value was $220,000. Stock prices had increased steadily until the market peaked at 995 on the Dow Jones Industrial Average (DJIA) in December 1968. When I joined St. Louis Union Trust Company on February 15, 1964, the DJIA was at 795. At the end of 1970, with the DJIA at 839, our holdings totaled $310,000 with the loan from the bank now up to $140,000. Accordingly the net value was $170,000, a decline of $50,000 in two years. Two years later, at the end of 1972, with the DJIA at 1020 (just before the move to Kansas City), the value of the portfolio was $332,000. I had reduced the loan slightly to $115,000, so the net value of $217,000 was about the same as it had been at the end of 1968. This meant we had made no progress for four years. Still, our investments did keep pace with the DJIA that closed out 1972 at 1020, having been at 995 at the end of 1968. My position in McDonald's that I had acquired in 1967 had appreciated steadily and amounted to $120,000; the St. Louis Union Trust Company investment amounted to $110,000. This meant that two-thirds of my portfolio, which had a market value of $332,000, was in two stocks.

In January 1973, the Dow moved up a small amount and peaked at 1052 as a bear market commenced that lasted for almost two years. In the early months of 1973, I was so involved with my decision to move to Kansas City and establish myself with Waddell & Reed that I completely neglected my investments. Then, when I decided to reduce my bank loan and liquidate some holdings, I was precluded from doing so because almost every stock I owned was in one or more of the mutual funds. Between July 1973 and January 1974, I did not even take the time to record the declining value of my portfolio. Although I was somewhat unhappy with what was happening to our net worth, it did not cost me a minute of sleep. Instead we placed a $35,000 mortgage on our house in Kansas City and borrowed another $35,000 with a loan against our house at the Lake of the Ozarks. Common stocks were at such bargain levels I wished we had more money than even these loans provided to put into the stock market.

When the DJIA reached its low point of 577.60 on October 4, 1974, the gross value of our common stocks was $114,721, against which I had borrowed $80,000, giving us a net worth of $34,721, excluding the equity in our two homes. The stock market had declined 45 percent, and my portfolio had declined 84 percent from its peak net value of $220,000 in December 1968. The risks associated with being heavily leveraged are obvious. Yet by being so fully invested when the market turned around and moved upward, the recovery was exceptionally gratifying. By the end of 1980, with the DJIA at the 1000 level, our investments in the stock market had a value of $429,000. This change in the DJIA was about a 73 percent increase from its low of 578 on October 4, 1974. From then until the present, which is the final quarter of 1996, the DJIA has been in a strong uptrend, with the only meaningful interruption being the short-lived collapse of the stock market in the fall of 1987. With the DJIA now at the 6000 level, the change in stock prices has presented a tremendous opportunity to make money. The last time the DJIA was at the 1000 level was near the end of 1982. The move to reach the 6000 level over a period of 13 years has truly been phenomenal.

During this period, I have not deviated from being fully invested in common stocks and have continued my policy of concentrating investments in companies with which I am very familiar. Investment advisors, like myself, are usually correct when they advise investors to become more conservative after they have retired; however every situation is somewhat different, and generalizations can be misleading. Since it has never been necessary for me to obtain income from my investments, I have always concentrated on owning the common stocks of companies that are growing rapidly and paying a small amount of their earnings to shareholders as dividends. The increase in our net worth had no impact on our life-style while Mary was alive and none on me since her death.

CHAPTER 21

◆

Mary's Illness And AIDS

We did not discover that Mary had a serious blood problem until she had a hysterectomy on August 26, 1959. As a child she had suffered from nose bleeds without apparent provocation, but it was controllable, albeit with difficulty. In hindsight, the difficulties with Barbara's birth on December 9, 1943, should have alerted us that Mary's blood did not coagulate as readily as is normal. After the birth, Mary required more than 60 stitches and a prolonged stay of close to six weeks in the hospital. She also experienced some bleeding after the birth of our son, John, on January 23, 1951; however, it was not excessive.

The 1959 surgery was performed at Delnor Hospital, located near St. Charles, Illinois, about 15 miles west of our home in Glen Ellyn. This was a small regional hospital, but we felt comfortable with its head surgeon, Dr. Wyngarden, performing the hysterectomy. It seemed to be an uneventful operation, and she was released on September 7 only to be readmitted on September 16 when she began to bleed excessively. The doctor's solution was to pack her, believing sufficient pressure would halt the bleeding. He was not successful, and with the loss of a large amount of blood, transfusions were mandatory.

Rolly Davis organized a blood donation program with the members of the Glen Ellyn Kiwanis Club. For about six weeks, they were a continuing source of blood for Mary.

As time passed, I decided our doctor had exhausted his skills to treat Mary and asked for help from The Northern Trust Company. The Northern managed the endowment fund of the Presbyterian-St. Luke's Hospital in Chicago, and, through that contact, I learned of Dr. Albala, a highly regarded blood specialist in the city. I contacted him, arranged for an ambulance to move her and notified the physician at Delnor. He did not object and was obviously happy to be relieved of the responsibility. I rode in the ambulance with Mary for the one-hour trip into downtown Chicago.

The hospital staff began a series of tests, and, shortly after we arrived, Dr. Albala examined her for the first time. He removed the packing and immediately said it was doing more harm than good. He also told Mary she should not worry about the bleeding since she would not bleed to death. He believed her body would heal naturally if left alone. The psychological and physical results were both impressive, and Mary was out of the hospital in less than a week.

The cause of her bleeding necessitated extensive research, and, coincidental with her release, we were told the problem was hyperheparinemia. Heparin is a natural blood-thinning substance produced by the body, and Mary's heparin levels were excessive. There is a treatment for it, and from then until 1984, Mary carried a card with her describing the procedure to be followed to control any bleeding she might have.

After that diagnosis, Mary had several scary experiences. One was in March 1962, when an oral surgeon ignored our request and used naturally dissolving stitches following the removal of a tooth. After the stitches dissolved, she began bleeding heavily. I rushed her to the hospital; new stitches were applied, and she healed in a satisfactory manner. Another time in the middle of the night, Mary began to vomit and excrete blood. I called the Davises who lived several blocks away, and they arrived in just a few minutes. I carried her to the car, and we were at Delnor hospital in almost 30 minutes. Barbara was old enough to take care of Lynne and John. The bleeding persisted for a few hours, but it stopped without treatment. The exact cause of the bleeding was not determined; however, we had been at a party the previous evening when, over a period of about three hours, she had two alcoholic drinks. Quite unscientifically but perhaps logically, the doctor recommended she limit herself to one mild drink in the future. Mary never violated that suggestion and in fact rarely ever took an alcoholic drink.

On November 5, 1975, Mary had another tooth extracted, and, despite our warnings to the dentist, bleeding commenced as soon as the stitches dissolved. She was admitted to the Research Medical Center in Kansas City where they followed the treatment prescribed in 1959. It proved to be ineffective, and as before, new stitches were eventually successful. This event led to our search for a specialist to test Mary's blood. As a result we were directed to Dr. Marjorie Sirridge, a specialist in hematology at the University of Kansas. Her tests were conducted on May 19, 1977, and she concluded the problem was not caused by heparin. Instead she diagnosed Mary as having a mild case of Von Willebrands disease, a problem with coagulation caused by deficiency of factor VIII.

This diagnosis was confirmed by Dr. Amare at the University of Kansas on November 24, 1980, and again by Dr. Sirridge, on May 25, 1983.

August 31, 1984

As I said in Chapter 17, I was highly honored to be the guest speaker on "Wall Street Week" on August 31, 1984. Since the audience was national in scope, the interview was important to my company because we operated in 50 states with more than 3,000 salespeople who could benefit from the publicity. From a personal viewpoint, it was a recognition of my stature in the investment industry.

Mary was proud of me and sensitive to this honor's importance in our lives. Accordingly when I left the house around 7:00 in the morning to drive to the airport for the trip to Washington, D.C., I was unaware that, during the night, she had been experiencing excruciating intestinal pains. As soon as I left the house, she drove herself to our internist, Dr. William Eubank, whose office was located in Kansas City's Research Medical Center complex. She was immediately admitted to the hospital, where they sedated her while beginning a series of tests to determine the cause of the pain. John and my secretary were notified and followed Mary's wish not to let me know until after the program, which was at 6:30 in the evening Kansas City time. I could not leave for home until the next morning.

It took until September 4 to determine the cause of her pain to be adhesions in her small intestine, which were probably the result of the hysterectomy performed in 1959. Dr. Eubank introduced Dr. Nancy Abdou, a hematologist and oncologist, into the picture, and they began to prepare for surgery by giving her five units of cryoprecipitate that would correct the factor VIII deficiency and increase her platelet count. The surgery, performed by a golfing friend, Eric Quer, was quite minor. It was performed on September 5 with more units of cryoprecipitate being given over a four-day period. Mary had some internal bleeding on September 8, so in addition, they started her on Amicar (a drug formulated to control serious bleeding) while also giving her 10 units of platelets. The bleeding, which was mild, ceased on September 12, and Amicar was continued until September 17 when she was released.

Mary did not feel well after she returned home, but when we saw Dr. Nancy Abdou on September 28 about her dry mouth, Dr. Abdou said she had a mild case of leukopenia, a disease that reduces the number of white blood corpuscles. She saw Dr. Eubank on October 15 about pain between her shoulders, but no conclusions were reached, although he then noted enlargement of several lymph nodes. The pain between her shoulder blades interfered with her sleep, although Darvon, an effective painkiller, helped. When she saw Dr. Abdou on October 15, a CAT scan of her chest did not provide any explanation of her pain. When Dr. Abdou examined Mary on October 24, her conclusion in regard to the lymph nodes was that Mary had mononucleosis, possibly induced by the blood transfusions and blood products. Visits on October 30, November 6, November 20 and December 11 were unproductive. When we visited Dr. Abdou on January 14, 1985, the pain had disappeared from her back. Mary and I had played golf over Christmas and during the first week in January in Texas, and she did not complain of anything except a slight swelling in some of her lymph nodes. Barbara and her husband joined us for several days of golf while we were at the Rancho Viejo resort near Brownsville, Texas.

At our February visit with Dr. Abdou, she recommended we go through the Mayo Clinic in Rochester, Minnesota, to see if they could explain the problem with the lymph glands. They were also to evaluate the advisability of surgery for a urethral prolapse.

The Mayo Clinic

We were in Rochester for three days from February 25-27. The physician assigned to us was Dr. Letendre; however, our only contacts with him were the opening and closing interviews. The testing procedure was well organized and, as might be expected, very professional and impressive. They did not do a biopsy on the lymph nodes, but they did conduct a biopsy of her bone marrow. Their diagnosis was that Mary had a low-grade B-cell lymphoma. Dr. Letendre discussed the prognosis at length, explaining the difference between leukemia and lymphoma and advising us Mary could live anywhere from three to ten years without the necessity of chemotherapy. We were also reassured that the treatment would control the growth of the cancer so that her life expectancy was very good. We left with the feeling Mary's situation could have been more frightening, even though we had not anticipated anything this serious. Dr. Abdou's reaction to this report was rather noncommittal.

The USC-Kenneth Norris, Jr., Cancer Hospital

My next contact with Dr. Abdou was a telephone call I received on April 30. I visited with her, and she let me read a letter she had received from the University of Southern California-Kenneth Norris, Jr., Cancer Hospital and Research Institute. The letter reported on the evaluation of the pathological material she sent to them following our visit to Mayo. Their letter stated the B-cell lymphomas occurred in homosexual men at risk for AIDS, but that Mary's low-grade lymphoma was different from the high-grade pathologic type in homosexual men who had a high incidence of central nervous system involvement during the course of the disease. The doctor who wrote the letter was Alexandra Levine, and in the letter, she said she did not believe Mary's lymphoma was related to AIDS. She also requested that we visit them for complete testing as soon as possible. Dr. Abdou agreed and thought I would want to break the news to Mary before the trip was arranged.

I was shocked, yet hopeful, because of the tone of the letter. However, by the spring of 1985, there was so much publicity about the severity of AIDS, it was impossible to be optimistic. I simply could not show the letter to Mary and delayed talking to her about the letter and making the arrangements for the trip. Dr. Abdou had told me she had initiated contact with Norris because the hospital had a lymphoma specialist on their staff. This is how I approached Mary to decide when we should go. I do not recall when I told her she might have the human immunodeficiency virus (HIV) and could eventually develop AIDS. I do know that Mary treated it as a non-event. There were no tears and no visible emotion. I did my best to be casual and nonchalant; perhaps I was convincing. Mary had always believed her blood disease would shorten her life. It is conceivable she combined that with her belief that death, when it came, would be God's will for her life. She was not fatalistic in the sense that God would cause it to happen. She had more of a feeling that one did everything possible in order to stay alive, but a person should accept what life brings.

At 11:00 A.M. on June 20, 1985, we met Dr. Alexandra M. Levine. Our initial meeting with her was relatively short and simply a preliminary to four days of testing and interviews with a variety of specialists. Their testing included another bone marrow test and, for the first time, a biopsy of a lymph node. Mary had also been complaining of some visual problems, so she underwent a thorough examination of her eyesight.

At the conclusion of the four days of testing, Dr. Levine again met with us and was emphatic in reassuring us that HTLV3 (now shortened to HIV) did not necessarily cause AIDS, and, in Mary's case, she did not expect AIDS to develop. In her opinion, Mary had "persistent, generalized lymphadenopathy," which was characterized by fatigue, malaise, fever and swollen lymph nodes. She reassured us that, before long, all those symptoms would disappear. Furthermore, the lymphoma would never be a serious problem because, when the time came, the chemotherapy treatment would be one pill a day, with no side effects, that would completely control the disease. Her advice to Mary was to take care of herself, to listen to her body and, if she felt tired, rest and not push it, etc. Although she hoped and believed Mary would not develop AIDS, she cautioned us not to be too optimistic because they still had a great deal to learn about the HIV virus. We were also told that their analysis of Mary's bleeding problem indicated a different cause than the one determined by Dr. Sirridge in Kansas City. After we returned to Kansas City, Dr. Sirridge refuted their conclusions. Their testing of Mary's eyes did not indicate any cause for our being concerned.

From the University of California campus to Mission Viejo was only about an hour's drive. We left feeling much relieved and thoroughly enjoyed a long weekend with our daughter Lynne and her family. Dr. Levine sent the results of the tests to Dr. Abdou, and not much later, we were told that the blood bank had traced the source of Mary's transfusions to a homosexual who had given the blood as a part of a company's program of cooperating with the blood bank.

During our week at the hospital, we learned some things about the sexual habits of homosexual men that apparently accelerated the spread of AIDS. At that time and for several years before, there were places of business in some large cities like San Francisco and New York that were called "bath houses." Inside were open door cubicles where men would be available for anal intercourse with multiple sex partners. It is my understanding that homosexual men might have been vulnerable to the development of AIDS because their immune systems were weakened, as their bodies had to fight off infections from the abuse of anal intercourse. I believe studies have indicated that the rapid spread of the virus in the United States among homosexual men was facilitated by a combination of the mobility of our society and the large numbers of men who frequented the "bath houses."

However, that has nothing to do with the fact that once the HIV virus became active in humans, it was just a matter of time before it would spread throughout the United States. More than 12 years have passed since Mary became a victim of this terrible disease, and all over the world the disease is spreading rapidly. The life-style of some homosexual men is no longer the focal point of the spread of this disease. It is the moral weakness of many segments of our society, heterosexual adults and young people included, that make the spread of the disease so pervasive and frightening. The tainted blood that came from a homosexual killed Mary. I can never forget that. But organizations like the American Red Cross, the Centers for Disease Control and many people in our government could have moved more quickly to test our blood supplies. Mary would not have been a victim, and her life would have been spared. One reason for not testing the blood at an earlier date was the cost, which was quite nominal. In my view it was an inexcusable delay. Books that analyze the excuses have been written on this subject. The fact is they had the technological knowledge to commence testing blood for the presence of the HIV virus early in 1984 instead of early in 1985. But being bitter solves nothing, and Mary felt the same way.

Living With The AIDS Virus

In a normal person's blood, there are twice as many T4 helper cells as there are T8 suppressor cells. Just before we departed for California, Mary's ratio was tested for the first time and proved to be drastically reversed, with a percentage of 13 percent T4s instead of the 200 percent that is normal. In effect, she had no immune system.

Mary's visits to Dr. Abdou were at least monthly, and periodically the T4:T8 ratio was analyzed and showed no improvement. In November 1985, the ratio was 6 percent and remained in that area. Accordingly, we knew that, without an immune system, Mary was vulnerable to almost any kind of infection. Dr. Abdou expressed some encouragement in the numbers by stressing the fact we did not know what Mary's T4:T8 ratio was prior to her getting the virus. Other than always having this concern with us, Mary was able to live a fairly normal life until November 1986. She played golf, traveled with me and outwardly seemed to be happy about life in general.

She had decided not to tell anyone about the HIV virus and, instead, cited the lymphoma as the only health problem she had of any consequence. At the same time, she and I could not ignore the fact that radio, newspapers, magazines and television were constant reminders of the increasing evidence of the fatal nature of the HIV virus. Her only reason for not telling the family, relatives and friends about the virus was the widespread misunderstanding of how the infection is spread from one to another. Actual contact with an infected person's blood and sexual intercourse were the means of transmittal. We were told not to be afraid of kissing, with a word of warning that contact with saliva should be minimized. Sneezing and coughing were said not to be a means of transmittal. Mary and I slept together, carefully followed their instructions and, other than not having any sexual intercourse, had a normal husband-wife relationship. In her contact with the grandchildren, Mary avoided kissing them but held them without any fear of transmitting the virus.

Mary's Other Health Problems

During Mary's hospital stay in the first week of September 1984, it was determined she had a potentially serious gallstone problem. This conclusion was based on the realization that the stones could break loose and cause considerable pain at almost any time. Accordingly, those doctors familiar with her condition, specifically the HIV virus and potential bleeding, were looking for an opportune moment for gallstone surgery. Also, as a result of difficulties with the birth of our children, Mary was in need of surgery in the vaginal area. The various doctors involved recommended, and we approved, all the surgery at one time. Mary's health in the fall of 1985 was as good as could be expected, so she was in Research Medical Center Hospital in Kansas City from October 6 through October 22 for both operations. Dr. Quer and Dr. Doerring removed the gall bladder while Dr. Rodgers and his associate, Dr. Habib, performed the vaginal surgery. They were unable to correct the urethral prolapse because, they said, the tissue was so thin it would never hold. One night following surgery when Dr. Habib was on call, both he and I were contacted by the head nurse on duty to let us know that Mary was experiencing vaginal bleeding. When I arrived, he was not present. It wasn't until around 5:00 A.M. that he examined her and made the decision to try to handle the bleeding with additional sutures. To do this, Mary was moved to a nearby room where some facilities he needed were available. The nurse assigned to assist him was very nervous, and neither one of us could clearly understand his broken English. The correct needle, sutures and a few other items were ordered from the supply room, but the man on duty would not release them. Finally, the release was accomplished. But when they arrived after a much too lengthy delay of at least a half an hour, neither the needles nor the sutures were as ordered. In the meantime Mary was wide awake, apprehensive and a bundle of nerves. I held her in my arms at times to reassure her, and when the suturing was done without anything to numb the pain, she simply held my hands and squeezed as hard as she could as he closed off the blood vessels that were responsible. Whether the use of the wrong-sized needle made it more painful for her we never knew. However, he was successful, and Mary ended up spending 16 days in the hospital.

More Surgery—Then Europe

Another 10 days in the hospital were necessary from May 8 to May 17, 1986, when Mary had to be operated on for an obstruction in her small intestine. It proved to be a simple operation but, as usual, we were apprehensive. Having surgery on her birthday was not an enjoyable way to celebrate 65 years.

Mary was also concerned about the surgery interfering with a trip to Switzerland that was scheduled for May 22. The purpose of the business side of this trip was for our home office senior management and regional vice presidents to honor and reward the best sales representatives of the company. We looked forward to the seven days in Switzerland because the trip was an all-out effort to do something very special for the regional vice presidents and the salespeople. The format of our company's approach to recognizing our salespeople was to have six regional meetings around the country to recognize a large number of people and then do something special for the very best. In March, April and May, I was in Georgia, Arizona, Idaho, Oklahoma, Wisconsin and Pennsylvania for the regional meetings. Mary was with me for the Wisconsin and Oklahoma trips. During all these months, Mary was in the doctors' offices on a biweekly basis as they monitored her condition. My traveling was virtually continuous and included trips to Boston, Chicago, New York, Los Angeles and San Francisco for meetings with potential institutional investors in our initial public common stock offering of TMK United, the holding company for Waddell & Reed and United Investors Life Insurance Company. Travel to these cities was in a Torchmark plane, so it was a very efficient use of time.

Mary and I were able to make the trip to Europe, and her health was the best it had been since she contracted the virus. We were always on the move, riding buses, walking for hours, talking and visiting; in effect, we enjoyed every aspect of the trip.

After our week with the sales force, Mary and I took a train from Geneva to Zurich to show her some sights I had enjoyed on my previous business trips. From there we flew to Paris, and life could not have been nicer. We visited the Louvre, enjoyed the sidewalk cafes, took some sightseeing tours and had about three days happily filled with the simple pleasures of just being alive.

From there we flew to Amsterdam and did the usual sightseeing. Our plans called for three days in London, but, unfortunately, a fog closed in over the Amsterdam Airport and delayed our departure one day. With the turmoil and the language difficulty, both of us concluded another trip by us to a foreign country was highly unlikely.

When we arrived in London, we discovered our luggage had gone astray. We returned on the second day to search the airport lost and found areas but to no avail. The next day we left London, so the downtown area, Westminster, St. Paul's Cathedral and the Tower of London were about the extent of our sightseeing. Our luggage found its way to Kansas City two weeks later.

Reno, Nevada, And October 31, 1986

On March 19, 1986, Mary was with me as I made a trip west to speak at shareholder meetings organized by our sales force. Our first stop was in Reno, and from there, I went on to speak in Sacramento and San Jose. On this trip, Mary and I worked in a weekend in Grant's Pass, Oregon, to celebrate my 65th birthday with my sister Mary Grond and her family.

While in Reno, Mary was impressed with the Grand, a large hotel and gambling casino that had just been opened. We had not stayed there and only saw it as we had breakfast with some of our salespeople before we departed for Sacramento. After we left, Mary suggested that we celebrate our 45th wedding anniversary by coming back for a couple of days around October 31. It took some advance planning, but I was able to work in a speech at Oklahoma City on Thursday, October 30, and arrive in Reno to stay at the Grand Hotel on October 31. Neither of us did anything but play the 5, 10 and 25-cent slot machines for a few hours and attend the extravaganza show that night.

The next morning, we flew to Mission Viejo, California, to spend the weekend with Lynne, Steve and the three children they had at that time. The newest was Charles Thomas (CT), who was born on September 17 and was just six weeks old. Usually Mary would spend two weeks with Lynne after a child was born. This time Mary's health did not permit her to be there. It was difficult for Mary because she really wanted to help Lynne ... and besides that she loved babies. She was so good at rocking and holding them that Lynne tells her children she's sure " their Meme" loves and rocks the babies in heaven.

A day or two after we returned home from Mission Viejo, Mary's arms broke out with a reddish color, and before long, her face had a similar appearance. Her first thought was that the smoke at the casino was the culprit. We also thought it might be a reaction to Lynne's dog or cat. She made an appointment with our dermatologist, Dr. Gordon Sauer, and he described it as "contact dermatitis." Her appointments with him were weekly in November and December as he endeavored to bring it under control. The itching was severe, and the prescriptions were relatively ineffective. Later, another dermatologist, who saw her in the hospital in August 1987, prescribed a skin cream, but it was also to no avail. The redness was gradually replaced on her arms and legs by a leathery skin condition. In effect, with no immune system available, she could not recover from what should have been a minor problem.

I retired on December 31, 1986, and during the last two weeks in January, we were back at our favorite place in Hawaii, the Maui El Dorado. We played golf almost every day, usually starting before 8:00 A.M. so that we could be out of the sun before it was very high. From there we flew home for a couple of days and then on to Florida for a meeting of the board of governors of the Investment Company Institute at Naples, Florida. While there I developed a bad head cold and missed some of the meetings. We did play golf twice, and Mary was the relatively healthy person. As soon as we returned home, we left for our house at Lake of the Ozarks to begin some extensive remodeling on February 17. From then until late in May, we spent most of our time at the lake, making decisions and running errands for the contractor. It never occurred to us that dust from sawing wood and sanding the wallboard would be a problem, but on March 4, I took Mary to the Lake Ozark Hospital emergency room with one eye so inflamed she could not see with it. She was treated, and after keeping a patch over her eye for a few days, she healed satisfactorily. However, I soon noticed that Mary tired quite easily, and by the early part of April, she was avoiding something as simple as walking down to the lakefront where they were doing a great deal of landscaping and building the basketball court.

In retrospect, we should have been more aggressive in our contacts with her doctors during this period of declining health. On February 24, we had seen Dr. Richard Butin, an associate of Dr. Eubanks, but at that time, Mary was feeling quite good. Her next appointment with Dr. Abdou was set for May 15. On April 3 and on May 7, she had appointments with her eye doctor, but we both considered them routine.

She saw Dr. Gordon Sauer, her skin specialist, on May 8 and

May 15 and had an appointment with Dr. Abdou on May 15. Mary's weakness was becoming quite apparent, and Dr. Abdou and Dr. Eubank scheduled a series of extensive tests, focusing on the diarrhea problem that had gradually developed. We knew and they knew it was related to the HIV virus. At this time, the ratio of Mary's T4 to T8 cells was 4 to 100 instead of a normal 200 to 100.

June 19, 1987, was the last time Mary played golf. It was a Sunday afternoon at Hillcrest Country Club with some good friends, Doris and Les Rist. She awakened that morning with a severe case of diarrhea and immediately took Pepto-Bismol tablets to bring it under control. She did not want to let them down, and by the time we left the house around 12:30 P.M., it was under control. However Mary's coordination had worsened so much that, on two or three holes, she picked up the ball and did not finish the holes. That was highly unusual for her. We had a pleasant dinner and evening, and I know the Rists never suspected the extent or nature of Mary's medical problems.

Both Lynne and John's families were with us at the Lake of the Ozarks for the July 4 holiday. Barbara and Jim came on the fifth. Lynne, Steve and family had been at the lake for some time on vacation, and the rest of us joined them for the weekend. On Sunday a severe storm, actually a tornado, moved over our house and took the top of a tree and laid it across our car and part of the house. At the peak of the storm everyone, except Mary and I, went to the lower level. She refused to go, for reasons we never discussed. It was during that weekend that Lynne, John and Barbara became aware of how easily Mary tired.

On July 17, she had an appointment with Dr. Donald Black, an associate of Dr. Eubank, to see if he could help with the diarrhea problem. She had previously seen Dr. Eubank on June 26 when he had her colon X-rayed while conducting other tests. When Mary met with Dr. Abdou on July 29, they conducted another extensive series of tests. On August 4, the Research Radiological Group, Inc. conducted additional tests. By this time, Mary had become so weak that I had to place her in a wheelchair to take her from one area of the hospital to another.

Finally, on August 7, Mary and I met with Dr. David Smith, the head of the infectious disease department at the hospital. It was on a Friday, and he arranged for her to be admitted on August 10. The decision he immediately made was to contact the Burroughs-Wellcome Drug Company to ask permission to give her AZT, the only drug known to delay death for those afflicted with the virus. He was hopeful they would consent, but he did not believe the drug would be available for about three weeks. I was dismayed, but over the weekend, we both tried to be optimistic. Dr. Smith was recognized as one of the leading AIDS doctors in the city. I have often wondered whether consultation with him earlier in 1987 might have prolonged Mary's life. I console myself with the knowledge that even now, more than eight years later, little meaningful progress has been made against the disease.

I Told Barbara, Lynne And John

All that was accomplished for Mary during her stay in the hospital from August 7 to August 22 was to let her rest while every test that could be conceived was conducted. Specialists from every area were brought into the picture. They also began to focus on the probability that the virus had invaded her central nervous system. Since Mary had the HIV virus, a warning was placed on the door to her room that made it impossible to hide the cause of Mary's problems from our children and their spouses. I decided to make telephone calls to Barbara and Lynne to tell them, and a conversation with John followed.

During the first week of her stay in the hospital, I was with her all the time and in frequent contact with both Barbara and Lynne, who did not live in Kansas City. Barbara and her husband, Jim, decided to come down for the weekend, so I decided to play golf on Saturday morning. I thought it might help me handle the stress with which I was trying to cope. John arranged to stay at the hospital with Mary. Late in the morning, we were on the 12th fairway when my heart began to fibrillate. The "pro" at Indian Hills drove me to the emergency room; John was called to come down from Mary's room; and I was admitted to the hospital and placed in a room on her floor. About that time, Barbara and Jim arrived, and we agreed not to tell Mary. During the night, my heart became regular, and the next morning I was able to walk down to Mary's room. I was released on Monday, and she came home a week later.

When Mary was released, she also received word she could start taking AZT. Since she had to take a pill every four hours, she insisted on moving to a separate bedroom but remained on the same floor. Our routine from August 22 until she was readmitted on November 30 was almost the same every day. We set our clocks so that we were alerted every four hours. A side effect of AZT was nausea whenever she first stood up. She was determined to eat about a 1,000 calories a day, so, despite her weakness and loss of appetite, she fought for survival. A glass of Ensure and oatmeal for breakfast and a fish sandwich at McDonald's for lunch were consistently the only sources of calories she could swallow. Mary's illness soon resulted in the loss of most of her hair, and, since she was so sensitive about how she looked, to be fitted for a wig was an easy decision. On most days, as soon as she finished her breakfast around 8:30 A.M., she would return to her bed where she would no longer feel nauseous. She would get dressed for lunch, and we would drive to McDonald's, which was located about five miles away on Noland Road. After lunch she sat in the recliner and usually watched a movie on television. At 4:30 P.M. we would watch *Wheel of Fortune* as well as the news, etc. After her 8:00 P.M. pill, Mary was in bed. Our alarm clocks were set for midnight and 4:00 A.M. Sometimes she would have taken the pill and gone to the bathroom before I got to her room. Usually I would sit on the side of her bed, and we would talk for a few minutes. She liked that.

Physicians And Tests

My recovery from atrial fibrillation was not a smooth one. I had left the hospital on August 17 with a prescription for quinidine, the drug selected to control my heart. Three days after Mary came home on August 23, I was back in the emergency room with a violent reaction to my medicine in the form of chills and fever. The answer for me was to try another heart drug.

Our visits with Mary's doctors and the hospital's laboratories became frequent and lengthy. The table shows a reasonably accurate summary:

Treating Mary's Illness 1987

DATE	PHYSICIAN	PURPOSE
8/25	Smith	To start on AZT
9/1	Smith	Follow-up
9/9	Abdou	Lab tests
9/15	McKenzie*	Follow-up
9/22	Ginsberg	Liver specialist
9/28	McKenzie	Lab tests
10/5	Abdou	Lab tests
10/14	Abdou	Blood transfusion 9:00 A.M.-3:00 P.M.
10/20	Smith	Follow-up
11/2	Abdou	Lab tests
11/3	Abdou	Blood transfusion 9:00 A.M.-3:00 P.M.
11/10	Abdou	Blood transfusion 8:00 A.M.-4:00 P.M.
11/16	Smith	Follow-up

*Smith's assistant

I also took Mary to either the doctors' building or to the hospital several times for various kinds of tests without seeing a doctor. On every visit, Mary was so weak that I had to put her in a wheelchair to move her from one area to another. Near the end of October, at my suggestion, Dr. Smith reduced Mary's dosage of AZT to one-half of normal. The theory was that because of her small stature and weight, her body might not need as much. Unfortunately we could discern no improvement, and near the end of November, she could not walk by herself.

November 26 – Thanksgiving

Mary and I had celebrated Thanksgiving with her brother Don, his wife, Reve, and their two children, Jana and Jeanna, for many years. Despite her weakness, Mary was determined to spend it with them, as was our custom, at Indian Hills Country Club. Mary and I did not talk about dying, but that morning when I questioned her as to whether we should go, she said she wanted to be with them because it would be their last Thanksgiving together. I had to put almost all of her clothes on although, pathetically, she did her best. Her nylon stockings were the most difficult for both of us.

At the club, the management people and waitresses who knew her so well could not have been more considerate and thoughtful. I brought her food to her and remember nothing of the conversation that day. Don, Reve and the girls rode to the club with us, and shortly after we returned home, they left for their home in Macon, Missouri. After Mary went to bed, I called Dr. McKenzie to tell him how she was. Dr. Smith called me in the morning and asked for me to bring her to the hospital Monday morning, November 30, 1987.

Mary was still fighting for life and hoping they could find something to do for her. So with her wig in place, I helped her in the car. She was still wearing her night clothes and her robe. Neither one of us could talk about what was happening.

CHAPTER 22

◆

Mary's Death

When Mary was in the hospital in early August 1987, other specialists visited with her, ran certain tests and became familiar with her history and condition. As a result, when she was readmitted on November 30, they were once again involved.

When she was in the hospital in August, the neurologist who had become involved was Dr. John Sand, one of the specialists in Kansas City Clinical Neurology Associates. Although he remained somewhat involved when Mary was in the hospital after November 30, the principal physician assigned from that group was Dr. Woody Harlan.

Whether caused by her weakened physical condition or the damage to Mary's central nervous system by the invasion of the virus, it was obvious that her inability to remember and loss of the ability to stand and walk had become major aspects of Mary's failing health.

For a day or two after Mary was admitted, she tried to keep her wig in place, but it proved to be impossible. Mary's pride in herself was something she fought hard to preserve but to no avail. I remember as if it were yesterday the embarrassment in her face as she tried to answer the questions they asked in conjunction with the evaluation of her mental health. I knew how much it meant to Mary, who had not gone to college, never to have anyone question her mental prowess. Mary's dyslexia had always made it difficult for her to handle numbers, but her verbal skills were superb.

Before Lynne came from California on December 14, Mary was fairly articulate. Lynne's telephone conversations with her on December 11 and 12 had been reasonably satisfactory. When I told Mary that Lynne was coming to see her, my greatest concern was to avoid alarming her with any implication that the visit was related to her terminal condition. On December 13, Jeanna Schelle, Mary's niece (who had been with us at Thanksgiving), slipped away from her job as a parking attendant at a Chiefs game to spend a few minutes with Mary. She did not stay long, and Mary talked to her in what seemed to be a fairly logical way. But, after Jeanna left, Mary turned to me and asked who the visitor was. Barbara flew down on December 16 from Minneapolis, and Jim drove Schelle down on the 18th. Since John lives here, all Mary's children were with her until the 24th when Lynne returned to California.

It was fortunate that Lynne came when she did, because Mary could still talk during the first three or four days of that week. One day shortly after Lynne arrived, she had a VCR moved into the room to show Mary some pictures of their fourth child, Charles Thomas, who had been born on September 17, 1986, and was just a little more than a year old. As she was looking at the VCR, I knew Mary was confused, and after it was taken away, she asked me what it was all about.

Shortly after Barbara had arrived on December 16, Dr. Abdou and a doctor of psychology in the hospital met with Barbara, Lynne, John and me to ask us whether we wanted Mary to be revived in the event the hospital announced "Code Blue." If we did, it would mean they would do whatever possible to revive her. It did not take many minutes for all of us to agree and instruct them to not take action.

This was the first time I had made a decision that meant I believed the situation was hopeless. There would be two more times when I personally had to make such traumatic decisions.

Between August and November 30 when Mary was at home, it was necessary for her to have three blood transfusions. They put her in a room at the hospital where they did the procedure very slowly over a period of about six hours. Mary's red corpuscles were continually being destroyed, so platelets were a necessity.

During the 10 days Lynne was with us, the need for platelets became so great the blood bank had difficulty in supplying those that matched Mary's blood type. Both Lynne and John had matching blood types, so each of them was able to give blood, John twice and Lynne once. Because Barbara was taking aspirins, her blood was not acceptable, but her husband, Jim, donated platelets. Mary's brother, Don, had a blood type that did not match, however, his wife, Reve's, did. The process of removing platelets from blood was a lengthy procedure and involved several hours at the blood bank. Later in December, Mary's platelet level stabilized, and for a while, she did not need transfusions.

In the middle of December during all of the testing, Dr. William Ginsberg, the liver specialist, came to the conclusion a biopsy of her liver was advisable in order to understand why it was beginning to malfunction. After consultation with the surgeons and internists, they decided the difficulty of controlling bleeding was too critical. No biopsy was done.

One night just before Christmas after Lynne's arrival, we received a telephone call from the hospital telling us they thought Mary had experienced a seizure because her eyes were fixed. Lynne and I got there as soon as we could, and a short time later she had a grand mal seizure. Neither of us had been so frightened by anything as we were when that happened. They pushed us out of the room, and, as we looked at Mary through the door, Lynne said, "Dad, pray for her." I did, but I had such a helpless feeling. It just tore us apart to see it happening. If tears count as prayers, they said everything. Barbara, Jim and Schelle came to the hospital and arrived just after Lynne and I had to leave Mary's room. John had been called by Barbara and arrived a few minutes later. All of us were terrified with the thought that this was the end. In terms of any coherent communication with her, it was indeed.

I had not forgotten Dr. Alexandra Levine in California and on August 9 had written to her, summarizing events and advising her of our beginning treatment with AZT. Her reply was a thoughtful one and confirmed we were doing what should be done. On Christmas Day, I wrote her another letter so that she would know Mary was virtually comatose. When she replied on December 29, among her other comments about what was being learned about AIDS she said the following, "Never give up hope, and never stop fighting ... no one really knows what will happen except God."

All the month of December and during the first week in January, the neurologists were desperately endeavoring to discover what was happening in Mary's central nervous system. Periodically the procedures for analyzing brain waves and activity were conducted. CAT scans of her head seemed to be almost a weekly procedure, and her spinal column was tapped several times as they tested and analyzed her spinal fluid. One of their objectives was to discover the HIV virus in her spinal fluid, but they were never successful. Finally, during the first week in January, they told me they had learned of another test that might prove something. It meant growing a culture in the fluid and took three to four days. When that test came back from the laboratory and proved nothing, they finally had to say that circumstantial evidence was the only basis on which they could conclude the HIV virus was destroying her brain.

The Inevitable Decision

Lynne returned to California the day before Christmas in order to be with her family. Christmas was a quiet day of sadness as Mary was becoming semicomotose. My last communication with her was a couple of days after Christmas when she whispered something that I could not understand. When I asked her what she had said, she lifted her hand and feebly waved in a way that was obviously an expression of hopelessness and futility. The seventh day of January 1988 was when Abdou and Eubanks came to me and said it was time to give up. For more than a week, we had been unable to discern any reaction from her. We tried every way we knew to see if she could hear or understand us. They believed all they were doing by running additional tests was to abuse her body. They were convinced, and I believed them, when they said there was no hope for a recovery. We had previously made the decision to place her in the skilled nursing area of the hospital where every effort would be made to keep her comfortable. There were three nurses with Barbara and me when they put her on the cart to move her. All of us were crying, even the nurses, because it was really the beginning of the end.

When I left the room, I took with me the results of 39 different tests of the condition of her blood they had conducted that day. I did not then and do not now understand their medical implications. However, the data compared her numbers with those in the normal range and showed that 27 of them were abnormal in one way or another.

The skilled nursing unit was located on the same floor of the hospital but in a different wing. Mary's corner room was spacious and private. Of all the nurses who attended her, only one seemed to be afraid of the responsibility. Since Mary was incontinent and had to be turned frequently to avoid bed sores, the demands on the staff were substantial. I made arrangements for a special bed that circulated air through the mattress, but even that could not prevent such problems. The details of Mary's gradual deterioration are irrelevant except the one that culminated in my third traumatic decision.

Throughout Mary's illness, the loss of red blood corpuscles necessitated transfusions. One weekend early in March, a physician on duty on Sunday ordered an analysis of her blood. We had not been having her blood tested because there was no hope for her. His tests, particularly of her hemoglobin, resulted in his asking me for the authority for a transfusion. I talked to my children, prayed for God's guidance and made the decision to give her the blood. The next morning on Dr. Eubanks' daily visit, I asked him what he thought of my decision. He simply said I had done the right thing because we could see, once again, if it changed her situation. He agreed with my belief that, if nothing positive developed, there should be no further tests. They continued to feed her intravenously, and Mary continued to lose weight.

From January 8 until Mary's death, I was in the hospital every day during most of the day. I usually left near lunch time to go home and check the mail before I returned in the afternoon. It was close to a 25-minute drive to the hospital. Each and every trip, particularly to the hospital, was one of hope, prayer, tears and apprehension of what I would find. Being at home was worse than being in the hospital. At least when I was there, I could feel as if I were supporting her, and there was no uncertainty as to what was happening. John stopped by the hospital every day after work and often on weekends to spend time with his mother and me. A few times Barbara stayed with me for a week or two, but as time passed she and Jim just drove down from Minneapolis for the weekends. Lynne was in daily contact with me on the telephone.

During those agonizing weeks when I knew there was no hope, I made plans for Mary's funeral with great cooperation from the family. We visited with everyone who would be involved, selected songs and flowers we knew she loved, decided on the casket, and attended to a variety of other details. Services were to be held in Kansas City as well as in Lafayette, Indiana, where Mary was to be buried. I made all the necessary arrangements in advance so the stress of handling so many things could be done when there was time for careful planning. I did not want to have problems with my atrial fibrillation when I knew I faced a traumatic period.

On Sunday, May 8, it was apparent the end was near. John was with me during the afternoon and early evening before he went home for dinner. Around 9:00 P.M. I called and asked him to return, so he was with me when Mary died at 11:15 P.M. In Lafayette, Indiana, her birthplace, it was an hour later, so Mary gave up on the same day she had been born 67 years earlier. The two services conducted by Bryce Mensink in Lafayette and by Charles Holt at Mount Moriah in Kansas City were what I had hoped to hear. Charles had been our minister for five years and had stayed in close touch with me since August 1987, when I told him Mary was dying of AIDS. His comments were personal and very meaningful. Bryce was the minister of the Christian Reformed Church (my home church) and did not know Mary personally. After our family visited with him for two hours the day before the funeral, he knew enough about us and Mary to enable him to speak about Mary with sincere convictions as to her faith in Christ and the promise to her of eternal life. Her resting place in West Lafayette, Indiana, is very close to the elementary school where I first met her and where we spent the early years of life. I visit the mausoleum three or four times a year and live every day with beautiful memories of life with her.

My high school basketball coach, Bill Chase, lost his wife, Louise, shortly after Mary died and sent me the following verse. It expresses my feelings.

> You couldn't say "I'm Leaving."
> You couldn't say "Goodbye."
> You were gone. You didn't deserve it
> And only God knows why.
> A million times we cried.
> If love alone would have saved you,
> You never would have died.
> In life we loved you dearly.
> In death we love you still.
> In our hearts you hold a place
> No one could ever fill.
> It broke our hearts to lose you,
> But you did not go alone,
> For a part of us went with you.
> The day God took you home.

CHAPTER 23

◆

Living Alone

More than eight years have passed since Mary's death in 1988. Adjusting to life without her continues to be difficult, and perhaps it will always be that way. The torture of watching her die can never be forgotten. The loneliness and despair that followed, because I could not decide what I was living for, were like a darkness where there can be no joy or happiness. When she was alive, we did not talk at length about her death because there was too much hope it would not happen so soon. When we talked about what I would do, I just said that, between golf and my investments, I would be able to keep busy and be okay. How wrong I was could not have been anticipated, because nothing could prepare me for the experience of not being able to share every aspect of life with the person who had made my life so happy. As I sit back and think about what has happened in these seven and one-half years, I was fortunate in having several avenues of activities to keep me busy and positive about my future. Most important were the relationships I had with my children, my grandchildren and my sister Mary Grond.

The Family

Neither Mary nor I could have foreseen how important our children and grandchildren would be in helping me build a new life. When Mary became comatose in 1987, she did not know that our daughter Lynne Gooding, with Steve and their four children, would be leaving California to move to Kansas City. Their home is a 25-minute drive to the south side of Kansas City in Leawood. Lynne and Steve now have six children with the two youngest, Benjamin Calvin and Mary Catherine, born on September 11, 1990, and April 19, 1994, respectively. Ben is named after me, and Mary Catherine is named after her two grandmothers. Their first two children, Julia Marie, born on September 27, 1979, and Stephen Lee, born on May 18, 1981, were born in Austin, Texas. The next two were born in California, Annette Marie on October 6, 1983, and Charles Thomas on September 17, 1986.

Steve Gooding and Lynne met in 1970 when they were attending the University of Texas. Shortly after they were married in 1974, they moved to Corpus Christi, Texas, so Steve could pursue music studies at Del Mar College. After a great deal of soul-searching by Steve, he and Lynne moved back to Austin, and Steve started his career in real estate as a salesman. He was successful in this and soon organized his own agency as he pursued various courses in real estate investment and syndication. In April 1983, he joined Butterfield Securities Corporation, a subsidiary of Butterfield Savings and Loan Association in Santa Ana, California. Lynne and Steve lived in Mission Viejo, California until the company Steve worked for was sold. This was just before Mary's death.

For a variety of reasons, they then made the decision to sell their home, leave California and move to Kansas City. This made it quite logical for them to take advantage of the opportunity to live in my house at the Lake of the Ozarks while Steve looked for a position in the Kansas City area. There proved to be limited opportunities for Steve in Kansas City, and after an extensive search in the area, he expanded his search to other cities. He located an opportunity in real estate securities analysis with a firm in Houston, Texas, and they bought a home there. The day after they closed on the purchase of the home, Steve was offered a position as director of real estate asset management for Waddell & Reed in Kansas City. He took the position, and Steve, Lynne and their family moved to Kansas City. After being with Waddell & Reed for more than three years, Steve joined Midland Loan Services, a real estate subsidiary of Kansas City Southern Industries, Inc. With my encouragement, Steve enrolled in the Chartered Financial Analyst (CFA) program, which John had completed and which had been vitally important to me in my career. Accordingly Steve has greatly expanded his knowledge about investments in securities and obtained the CFA designation. Steve's background and experience in real estate investment combined with the CFA body of knowledge should prove very beneficial as the rapid growth of real estate securitization continues into the future. Early in 1995, he organized his own company, Gooding Partners, to utilize his expertise in both real estate and securities.

John and Susan have three children and live in Lakewood, about two miles from my house. John and Susan's first child, Amy Elizabeth, was born on January 6, 1982, while they were living in St. Louis. John Andrew was born on March 5, 1984, just before they moved to Kansas City. Mary and I had helped them find a house in Lakewood, and for the first time, we had part of our family near us. The youngest, Jacqueline Calla, was born on February 27, 1988, with the name Calla for a girl as close as they could come to my middle name.

In St. Louis, John had become a Certified Public Accountant (CPA) immediately after receiving his MBA from St. Louis University in June 1976. He did this because he believed it would be of value to him as a bank lending officer. During his eight-year business career in St. Louis, John was successful as a bank lending officer for the Commerce Bank and later the Mercantile Bank. He left the banking industry because he believed he could use the same expertise and earn a higher income with an investment banking firm. After careful investigation and interviews, he accepted a job in Kansas City with Stern Brothers. John was also becoming more knowledgeable about investments in securities so, in a three-year period, he took the three examinations required to become a Chartered Financial Analyst (CFA). His responsibility at Stern Brothers is development and management of a department that establishes values for nonmarketable corporations or businesses of any kind. This aspect of the securities business is not what I did during my career, but it requires similar expertise.

The marriage of Barbara to Craig Carver ended in 1982 after 16 years. On July 4, 1984, she married Jim Haehlen, a school teacher in Wayzata, Minnesota, a suburb of Minneapolis. Over the years, Barbara has had various jobs, but most of the time she was a substitute teacher. After her marriage to Jim, she spent most of her time teaching in the same school where Jim had taught for many years. Jim took early retirement in the fall of 1991, having been able to combine 35 years of teaching and his age to earn that reward. They have retired to Eureka Springs, Arkansas, having built a home on the shore line of Beaver Lake, on the lots Mary and I acquired in the real estate development we started in 1970.

In the meantime, Barbara's only child, Mischelle Marie (Schelle), had decided to major in graphic art and design and attended the University of Wisconsin at Eau Claire. She graduated just before Christmas 1990. While there she met Michael Glenn Miller, who was one year behind her in school. Mike had spent two years in the army. To my great surprise and immense pleasure, they decided to be married in Kansas City. The date was January 5, 1991, at St. John's United Methodist Church, with the reception at Indian Hills Country Club. They made the decision to be married here for many reasons. One was the convenience it would create with so many of Schelle's young cousins living here in Kansas City. Another was their plan to settle in Kansas City after Mike's graduation in December 1991. Just before Thanksgiving and Mike's graduation, Schelle came to Kansas City to live with me while she looked for a job. Mike came after his graduation and immediately found a job in his field. Schelle's search took longer, but she was also successful. They bought a house about five miles from my home and moved in during the second week in April 1992. The two months Schelle lived with me, as well as the additional four months with both of them, were a great pleasure and helped me adjust to being alone. At the beginning of this year, she and a friend Julie Luton, established their own writing and design firm, The Milton Company. Julie has been very helpful to me in the editing of this book.

I have looked for opportunities to do special things with my family that they could not afford financially. In January 1989, Barbara, Lynne and John (without their spouses), and my grand-daughter Schelle and step-granddaughter Suki Haehlen spent a week with me on the island of Kauai. Barbara's husband, Jim, then joined Barbara and me for a week of golf on Maui. In January 1993, my three children, their spouses, their children and I spent a week together at Disney World. Mary and I had tried to do similar things when she was alive, as in 1983 when all of us except Lynne's family were on Maui for two weeks around Christmas time. Having such a loving and cohesive family that can do things together adds immeasurably to the quality of my life.

A little more than seven months after Mary's death, my sister Mary's husband, Neal Grond, died on December 1, 1988, from lung cancer. Mary is seven years older than I am, having been born on July 11, 1914. As we were growing up, the years between us were not con-ducive to a close brother-sister relationship. A few years after their marriage, they moved to California. After their three children were grown and out of college, they moved to Grant's Pass, Oregon, where a son and a son-in-law developed a partnership in an automated dairy.

Not unexpectedly perhaps, Mary and I found many opportuni-ties to enjoy each other's company in ways that could never have been foreseen. She spent two weeks each summer in 1990 and 1991 with me, and we were together for a week in Hawaii in February 1990. I traveled to Oregon for family weddings, the first for one of Mary's grandsons, John VanLeeuwen, in February 1991 and another for his sister Cathy in June 1991. Earlier in 1991, Mary came to Kansas City for Schelle's wedding, and in January and February 1992, we traveled to Florida for a three-week vacation. We were in Hawaii for two weeks in January 1994, visited relatives in Clymer, New York, in May, and spent the first two weeks of August in Missouri and Arkansas before attending the annual Korschot family reunion in Lafayette. We were together again in the first two weeks of August 1995 to do pretty much the same things. Weekly, and sometimes more often, Mary and I have enjoyed lengthy telephone conversations. This companionship did not fill the void caused by the death of my Mary but added a dimension of great value to my life.

Mary and Neal had three children: Janet, Robert and Kay. Janet and her husband Jim Van Leeuwen, in addition to John and Cathy, have a daughter Kelly. Robert and Theresa Grond have three boys: Michael, David and Stephen. Kay and Andy DeVries also have three children: Jaime, Julie and Andrew. Mary and Neal have three great-grandchildren. As the result of Mary and I spending so much time together, I have had a great deal of contact with her nine grandchildren.

My sister Mary and I experienced another great loss when our sister Ruth Smith died of cancer on March 11, 1989. Ruth and her husband, Art Smith, had lived in Tucson ever since they left Lafayette, Indiana, shortly after World War II. Ruth had developed tuberculosis during the war, so, when the medical profession in Lafayette gave up on her, they went to Arizona with the hope that the change in climate would help. Not long after they arrived, a doctor treated her by injecting a fluid in her infected lung, which proved to be a cure. Apparently, the cancer which ultimately caused her death, commenced in her lung. My close relationship with Ruth since our childhood has been an important part of this book. In our adult lives, my business responsibilities provided us with numerous opportunities to visit with them in Tucson.

Ruth and Art had three children: Arthur (he has my middle name, Calvin) and his wife, Merlene, have three children: Dwight, Aleida and Kevin. Their daughter Sharon has two daughters, Sheila and Cristy. Their youngest son, Mark, and his wife, Lucille, have two children, Robert and Sherlyn. Since all of Ruth's family have spent most of their lives in the western part of the United States, most of our contacts with them have been my business trips, telephone calls, family reunions and the family letters. My brother-in-law, Art, continues to live in Tucson. Ruth and Art have 11 great-grandchildren.

Our sister Johanna (Jo) died on April 25, 1993, at 77 years of age while she was a patient of the Indiana State Hospital for the Mentally Disturbed at Logansport, Indiana. She had been there since shortly after the end of World War II. The story of her tragic life and death needs to be an important part of my autobiography.

When Jo was born on August 21, 1915, she had a cleft palate, that is, an opening in the soft palate between her mouth and her nasal passage. Fortunately, there was no outside or facial indication of the seriousness of the opening. My parents made two trips to Indianapolis for surgery to close the opening, but it was to no avail. Her crying would break open the closure, and nothing else could be done.

As she was growing up and attending school, her voice had a nasal sound that induced her schoolmates to tease her mercilessly. My parents, sisters and cousins, who were about her age, were continually reassuring her and telling her to ignore the taunting. Jo was a very pretty girl, which, combined with her intelligence and friendly, outgoing personality, made her a fun person to be with. When we moved to West Lafayette, she was just entering her first year in high school. In her new surroundings at Klondike with a new group of kids who had not grown up with her, the ridicule was too much to handle. So when she was 16. she withdrew from school and started doing housework to help our family financially. Along with others her age, she dated boys who were either members of our church or of the other Dutch church in Lafayette, the First Reformed Church. One of the boys she dated was Leonard Rhoda. About the same time, two of our cousins, Hilda and Helen Korschot, dated Len's two brothers, Jake and Stuart. The three cousins ended up marrying the three brothers.

Jo, as an older sister, always seemed to be perfectly normal to me. What I did not perceive was that, under this facade of being a happy-go-lucky girl, wife and mother, was a person with a serious inferiority complex. I later learned that my parents were keenly aware of this. Len and Jo had been married about six years when their third child, Robert, was born on December 22, 1943, just nine days after Barbara was born. Early the next year, Mary arranged a luncheon with Jo so they could talk about the two babies. Mary wrote to me immediately to let me know that something was wrong with Jo because she did not carry on a normal conversation and would smile or laugh at things not related to what they were discussing. Letters from my mother then began to tell me about Jo's strange behavior. About that time, Len had his mother come to live with them because Jo was not taking care of the three children or preparing meals. When I came home on leave from the Navy in April 1945, I did not see much of Jo and, as a result, did not think the problem was too serious. I believe the family purposely shielded me from knowing what was happening.

Later in 1945, I learned from my mother that she and Len had decided to place Jo in Pine Rest, a mental health facility managed by the Christian Reformed Church in Grand Rapids, Michigan. However they did not want to take action until I returned and could approve what they wanted to do. As soon as I returned home, I visited with Jo, and, without any delay, Len, Mom and I took her to Pine Rest. By that time, they had decided she was a schizophrenic. They immediately commenced to treat her with electric shocks, but it soon became apparent her condition was deteriorating and physical restraint was required to keep her under control.

Not too much time passed before we became aware of an operation called a pre-frontal lobotomy, which apparently was successful in situations like Jo's. The surgery severed the nerves in the front part of her brain, which, we were told, would make her more passive and not vulnerable to strong feelings of anger that could lead to violent behavior. We understood that after the operation Jo could return to her family with the prospect of a fairly normal life. My mother, my sisters, Len and I approved of the operation. My sister Mary accompanied Mom and Len to Indianapolis for the surgery. After the surgery, Jo returned to her home; however, Len still had his mother helping him, so it was not the completely natural situation that the doctors had encouraged us to establish. He and my mother then decided that perhaps it might work out better if Jo stayed with her. After a few months she began to withdraw from reality, go for long walks by herself, and do enough strange things (not violent) to make Len and my mother decide that she should be placed in the State of Indiana's mental health facility in Logansport. They did not take her back to Pine Rest, because it was expensive and there was no reason to expect them to do more for Jo than the staff at Logansport.

During the almost 50 years Jo was at Logansport, she lived a fairly comfortable and rather tranquil life, to some extent due to medicines designed for patients like her. In the earlier years of her confinement, the doctors and staff working with her seemed to have some hope that she could eventually be released. In the later years, it was obvious they knew they would not be successful. For many years, she was permitted the freedom to roam the grounds, visit with other people, buy things at the canteen, go swimming in the pool, accompanying others on various bus trips and having her meals in a cafeteria. When Mary and I visited her (once or twice a year), we would go shopping, eat at local restaurants and enjoy her company. One interesting thing always happened as soon as we left the hospital grounds. Without saying anything, except to chuckle, she would take Mary's visitor tag and put it on her coat or dress. It was always obvious to us that Jo never wanted to be thought of as an inmate. Sometime in her 60s, arthritis and diabetes necessitated her being confined at all times. As she grew older, the clarity of her speech deteriorated, and when she was asked to repeat something, she was visibly annoyed. Jo's memory of her life before the operation was good, but one of the aftereffects of the lobotomy was the inability to remember new developments. I believe that, if we had not approved the surgery, she would have been able to benefit from newer drugs and possibly return to her home. There is no doubt in my mind that I was the person primarily responsible for the operation. I feel that way because Len had complete confidence in my judgment. If I had said no, there would not have been an operation.

Prior to Jo's death, their first child, Mary Ann, died of a heart attack when she was only 50 years old. She had never married. Their second child, Len (who continues to be on the faculty of Dordt College), and his wife, Lee, have three children: Scott, Jill and Dawn. All three are married and each family has two children, so Jo and Len have six great- grandchildren. Bob, Jo's youngest, is a teacher in the Lafayette school system. He and his wife, Jane, have three children: Matt is a recent graduate of Purdue, Sara is a senior and Sally is in her first year at Purdue. My trips to Lafayette provide numerous opportunities to be with Bob, Jane, Matt, Sara and Sally.

My sister Alice died on September 23, 1985, when she was 74 years old. Alice and Clarence only had one child, Judy, who married a Purdue graduate, Garry Roorda. They have three sons: Steve, Mike and Doug. I encouraged Steve to enter the investment business and am pleased because he has been very successful. At present, he is in New York City. All three boys are married, and Alice and Clarence have six great-grandchildren Our family has always been indebted to Alice for remaining in Lafayette, staying close to our mother and answering her need for assistance and companionship in her later years. While my mother was alive, she seized every opportunity to go to Logansport, visit with Jo and show her love and compassion in a variety of ways. After Mom died, Alice took over the responsibility of being the guardian for Jo and monitoring the kind of care she received at Logansport.

After our mother died on February 18, 1963, Alice, Mary, Ruth and I decided it was important for us to keep in touch with each other. Without our mother as the focal point of our communications, something needed to be done. Our solution was a chain letter in which each of us would write a letter to enclose in the package with those of the others. My Mary did the writing for me, and the system worked perfectly. When my sister Alice died, her daughter, Judy, became the correspondent for her family. In recent years, Carolyn Roorda, Mikes wife, has joined the group and keeps us informed of what is happening in their family in Rochester, New York. My sister Mary always writes, and at times has her daughter, Janet, or her son, Bob, contribute to the chain of letters. My daughter Barbara and I both do our best to keep everyone aware of what is transpiring in my family. My sister Johanna's two sons, Len and Bob Rhoda, are included in the circle, as are Sharon Smith and Mark Smith, the daughter and one of the sons of my sister Ruth. So in total, today, there are seven or eight of us writing, and it takes about three or four months to complete the circle. We send pictures with the letters, so almost 100 of us in my parents' fam-

Barbara as a teenager.

Lynne as a teenager.

John as a teenager.

Mary on our 24th wedding anniversary.
October 31, 1955 in St. Louis.

Golf at Bellerive Country Club in St. Louis.

Rolly Davis took this picture of Mary and me.

With Rolly and Virginia Davis at Beaver Lake, Arkansas.

Lynne married Stephen Gooding on January 19, 1974.

John married Susan Skipton on June 11, 1976.

*With Mary on Maui, Hawaii Islands in
January 1983.*

With Bulldozer.

Barbara married Jim Haehlen on
July 4, 1984.

With our Glen Ellyn, Illinois, friends in 1985. (From left to right)
Maxine Hansen, Jan Earle, Ron Earle, Edie Rosenthal, Virginia Davis,
Ben Korschot, Evelyn Cherry, Howard Hansen, Mary Korschot, Henry
Rosenthal and Rolly Davis.

Lake of the Ozarks house.

Our home at Lakewood in Lee's Summit, Missouri.

Barbara and Jim with Schelle at her wedding on Januray 5, 1991. In front are Jim's daughters Suki and Heidi.

My grandaugter Mischelle (Schelle) and her husband, Michael Miller.

Mary and Jacob Schelle Jr.

Pauline and Charles Schelle.

Arevia (Reve) and Don Schelle.

Richard Schelle, deceased 3/30/72.

Mary's dad, Jacob Schelle.

My sister Alice and her husband Clarence Vanderkleed.

My sister Mary and Neal Grond on their 50th wedding anniversary.

My sister Johanna and her husband Len Rhoda.

My sister Ruth and her husband Art Smith.

*Our U.S.S. Knapp Plank Owners Reunion, September 1993, in Bath
Main and Boston, Massachusetts. (From left to right) Ben Korschot,
Alden Clayton, Robert Buck, John Morton, Donald Keigher and
Malcolm Thompson.*

*With my sister Mary Grond at Grant's Pass,
Oregon in 1992.*

The Goodings in 1995. (From left to right) Ben, Lee, Mary, Lynne, Annette, C.T., Steve and Julia.

The Korschots in 1995. (From left to right) Amy, Drew, John, Susan and Calla.

ily keep in touch with each other.

On the second Saturday in August 1992, the descendants of my grandparents' family celebrated the 80th family reunion in Lafayette, Indiana. The descendants of my parents were in charge, and 54 of us attended. There are more than 500 of us who are descendants of my grandparents. There were 24 of us grandchildren who grew up in Lafayette, Indiana. Three of my cousins are younger than I am, and 10 of the 24 are still alive. Our immediate family had a picnic dinner the night before the reunion, and it proved to be a meaningful occasion. Some of us played golf on Saturday morning before the reunion, which commenced around 3:00 P.M. The reunion was attended by about 140 people and concluded around 9:00 P.M.

I believe family relationships are vitally important in our society in which there are so many family-related problems. I believe our family has had some unique qualities. I choose to believe it comes from our Christian heritage. When I was admitted to *Who's Who in America,* I was asked to write a few words regarding what had been the major influences in my life. Below is what they have been printing for several years.

"A happy Christian home environment, the adversity of the Depression of the '30s, the challenges of competitive sports, the desire to achieve knowledge, recognition and responsibilities, and a devoted wife and three children who made our marriage most meaningful have been the dominant influences of my life."

Mary had four brothers, all younger than she. Three brothers, Don, Charles and Jacob, and their wives, Arevia (Reve), Pauline and Mary, have also continued to be an integral part of my life since Mary's death. Mary's other brother, Richard, died of a brain tumor when his two daughters, Nancy and Tina, were quite young. The two girls live in Lafayette, but Mary and I have never had much contact with either one of them or Dick's wife, Ann, who is now also deceased. Since Don and Reve and their two daughters, Jana and Jeanna, lived in Missouri, it was natural for Mary and me to visit with them frequently. Both girls are married, with Jeanna and her husband, Kevin Noblet, living quite close to me in Lee's Summit. Jana is married to Robert Norton, and they now live in Houston, Texas. Don's family continues to join with mine as often as possible for Thanksgiving each year.

Charles and Pauline and Jacob (Junior) and Mary have always lived in West Lafayette, so I continue to be with them two or three times a year. When we celebrated the Korschot reunion in August 1992, the Schelles gathered together so we could also have a reunion with them. Charles and Pauline have four children, Sandy, Randy, Gary and Teresa. Junior and Mary have two children, David and Donna. Each fall Mary's three brothers and their wives join me for a few days at my place at the Lake of the Ozarks. In the spring I join the three families in Macon, Misssouri (Don and Reves' home), to spend a couple of days with my three brother-in-laws looking for mushrooms and doing some fishing. The compatibility of the Schelles and my family continues to provide me with an important avenue of love and fellowship.

The Church, Golf, Movies And Basketball

Prior to my retirement and before Mary's death, we were as active in St. John's United Methodist church as we could be when living 30 minutes away from the church and involved in a myriad of business activities that kept us out of town on a very frequent basis. At one time in the early 1980s, we devoted more than two years in an effort to establish a facsimile of the "60-60" Club that had meant so much to us in the 1950s in Glen Ellyn, Illinois. It failed ultimately when Mary and I had to give up the management of the new club in order to do the traveling required by my business responsibilities. Since Mary's death and with my retirement, I have become more active in the church. A program named "Dinner for Eight" has been developed by the church and has some of the attributes of the "60-60" ... Club concept. During the past eight years, the church has completed a major remodeling program and, in recognition of my financial support, has dedicated a meeting room called the "Assembly Room" to Mary. The wording on the plaque at the entrance to the room was important to us. After much thought, it reads "A Loving Wife and Mother Who Endeared Herself To All Who Met Her."

An unexpected source of enjoyment for me has been high school basketball. Mary and I had been avid supporters of the Kansas City Kings from the time we came to Kansas City until the franchise was moved to Sacramento, California, in the middle 1980s. During those years, high school basketball was not as important to us because we were too busy with other activities and the Kings filled our desire to watch basketball. After Mary died, I began to attend the games being played by Lee's Summit girls and boys, both varsity and junior varsity. So during the past seven years, two or three winter evenings each week have been spent watching the games, getting to know the parents of the players and developing a strong interest in the players' abilities and lives in general. Several players have been good enough to play in college, so keeping tabs on their progress has been of interest to me. My enjoyment of basketball extends to the Missouri State Tournaments and watching college basketball, either in person or in front of a television set.

Playing golf as much as possible has also filled hours that otherwise would have been very lonely. Fortunately, some of my friends who have retired are also avid golfers, so a group of us plays at Indian Hills Country Club two or three times a week, and another group plays twice a week at Lakewood Oaks. A national golf organization, "Senior Golfers of America," holds tournaments around the country several times a year, so I go to some of those. I also participate in numerous golf tournaments that benefit charitable organizations.

Early in this book, I mentioned my enjoyment of movies. During my more than 40 years in the business and investment world, the only time Mary and I could find time for movies was on television. Since her death, I attend movies whenever the mood strikes me, even if it's the middle of the afternoon or at dinnertime. They have truly been therapeutic as well as enjoyable.

Not long after Mary died, my children persuaded me once again to see if I might enjoy having a dog to keep me company. I was not enthusiastic about the idea, but when Lynne offered me the opportunity to take a dog they had, which I had come to like, I succumbed to the temptation. The dog was a small Sheltie with the name Sheena.

She was an easy dog to have around the house, in that she was very quiet and liked to lie alone, not necessarily in the room where I was sitting. She was not the kind of dog that liked to be held, so that was not a part of our companionship. She enjoyed the long walks we took several times each week, and with her as the motivation, I was once again fairly faithful in exercising on a regular basis. However, I had one problem with Sheena, which after a couple of years convinced me she needed a different home. My life-style, which dictated my being away from the house ten or more hours a day, two or three times each week, meant that my life began to be controlled by the necessity to get home to take care of Sheena's bodily needs. She never had an accident because of this, but I frequently had to break away from something I was doing to take care of her. When a woman at a nearby animal clinic asked me if I would ever sell Sheena, I seized the opportunity to give Sheena a new home. This woman had been grooming Sheena for several months, and I knew she was very fond of her. Several years have passed since then, and I do not intend to find out if some dog somewhere needs my company.

In endeavoring to overcome the paralysis of mind and body that comes with grief, I have pursued every avenue that might lead to an answer. The minister of the Christian Reformed Church in Lafayette, Indiana, who conducted the funeral service for Mary preached five consecutive sermons on the subject and sent me the tapes. I read several pamphlets and about six books that were of some value, but the one that reached me was written by Harold Kushner, a rabbi, with the title *When Bad Things Happen to Good People*. Recently, I have benefited from his thoughts as expressed in his book, *When All You've Ever Wanted Isn't Enough*.

From all this, I found the best answer for me was to help time pass by seeking ways to be active doing that which I enjoy. For those who do not have a family or hobbies and other ways to be active, it must be a more difficult challenge than mine. Many people are so lonely the only answer for them is to marry again. I have not needed this answer or wanted to find someone to replace Mary. In the years ahead, I may feel differently, but for now I am satisfied.

Still In The Business World

I did not want to retire. I had structured my work so that, with a great staff of highly-qualified people behind me, it was all pleasure. Actually, my commitment to Roosevelt Financial Group, Inc. by itself should have allayed all of my fears about retirement, but it did not. When Mary was still quite healthy in 1986, I was asked by the American Red Cross to become chairman of the investment committee responsible for supervising the management of all of the assets in their employee benefit funds. Without hesitation I accepted the invitation and attended my first meeting on September 3, 1986, in their head-quarters in Washington, D.C. It was a good committee, and through-out 1987, we gave serious thought to the strengths and weaknesses of our present money managers while interviewing other firms that might help us be even more successful in the future. However, as Mary's health worsened in the fall and early winter and my atrial fibrillation impacted my health, I had no alternative but to resign.

If I had rejoined the investment committee of the American Red Cross after Mary's death, that responsibility would undoubtedly have helped me adjust to living without her. However, I did not consider taking that step because, shortly after she died, I was invited to become a member of the board of directors of the Helping Hand of Goodwill Industries. I accepted because I would not need to travel and believed I could help them with supervision of their investments. With the passage of time, I accepted the responsibilities of treasurer and membership on the finance and investment committees, the result being some additional demands upon my time.

In 1994 and 1995, I gradually became familiar with an orga-nization of the United Methodist churches in Missouri, which has the responsibility for managing various kinds of financial assets. The name of the organization is Missouri United Methodist Foundation, Incorporated. The fund is growing quite rapidly, so when I was invited to become a member of the board and their investment committee, I could not resist the temptation to become involved. I attended my first meeting on July 22, 1995.

The weekly meetings and activities of the Kiwanis Club of

Downtown Kansas City have proven to be a source of great enjoyment. I have been a Kiwanian for more than 42 years. Another long-term relationship that has been very important is my membership in the Kansas City Chapter of the Financial Executives Institute. As I mentioned earlier, my membership started in 1972 in St. Louis. It was transferred to Kansas City immediately after I moved, so for the past 25 years, the activities and meetings have been an integral part of my life. Those things that interest the chief financial officers of corporations are directly related to my interests. Some close personal friendships have had their inception in these two organizations.

Management Of A Portfolio

When you have spent a lifetime managing and making money for other people and have been fortunate in accumulating some for yourself, it is easy to continue managing money for your own personal satisfaction. I use the word satisfaction because I do not need more money to live as I wish. My needs are very simple, with the exception of what I spend on golf and at the Lake of the Ozarks. The money I have made since Mary's death has been for my family, my church and for organizations that I believe are contributing to the needs of our society. If I have any regrets about not attempting to make more money while I was working, it is that I could have put myself in a position to do more for those organizations our society needs and that depend on the generosity of individuals.

Since I have said it is easy to make money once some has been accumulated, it seems not only logical but almost mandatory for me to provide some details. When I made the decision to accept lump sum settlements (instead of monthly payments) from our pension and thrift funds, I eagerly looked forward (for the first time in 40 years) to making investment decisions with the freedom to buy, hold and sell whatever and whenever I wanted to do so.

I received my distributions around the middle of 1987. Approximately two months later, the stock market commenced declining, with the Dow Jones Industrial Average dropping 36.1 percent from its high of 2722.42 on August 25, 1987, to 1738.74 on October 19,

1987. This short period of sharply declining common stock prices coincided with the period from the middle of August to the end of November when Mary entered the hospital for the last time. When I was not taking care of her, I buried myself in the challenge of coping with the weakness in the market. I made numerous changes in my holdings, but, in hindsight, I must say some of them were not very logical. From November 30, 1987, when Mary entered the hospital and became semicomatose, and until she was buried on May 13, 1988, my portfolios were relatively untouched and unimportant to me.

But after the funeral and when I was home alone, I began to watch the ticker tape and spent some time each day reading annual reports of corporations and utilizing various sources of financial information to make investment decisions. I subscribed to The Value Line Investment Survey, about eight business magazines, and the chart services of Securities Research Company. I also received the investment research reports of several research firms with which we had a working relationship at Waddell & Reed. After about two months, I decided the research from so many organizations was unnecessary. Instead I concentrated my attention on one firm, Kidder Peabody (now Paine Webber), not because their research material was the best, but because I believed by working closely with a good friend, Richard Jensen, a very good broker, I could learn as much as I needed about Wall Street's recommendations. I soon found that, between the statistical information provided by Value Line and the charts provided by Securities Research Company, I had all the tools I needed in order to be successful. I should qualify that statement by also emphasizing the value of the ideas presented on "CNBC" by their own staff as well as their interviews of a host of investment people from Wall Street firms, many of whom I had the opportunity to know during my working years. In effect, the challenges of my responsibility at Roosevelt Financial Group, Inc. and the management of my portfolios' meant I was still a working man. The big difference was that my home became my office. Being retired and enjoying the investment business so much made it very easy and comfortable to move into a life-style I enjoy.

The eight-year period from December 31, 1987, to December

31, 1995, is a period long enough to indicate what I have accomplished in an important personal portfolio. The portfolio was created as an IRA rollover account so that no taxes were paid on income or capital gains. In this situation, I normally held from 35 to 50 common stocks and traded them actively with emphasis on owning common stocks with above-average growth in sales and earnings. Dividends were unimportant, and capital appreciation was the primary objective. No bonds were owned.

During this eight-year period, the DJIA increased from 1939 to 5117, an increase of 164 percent, which was equivalent to an average annual increase of 12.89 percent per year. The S&P 500 index did not do quite as well, so the annual increase was 12.1 percent. Including the reinvestment of income from the DJIA index, the total return (income and appreciation) of the DJIA was 16.6 percent annually. Since income was retained and reinvested in the IRA portfolio, this is the valid way to compare performances. The IRA portfolio appreciated 363 percent during the eight years for an annual rate of 21.4 percent each year. The turnover in the portfolio was heavy and received my attention on a daily basis. I also concentrated in those issues that continued to perform well, so at the end of the eight-year period, about 40 percent of the portfolio was in 10 of the 50 stocks held. In 1996, the portfolio appreciated 31.2 percent. The S & P 500 was up 20.3 percent.

My Sister Mary Grond's Death

Early in the morning on April 19, 1996, my sister Mary had a massive heart attack. She died before the day was over, never having recovered from a deep coma. She and I talked about death many times, and, since she had experienced a coronary occlusion many years earlier, Mary believed a heart attack would cause her death. Although she was almost 82 years old and not in perfect health, the reality of a loved one's death is still devastating. After hearing the news, I left immediately to join her children, grandchildren, great grandchildren, other relatives and friends in Grant's Pass, Oregon, for a beautiful memorial service in the First Baptist Church. Her grandson John Van Leeuwen read the eulogy; her daughter Kay DeVries read several of

Mary's spiritual beliefs; her son-in-law Andy DeVries read several of her favorite passages from the Bible; and her singing group (about 30 elderly members), the Pacemakers, sang three songs. Many people in the congregation stood to mention what Mary meant to them.

As is obvious from what I have said, Mary was a deeply religious person who read and studied the Bible as if it were her vocation. Her compassion and love for her family, relatives and friends made her a very special person. In my quest for an enjoyable, worthwhile life, I have lost a very precious sister who helped me immeasurably during the eight years that have passed since my wife died. Many times, Mary expressed to me and others how our seeing so much of each other during the years since her husband Neal died also helped her as she lived alone. The weekly telephone calls when we shared our thoughts, beliefs and aspirations and the numerous trips we made to places such as Hawaii, Florida, New York, Michigan, Indiana and Arkansas can never be duplicated. I treasure the memories, and I shall miss her.

About The Epilogue

As I was writing this book, I wanted to include my thoughts on how money could be managed in today's environment, and to do so I interspersed suggestions as they occurred to me when I was writing about my experiences. Eventually, after finding that approach to be unsatisfactory, I decided to change my approach and consolidate my beliefs in the hope they would be more coherent and of greater value to my readers.

So in the epilogue to this book, I have attempted to provide some general advice and guidelines individual investors may choose to follow in managing money. So much information is available from magazines, television programs and a multitude of investment organizations and services that confusion as to what to do has become a great challenge to those who save money. I believe my thoughts and some of my actions could be helpful to people who wish to accumulate financial assets.

EPILOGUE

◆

Managing Money

This chapter is not intended to be a comprehensive text-
book on how to manage money, but it is a condensation of what I
believe individuals should understand and recognize as basic information, which can be used in making decisions as how to invest savings
and accumulate assets.

Investing In Mutual Funds

For most individuals, the answer lies with mutual funds
because they provide full-time management of diversified portfolios by
excellent money managers. There is no way the individual investor can
obtain this kind of money management unless he or she has many millions of dollars ... and even then it is questionable. In my experience,
too many individual investors, as well as many small- to medium-sized
organizations, have the belief they must have their own portfolio of
stocks and bonds if they are to achieve superior investment results.
This is an emotional, not a logical, approach to managing money.

In a discussion of the role of mutual funds in managing money,
there is some value derived from discussing equity (common stock)

funds separately from fixed-income (bond funds). However, it is important to note that a great many funds are designed to use both types of
securities in the same fund. It has only been in the last 15 years that
fixed-income funds have become an important segment of the mutual
fund industry. As I said earlier, the development of money market
funds opened the door to the use of mutual funds (including bond
funds) for managing every part of an investment portfolio. A starting
point on understanding common stock mutual funds is an examination
of the different types of funds. The differentiation between these funds
comes from a combination of what is said in the prospectus and the
exact way that the objectives are accomplished. First, I will briefly
describe only those fund groups that the individual needs to consider.
This is one way to begin to reduce the number of funds that deserve
the attention of the individual investor.

COMMON STOCK MUTUAL FUNDS

Aggressive Growth and Growth Funds

Aggressive Growth Funds are funds whose objective is above-
average appreciation in common stocks. To accomplish this objective, they
often take above-average risks by the use of leveraging (borrowing
money), trading in options and a high level of trading activity. Many times
these funds place great emphasis on younger and smaller companies.
Growth Funds are the same as Aggressive Growth Funds but probably
experience less volatile market fluctuations because of more conservative
management. Some Growth Funds are called Mid-Cap Funds because
they only invest in medium-sized companies in an effort to obtain greater
growth than might be achieved in larger companies. To some extent, this
is a sales tool. Growth Funds are more suitable than Aggressive Growth
Funds for most individual investors. The appreciation in Growth Funds is
often superior to a fund managed more aggressively.

Small Company Growth Funds

These funds concentrate on younger and smaller companies in
an attempt to obtain more appreciation than might be available from

larger companies. History has proven that the marketplace goes through periods when this type of a fund acts either much better or much worse than funds that invest in larger, more established companies. Small companies have less depth and breadth in their management and product lines. This makes them riskier investments. Managers of these funds offset this risk with the ownership of a large number of companies in their portfolios.

Growth and Income and Equity Income Funds

The prospectuses of these two types of funds justify identifying them as distinctly different types, yet in practice they attempt to accomplish the same goal. Specifically they invest in common stocks that provide slightly more income than is normally available from common stocks. However, the difference is very small. The managers sometimes use preferred stocks and bonds as an avenue for obtaining slightly more income. Make no mistake in evaluating the attractiveness of these funds. Many of them obtain excellent results that compare favorably with funds classified as Aggressive Growth or Growth Funds.

International and Global Funds

International and Global Funds invest in countries other than the United States, but, depending on the wording in the prospectus, at times these funds may have a significant proportion of their investments in our country. The attraction of investing internationally is based on the belief that companies in other parts of the world are obtaining greater growth in revenues and earnings than is available at home. It is also important to know that foreign markets move in different cyclical patterns than ours. These two factors justify consideration of having some money invested outside the United States. However there are risks that should not be ignored. One is the difficulty a money management organization faces in staying on top of everything happening in countries around the world. There are accounting and cultural differences that can create unpleasant surprises. It is my personal conviction that, at this time, most individual investors should limit investments outside the United States to perhaps 15 percent of a portfolio. Many investment advisors believe a larger investment outside the United States will produce superior results. I prefer to be more conservative.

Science and Technology Funds

These are specialty types of common stock funds that deserve a great deal of attention. Technological obsolescence is perhaps the most difficult analytical problem a money manager can face. The companies are of all sizes ... a new idea can create a large, new company in just a few years ... large companies can find themselves struggling for survival. Diligent, close and expert attention by an analyst is mandatory. The safe way to participate in this industry and its potential growth is in a mutual fund. Today, technology very definitely includes parts of the telecommunications industry.

Discussed below are groups of common stock funds that have some, but not as much, attraction for most individual investors. They can, and do, provide very satisfactory investment results. In my opinion (with the exception of index funds), they tend to complicate the challenge of selecting mutual funds. I have no need for them myself, and, as would be expected, this influences my comments.

Balanced Funds

These funds invest in both stocks and bonds and may make substantial changes in the proportions in the two categories. They are designed with the objective of being a complete package for the investor. If the manager has the ability to identify those periods when one group or the other has the best outlook — and acts accordingly — the results can be very impressive. Generally, the investor should think of this type of fund as a conservative way to own some common stocks. I believe most individual investors should achieve diversification between stocks and bonds by the multiple ownerships of funds. If an investor only owns one fund, balanced funds have merit.

S&P 500-Stock Index Funds

These funds endeavor to hold all of the 500 stocks in the index in proportions that will duplicate the index and, therefore, the market as a whole. They operate with significantly lower fees than other funds. It should be realized that all money managers cannot outperform the market as a whole. Some will do better; some will do worse. On balance the expenses and transaction costs of managing mutual funds mean that more funds will do worse than the market than better. Accordingly, S&P 500-Stock Index Funds are very popular with those corporations or organizations with large amounts of money. They often work on the theory that, if they have their money invested in a diversified group of mutual funds, or with several money managers, the superior results of some will be offset by the poor results of others. An individual investor does not need to feel the same way and instead, should strive for good results with a combination of different kinds of actively managed funds. There are other index funds, but I believe they should also be ignored by most individual investors.

Convertible Securities Funds

These funds invest their assets in securities that are convertible into common stocks, namely, either preferred stocks or corporate bonds. A fund invested in these securities should produce significantly more income than is available from common stocks. Preferred stocks (have no maturity date) and bonds that are convertible into common stocks provide a stated level of income that is greater than the income from the common stock into which they are converted. However, the investor gives up some of the appreciation that is achieved by the common stock of the company into which the shares may be converted when it is advantageous to do so. I look upon these funds as another way to obtain diversification that is not needed by an individual.

Specialty Domestic Funds

There are many funds thought of as specialty funds because their investments are concentrated in a fairly narrowly defined group of companies. Some examples are: Natural Resource, Environmental, Food, Industrial Materials, Retail, Health, Auto, Paper, Financial

Services, Real Estate, Gold Oriented and a great many funds that identify their objectives on a narrowly defined industry basis. These are often called Sector Funds. Those mutual fund organizations that offer a large number of these funds to investors do so as an appeal to individual and institutional investors who believe they have the ability to concentrate successfully their investments in selected sectors of the market. I question whether many investors can "time" their entry or exit from specific areas successfully. I believe most investors should leave the selection of specific sectors of the market to professional money managers. My belief is based on the assumption that most individual investors do not have the time or background knowledge to devote to a thorough understanding of the outlook for the various sectors they wish to own. One of the great dangers is the tendency to follow the crowd and rush into the popular sectors. The money managers of narrowly defined industry sectors are also vulnerable to either having more money than they want to invest or not having even enough to handle their withdrawals without selling stocks they would prefer to hold. This can have an adverse impact on their performance.

Specialty International Funds

Most of the comments I have made about Specialty Domestic Funds apply also to the international area. Some of the sectors that have been developed are: International Small Company Funds, European Region Funds, Pacific Region Funds, Japanese Funds, Latin American Funds, Emerging Market Funds and Global Flexible Portfolio Funds. I believe most individual investors should not attempt to select these funds. Investing in a broadly diversified international fund is all the risk most individual investors should assume. Some time in the future I might change my mind, but I doubt it.

FIXED-INCOME MUTUAL FUNDS

The above listing of common stock funds is not entirely complete, but hopefully it provides enough of an overview to enable the reader to feel comfortable about the kinds of decisions that can be made in selecting common stock mutual funds. Next it is necessary to examine how the investor can come to grips with the usage of fixed-income (bond) funds.

Money Market Funds

This type of fund invests in securities that mature in less than one year; the price of a fund does not fluctuate. This feature, when combined with a check writing privilege, has enabled the mutual fund industry to compete aggressively for the savings of individuals and the cash reserves of institutions. This type of fund is also highly suitable as a temporary investment pending a more attractive longer-term investment. The yields (income), most of the time, make them less attractive than bond investments.

Government and/or Government Agency Funds

The bonds issued by the different agencies of the United States government are not guaranteed, but it is unlikely that the government would allow them to default on principal and interest payments. The risk of default is great enough to expect a somewhat higher yield from U.S. Government Agency bonds than from U.S. Government Bonds. The primary attraction of these two types of mutual funds, most of the time, is their high quality. Their appeal is to extremely conservative investors. In addition to U.S. Government Bonds, securities of the U.S. government include U.S. Government Notes, which mature in less than 10 years, and U.S. Treasury Bills, which mature in less than one year.

Taxable Bond Funds

The quality of bonds issued by corporations differs widely, but when a fund does most of its investing in good quality issues, A1, A2, A3 and B1, it falls into the high-quality category. The managers of these funds strive for above-average results by obtaining favorable price action and good income. To obtain this goal, they frequently switch their holdings among different industries (including government and government agency issues) while shortening or lengthening the maturities of the bonds they own. This type of fund should be thought of as a sound approach towards obtaining satisfactory income.

High-Yield Taxable Funds

The bonds held in these funds are lower in quality with the risk that some of the corporations may become bankrupt. However, there is great safety in a widely diversified portfolio. These funds came into existence about 15 years ago. The price fluctuations of their portfolios are similar to higher quality bond portfolios and are not a cause for concern. Most of the bonds have shorter maturities than the bonds held in the better quality bond funds, and when this is true, the price volatility of a fund is softened. At times these funds are called "Junk Bond Funds." This is a misnomer because this type of bond fund provides a vehicle for younger companies to obtain the capital they need to grow. Historically small companies had to rely entirely on loans from banking institutions. These funds also provide a level of income that otherwise would not be available to individual investors. Most individuals do not have the time, knowledge or assets to enable them to select these bonds directly and own enough of them to have a diversified portfolio. This type of mutual fund reduces risk by owning hundreds of companies in its portfolio.

Medium Maturity Taxable Funds

As the name implies, these funds give up some income in order to moderate the price fluctuations of their funds. There is nothing wrong with this concept, which has merit for conservative investors.

Tax-Exempt Bond Funds

These funds are often called municipal bond funds. From a quality viewpoint, they usually hold issues that are rated B1 or better. Their investments are in the securities of school districts, cities, states and other approaches to tax exemption, such as industrial revenue bonds. The decision to buy this type of fund depends upon tax considerations. It is also logical to consider a fund that limits its investments to the state in which the investor is domiciled. Such a fund may produce even greater tax exemption.

High-Yield Tax-Exempt Bond Funds

The objective of these funds, as the name implies, is to lower quality and obtain more income. The bonds owned are usually lower than B1 in quality. This type of fund is attractive for the same reasons I mentioned for high-yield taxable bonds.

A MUTUAL FUND PORTFOLIO

An individual investor should own several common stock funds but not as many bond funds. Specifically, I recommend five stock funds and two bond funds. There probably is no such a thing as a typical investor in mutual funds, because at different ages, under different market conditions, with more accumulated wealth and perhaps a higher level of income, the needs and objectives of every investor change. Nevertheless, I believe the following diversification is logical for most people:

Type of Fund	Percent of Total
Aggressive Growth or Growth Fund	15
Growth and Income or Equity Income Fund	15
Small Company Growth Fund	15
Science and Technology Fund	15
International Fund	15
Total Stock Funds	**75**
Taxable or Tax-Exempt Bond Fund	10
High-Yield Taxable or Tax-Exempt Bond Fund	15
Total Bond Funds	**25**
Total Funds	**100**

My comments in regard to each type of fund explain my reasoning behind the proportion of each type of fund in the portfolio. This applies particularly to the types of funds that have been excluded. The proportion between stock and bond funds will differ for individual investors and depend on the need for current income, risk tolerance and other personal goals. The objective of every investor should be to attempt to justify having all investments in common stock funds, because over a lifetime, more money will be accumulated.

How Mutual Funds Manage Money

Since I have placed so much emphasis on common stock mutual funds, my thoughts about how mutual fund organizations manage common stock money may be of value in selecting a mutual fund or a group of funds. First it should be recognized that it is very difficult for those who manage very large sums of money to produce superior results indefinitely into the future. However, results somewhat superior to the market averages are achievable for a great many money managers if they have put in place an investment philosophy and organization that in itself is superior. Continuity of management and fund managers is a vitally important ingredient. The investment philosophies of successful organizations do not need to be identical. Here are some of them:

1. Selection of common stocks using a value approach that stresses such fundamental factors as low prices relative to earnings and book values.

2. Use of a sophisticated computerized approach to estimate future earnings and dividends as the basis for selecting common stocks.

3. Less emphasis on the relationship of prices as they relate to price-earnings ratios; instead, greater emphasis on growth in earnings and sales.

4. Concentration on smaller companies and medium-sized companies in the belief they can grow faster.

5. Use of a multiple-manager approach where emphasis is placed on making each analyst who follows a group of companies in an industry the portfolio manager of those stocks for which the analyst is responsible.

6. Emphasis on a variety of technical factors (meaning those related to the price action of common stocks) ... not their

sales, earnings, financial strength or fundamental factors such as price-earnings ratios.

7. Use of multiple managers where a computerized base of thousands of companies enables the managers to select those common stocks whose quarterly growth in sales and earnings is superior. In this approach, very little emphasis is placed on direct contact with the companies whose stocks are acquired.

In the first five approaches listed above, considerable emphasis is placed on having investment analysts personally visit the headquarters and facilities of the corporations being considered for purchase. Frequently investment analysts will have the responsibility for only following 15 or even just a handful of companies.

There are other approaches, or variations or combinations of two or three of these, that can be made to work successfully. What is important in all of this is the necessity for the organization to adhere to its philosophy and never cease working to produce above-average results. There is no one infallible way to manage a portfolio of common stocks.

At this time, the Securities and Exchange Commission is in the process of requiring disclosure of some of the information (to which I have alluded) in every prospectus. The SEC is particularly concerned with continuity in regard to any changes in responsibility for managing the fund. This is of considerable importance in selecting a mutual fund and deciding to stay with an investment.

I have discussed at some length the various kinds of mutual funds, and, as I have said earlier, I strongly believe in the advisability of working with one family of mutual funds when putting together a package of funds. A specific family of funds may not have a particular type of fund an investor wishes to own, and, in those instances, it is necessary to go to another investment management organization. A few comments on alternative approaches to selecting a fund manager may be helpful.

SELECTING THE FUND MANAGER

1. Utilize a mutual fund management company with a family of funds and a captive sales force such as those employed by American

Express Financial Advisors (formerly Investors Diversified Services), Waddell & Reed and many insurance companies. In these organizations, an investor is assigned a sales representative who can continually provide information about the mutual funds and how those suggested for purchase should achieve the objectives of the investor. These representatives are paid commissions on sales, and when one is working with a capable salesperson, the results can be quite satisfactory. These organizations promote themselves as "financial planners" and provide numerous services, such as the need for insurance, which can be important to the investor. The ease and absence of any meaningful cost to switching among the funds in the family makes this approach attractive to many investors.

2. Utilize a broker with a large brokerage firm. A broker's approach will be to recommend those funds that provide a sales commission because that is how one survives in that business. It is unlikely that a broker will limit the recommendations to one family of funds. This means another commission must be paid when, and if, an investor switches a fund into another family of funds. If the investor has confidence in the ethical standards, knowledge and judgment of the broker, very satisfactory results may be achieved. The managements of brokerage organizations endeavor to make available to their brokers those funds that they have investigated and believe will provide good results in the future. Frequently they also have their own family of mutual funds that they promote aggressively and where switching may be free. They often do a very good job of managing their own funds.

3. A third approach is to utilize those fund complexes that have no up-front sales charges and rely upon advertising to promote their funds, such as T. Rowe Price, Vanguard and Twentieth Century Investors. To a great extent, these organizations depend upon their reputation and past performance as a primary sales tool. Many of them are large organizations that manage a large number of funds in their family of funds. Paid advertising, direct mail solicitation, plus favorably written newspaper and magazine articles, are vitally important in promoting sales. There is nothing wrong with this. The chal-

lenge the investor faces is to know what is going on within the organization. How do managers make their decisions? What changes have been made among fund managers? Has the organization lost people and why? How did they get their good performance?

4. A viable approach that is widely used is to pay a fee to a "financial planner" who selects specific funds for an investor. Financial planners are also trained to provide assistance in many other matters, such as estate planning and taxes. The fees can be quite high. Normally planners stress their ability to select funds that have no up-front sales charges. Understandably, this is one of the ways they sell their services. I suspect they tend to avoid placing as much emphasis as I would on the fact that front-end sales charges on mutual funds are not relevant after one or two years as performance becomes the overriding consideration. In my experience, they also do not hesitate to have their customers invest in several different families of funds. They promote their judgment and knowledge of the industry as something the investor needs. It is up to the investor to evaluate whether the advice received is satisfactory and justifies the fees paid. There is a great need for capable financial planners, particularly Certified Financial Planners. I was on the Board of the College for Financial Planning from 1974 to 1977 when it developed and promoted this very important professional designation. I wholeheartedly endorse its value.

5. In recent years, another approach toward guiding investors in their selection of mutual funds has become very important. This is the development by organizations, such as Morningstar Mutual Funds and Value Line Mutual Fund Survey, of background information on individual mutual funds in a form where analysis of important data enables an investor to make intelligent decisions. The information provided by Value Line and Morningstar on individual mutual funds is superb, valuable and unique. Their development has been important for individual investors because of the wealth of data and periodic contact with the portfolio managers. These two organizations also make specific recommendations that the investor may evaluate. Since investing in mutual funds should always be thought of as a long-term approach toward the management of money, it is important not to lose

sight of that basic principle. One concern I have about these two services is that some investors will conclude that changes in the number of stars or numerical ranking by the service organization should be the reason for switching from one fund to another. Read what is being said by the service; evaluate it with good judgment; and plan on staying with a selection for at least five years. Also, to be better informed, one should subscribe to several magazines that publish articles on the industry and performance information. *Forbes*, *Fortune*, *Money* and *Barron's* are good examples. There are others, but these are enough to enable one to ask intelligent questions and make better decisions.

6. In 1991, a discount brokerage firm, Charles Schwab Corporation, introduced an approach to buying "no load" mutual funds that is attractive for some investors. It is named "OneSource." Charles Schwab has made arrangements with numerous mutual fund organizations where, for a small fee, funds can be bought and sold through Schwab. This system's ease of switching feature makes Schwab's approach attractive, but it may not provide quite the same personal touch achievable by investing directly in a single family of funds. Other variations of this approach will undoubtedly develop in the future. Some brokerage firms are alreading moving in that direction.

7. There are also a tremendous number of mutual fund newsletters that make a living by providing recommendations on the attractiveness or unattractiveness of selected mutual funds. I have no knowledge of which ones are superior now and will be superior in the future. Subscribing to Morningstar or Value Line could be a good backup to reliance on a specific newsletter.

Transaction Costs

In regard to sales expenses, one should not forget that, over a period of time, mutual fund sales charges are much less than the costs of trading in and out of individual securities. Frequently the cost of just one purchase of an individual stock can be as much as two or three percent. A front-end sales charge by a mutual fund of around five percent may adversely affect investment performance (as I have mentioned before) in the first year or two, but after that, it is not relevant because the ability of the fund manager and the total organization will determine the relative performance of the fund. Sales expenses may be covered in a variety of ways by mutual funds, including those described as annual and back-end charges. The investor should be knowledgeable on how the charges are made but should not let the specific charge, whether it is on the front end or charged later, determine which funds to buy.

In my opinion, too many financial newsletter writers and investment advisors, unfortunately for investors, find it necessary to promote themselves with complete emphasis on the ability to select no-load funds. Their motive is understandable because investors have a natural tendency to react favorably to something that will save them money. To make sure investors are well-informed on front-end sales charges, one of the disclosure requirements of the SEC is that mutual fund prospectuses and reports to shareholders reflect investment performance with the front-end sales charge added to the cost. Organizations that have a front-end sales load attempt to prove the longer-term unimportance of the sales charge by showing performance numbers over different periods of time without a front-end charge alongside the figures required by the SEC. The justification of a front-end sales charge is the price paid for obtaining personal financial help that includes guidance on which funds to own along with the amount and type of insurance appropriate for a family. In other words, these organizations provide advice on financial planning and a personal relationship with the person or organization providing the advice.

MUTUAL FUND BOARDS ARE VITAL

Each mutual fund has a board of directors responsible for continually monitoring the management company, which has the obligation to fulfill the objectives established for each fund. If the management company fails to handle its responsibilities to the satisfaction of the board of directors, they can terminate the contract that gives the management company its responsibility for the fund. This seldom happens because the management company will satisfy the concerns of the board of directors by changing portfolio managers, adding new people, terminating individuals who are not performing, changing their investment policies or philosophy, or anything else that is needed to rectify an unsatisfactory situation. It is most important not to lose sight of this constant evaluation process that goes on within every mutual fund complex as it analyzes its successes and failures and attempts to improve the performance of a specific fund in the future. This in itself is a vitally important safety factor for the investor and the reason why it is not necessary, and usually inadvisable, to switch from one family of funds to another family. This organizational concept is also one of the more important reasons the mutual fund industry is growing so rapidly. It is a regulated industry that produces very good results. Mutual funds provide all-day, everyday management of their portfolios, and the companies that manage each family of funds are highly motivated to make sure investors are satisfied. It has been my experience that dissatisfaction by an investor is, almost always, caused by the investor having selected the wrong type of fund or funds.

Unit Investment Trusts and Closed-End Funds

This discussion of mutual funds would not be complete if I did not comment on "Unit Investment Trusts" (UIT) and "Closed-End Funds." They differ from each other in many ways, but they have one thing in common; namely, they are created with a fixed amount of dollars with no additions of cash to the funds after the initial sale. They are not open-ended for new money. UITs are funds designed to provide higher income and total returns by not being managed and, thus, requiring no management fee. To accomplish this, all investments are made when the fund is created with a fixed amount of dollars. They are portfolios bundled together (usually by brokerage firms) with virtually no changes ever made in the portfolios during the years the fund is designed to remain in existence. What the investor buys is what he or she must live with until the portfolio is liquidated after a pre-determined number of years. Typically, these trusts have an initial sales charge that may be around five percent. If the individual investor wishes to liquidate part or all of his or her shares, the sponsor of a UIT will try to find a buyer, but it may be at an uncertain redemption price and fee. As a fixed-income type of UIT experiences maturities or the "call" of its bond holdings, the investor must cope with the accounting and tax implications of these developments. With close to 14,000 of these trusts having been sold, one cannot argue with their popularity, but I have never come across a way to compare their performances with open-end funds. Most of the UITs are bond funds, and their primary appeal is to investors in tax-exempt bonds, where it is more difficult to prove that active management is valuable. The absence of a ready market for the shares of a UIT and the fact that the investor gives up the ability to switch funds in a family of funds are the most important considerations and the reason why open-end mutual funds appeal to most investors.

"Closed-end funds" are similar to UITs in the way they are offered but differ in terms of liquidity and management. First appearing in the 1920s, these funds provided a new way to invest in common stocks. Today, both equity and fixed-income funds, including many concentrating in either foreign stocks or bonds, are being sold. Most closed-end funds are listed on the New York Stock Exchange, but both the American Stock Exchange and NASDAQ (the over-the-counter market) have listings. These listings are important to closed-end funds because a ready market is continually provided. The appeal of these funds to investors is active management, but the disadvantage of owning them is they tend to trade at a discount to the net asset value. This means buying or selling the shares requires a careful analysis of the size of the discount. Many brokers who follow these funds look for deviations in the discount and recommend a fund to interested buyers when the discount is unusually large compared with what is considered a normal or typical discount. Sometimes, but rarely, the shares trade at a premium price relative to their net asset value. This is very difficult to understand, for a premium infers a scarcity value that is probably short-lived. I would sum up my feelings by once again calling attention to the family of funds concept and its free exchange privilege between funds in the family. The uncertainty of what will happen to the discount is just another fact that makes the open-end funds, which always trade at their net asset value, more attractive.

Buying Your Own Bonds

I do not believe many individual investors should attempt to invest in individual fixed-income securities. A capable broker can guide an investor into specific bonds with satisfactory results, but there are risks, particularly credit or quality risks, that cannot be ignored. Most investors in individual bonds buy in the belief nothing can go wrong. This attitude can lead to disappointments; however, the risk can be reduced, if not eliminated, by buying high-quality corporate or tax-exempt bonds and securities of the federal government or its agencies. This does not solve the question of which maturities should be acquired. In my experience, most individuals solve this problem by buying relatively short maturities. This, of course, means they are obtaining less income and reducing the amount of appreciation in value that comes from longer maturities when interest rates are declining. The concentration on quality and short or even medium maturities is certainly not the best way to manage a bond portfolio, but it can be done.

With few exceptions, it is my belief individual investors should take advantage of the tremendous variety of well-managed fixed-income mutual funds. The costs are not prohibitive and the investment results likely to be quite satisfactory. As I said earlier, one of the attractive segments of the fixed-income environment is low-quality, high-yielding bonds. By diversifying away the credit risk, these funds make available a much higher level of income that, otherwise, would not be available to investors. In my opinion, it would be foolhardy for an individual to select his or her own individual low-quality bonds. But even more important is the active management by highly competent portfolio managers of all kinds of fixed-income funds. They take advantage of opportunities to switch their holdings to accomplish a variety of objectives. Sometimes it is to shorten or lengthen maturities; sometimes it is to move from one group, such as utilities, into another, such as industrials or governments. The fact is that the bond market is in a constant state of flux, and capable people can, and do, achieve results that are superior to a simple buy-and-hold approach that an individual investor would probably follow. There are other factors, such as greater liquidity, that could also be emphasized. Obviously, I am a believer when it comes to the use of mutual funds when managing fixed-income money.

Managing Your Own Stock Portfolio

The management of a personal common stock portfolio can be a source of great satisfaction. This is when one wants to have the enjoyment associated with learning how to make specific investment decisions. It adds a new dimension to life if one likes to be involved with such decisions, for example, as to whether Wal-Mart or Kmart is going to be the most successful in the future. Every day, new things are happening that will affect the future and create investment opportunities. Anyone who invests in individual common stocks comes to realize that making investment decisions means one automatically becomes involved with every aspect of life. This is a challenge, but it should not be something to fear. If the opportunity is presented to join an investment club, take advantage of it as soon as possible. A group of people with the same objective of making money in the stock market should only add to the enjoyment.

As the investor approaches the selection of common stocks, it is important to be sensitive to what is happening in the economy and the government as well as in the various industries in which investments may be evaluated. This is often described as a "top down" approach and is in direct contrast with simply placing primary attention on the outlook for specific companies. In the final analysis, an investor must have a good understanding of all aspects of the environment in which a company functions. The following are examples of the kinds of things that should be of interest to the investor: the trend of interest rates; the policies of the Federal Reserve Board; the new drug products of the pharmaceutical firms; the power of nicotine in the sales of tobacco products; the impact of the acceptance of soft drinks around the world; the effect of the concerns about fat, sodium and cholesterol on the restaurant and food industries; the need for large discount stores in rural and suburban environments; the importance of fast-food restaurants in a mobile and aggressive society; the opportunity to take advantage of the growth in the usage of personal computers; the growth of the Internet; the tremendous expansion of the mutual fund industry; the satisfaction of having good advice and materials available as one maintains the home; the impact of cellular telephones on the telephone industry; the foot traffic in the shopping centers as specialty stores take business from large department stores; the building of motels on the interstate highway system; and the significance of parents reacting to the television-inspired demands of children for all kinds of toys.

To bring some meaning to the above listing, the following are some common stocks that have become more attractive by these trends: Federal National Mortgage Association, Merck, Philip Morris, Kellogg, Coca-Cola, Home Depot, Wal-Mart, McDonald's, Intel, Microsoft, Compaq Computer, T. Rowe Price, Franklin Resources, AT&T, the baby Bells, Toys "R" Us, and The Gap. These are just some of the companies one might have placed in a portfolio. Many other everyday developments have been, and will be, there to trigger the curious investor into taking just enough time to investigate and react with the dollars that have been saved.

At the same time, many political and economic developments say to avoid some industries and companies: the closing down of defense plants; the competitive environment of the airlines; the impact of union power on the steel and automobile industries; the passage of legislation that can decimate an industry; and the development of a serious business recession. I hasten to say, however, that in the depths of a recession, those companies that are vulnerable to the cyclical downturn can be on the bargain counter. This means one must be right two times, once when selling and again when buying. This is difficult to accomplish, and the average investor is more likely to be successful if investments in cyclical industries are avoided. Most investors should look for companies that can grow in any economic environment. The trend of sales and earnings readily provides this insight into the nature of the business.

There is also much to be said for the part-time investor to concentrate on well-established, highly visible companies like General

Electric, McDonald's, J.C. Penney, Wal-Mart, AT&T, Texaco, Disney, IBM, Eastman Kodak and other household names. The last two names are included despite the fact that difficult industry conditions produced unimpressive market action for a prolonged period of time. This is exactly the reason one should have a diversified portfolio. It does not matter how much an investor knows (or thinks he or she knows) about an industry or a specific company. Surprises seem to come from many unforeseen sources or actions that one does not believe will be serious, even when he or she knows what is happening. For most individuals, 15 to 20 names, as a goal, is enough companies to obtain adequate diversification.

However, before going any further, it is important for me to emphasize that, if an individual or family has the opportunity to concentrate on one company, they should give the idea careful consideration. If it is a company they know and are convinced it has a good future, it might be a wise decision. However, the decision to concentrate must not be based on emotions. After Torchmark bought Waddell & Reed, our thrift plan permitted us to buy either the mutual funds or Torchmark common stock. It was easy for me to make the decision to buy Torchmark because the company was doing well. Consequently from 1982 through 1986, I placed as much of my earnings as was permitted into the thrift plan and Torchmark. One stock growing at an above-average rate will usually perform better than a diversified mutual fund or a diversified portfolio of individual stocks. The per-share price of Torchmark increased (as adjusted for two two-for-one splits) from trading around $4 per share to $20 per share during this five-year period.

Investors in common stocks should realize how important it is to take a long-term view of what one can achieve by ignoring the ups and downs of the market. During this century, common stocks have provided about a 9 percent annual return on average while fixed-income investments have provided a total return (income plus appreciation) of less than 6 percent. Obviously there are five and even 10-year periods when the results have differed from these. In a study discussed earlier that I commenced in the early 1950s and that we updated before I retired, there was only one period of five years' duration since 1900 (when equal dollars were invested each year) when bonds provided a greater total return than common stocks. Fluctuations in the prices of common stocks will always be volatile and can be frightening, but this should never discourage one from using them as the vehicle for participating in the long-term growth of our country. The United States has lost some of the ability of free enterprise to function effectively, but the ingenuity and aggressiveness of individuals continues to offset the burden of too much federal government intervention.

Even when an investor wishes to become involved with the selection of individual common stocks, it is not logical or wise for many investors to attempt to select common stocks that are difficult to analyze and follow. Specifically I would again emphasize and caution against three areas: international, technological and small companies. To have representation in a portfolio in these areas, the use of mutual funds is the safest approach and one that is much more likely to produce superior results. The following comments are somewhat repetitive, but they are appropriate.

The difficulty with foreign companies is the absence of readily available current information (both financial and general) comparable to what we have on companies domiciled in the United States. There are also accounting differences that the investor needs to understand. The currency risk (changes in the value of the dollar relative to the currency of the foreign country) can be removed by buying American Depository Receipts (ADR), which are available for many foreign companies. Nevertheless, in a global economy, it is wise to have some investments outside the United States, particularly to participate in the freedom and growth of the market environment of the Far East. However, as I said earlier, I believe the conservative individual investor should not have much more than 15 percent of an investment portfolio in securities of other countries. The problem with investing in technological companies is technological obsolescence and unforeseen fluctuations in the prices of their products. It is an extremely difficult job, even for a full-time, highly qualified analyst, to know when, and if, these kinds of developments will impact individual companies.

Investing in small companies is hazardous, because by their very nature, their future is less predictable than it is for large well-diversified companies. Usually, the managements of small companies do not have much breadth, and the product lines are narrow and vulnerable to unexpected competition.

Does my emphasis on taking a long-term approach toward owning common stocks mean that an investor should "never" try to benefit from the ups and downs of the stock market? The word "never" is inappropriate because "timing" can be done successfully and profitably. However, it requires great discipline and a lot of just plain luck. For most individual and institutional investors, it is better to buy for the long-term and not try to sell at the top and buy at the bottom. When I say that, I have in mind the investor making a very substantial shift in the diversification of the portfolio between stocks, bonds and some reserves. Modest changes in the percentage of the portfolio in common stocks should be expected, as an investor finds it either easy or very difficult to find attractively priced stocks. But do not forget that all it takes for the stock market to begin to move in a different direction is "something" that makes either the buyers or the sellers more aggressive than the other in their attitude toward owning common stocks, and there is no consistently reliable approach to predicting that "something."

When I was teaching at DePaul University in the evening school in the late 1940s, we had lived through the period from the 1920s when there had been no long-term uptrend in common stocks. Many institutional investors like the Commonwealth Edison Pension Fund and the Keystone Group of Mutual Funds in Boston were being managed with disciplined, formulaic, market-timing plans in the belief it was the only way to produce a satisfactory return from investing in common stocks. In the graduate program at the University of Chicago, one of the courses I took emphasized "Market Timing Plans." With this background, it was logical for me to teach this course at DePaul University. In the late 1940s, as the market began a strong upward trend that did not end until 1969, it was very difficult to be successful by trying to sell high and buy low. It was a time to concentrate on buying and holding common stocks and forget about market timing. The stock market declines in 1970 and from January 1973 to December 1974 were followed by another period in which common stocks did not seem to be attractive unless one could take advantage of the market's volatility by emphasizing market timing. The DJIA had reached the 1000 level in 1965 but did not return to that level until near the end of 1982, a period of 17 years. During those years, largely because of the high rate of inflation, investments in fixed-income securities and real estate were attractive alternative investments. By the end of the 3rd quarter of 1996, a period of 14 years, the DJIA moved to the 5900 level. Some individual investors did not participate in this upward trend, because the decline in 1987 and ongoing publicity about the volatility of the market kept them from a strong commitment to common stocks. Fortunately, the good results produced by the mutual fund industry have induced millions of investors to invest in common stock mutual funds and participate fully in an unbelievably strong stock market.

Today, as in the past, almost all money managers, investment advisory organizations, investment newsletter writers, portfolio strategists with brokerage firms, bank trust departments and mutual funds spend a heavy proportion of their time in attempting to decide (1) whether stocks are more attractive than bonds or cash reserves; (2) whether stocks in general are overvalued or undervalued; and (3) whether, because of the business outlook and other factors, some stocks in some industries are more attractive than stocks in other industries. If one has access to several sources of advice, recommendations will differ widely. The publicity that all kinds of news media give to this kind of material is interesting to read and hear, but it can be very misleading to an individual investor. Do not be misled. Most investors should place almost all of their attention on the factors and developments that can impact the securities they own or plan to buy not the above three portfolio management questions that dominate the attention of professional money managers and the media. Whether the answer for an individual is common stock mutual funds or the selection of individual common stocks, the best approach should be to stay in the stock market and invest for the long-term ... by that, I mean for an entire lifetime.

My confidence in common stocks does not mean that reserves in money market funds and investment in fixed-income securities are not important. The amount or proportion of one's investments in these two areas depends on a careful analysis of how much income one needs and how much risk one should assume. Money market funds (reserves) and fixed-income securities with different maturities should be held in whatever proportion the investor needs for liquidity, safety and income, not because one thinks they are the best vehicles for making money. That is the role of common stocks and common stock mutual funds that grow in value over time. The proportion of the portfolio to be invested in fixed-income securities should be related to the need for income and the advisability of being conservative and defensive. The proportion held in reserves, such as money market mutual funds, under most circumstances should depend upon how soon the investment needs to be turned into cash and spent. Money in savings accounts, very short-term certificates of deposits and money market funds are important for providing the answer for some needs, but they may not even produce enough income to protect an investor against inflation.

Picking Stocks

In a general way, I have alluded to trends and developments that can trigger an investor's interests and lead to specific decisions, but I have left a big void by not being more specific about what to consider when selecting an individual common stock. It may be helpful to go to a community college or wherever adult education classes are available and take some basic subjects, such as the analysis of financial statements and portfolio management. However, it is not necessary. Self-education can be sufficient.

In retirement I have not had available any more services or information than is available to any individual investor. My 49 years of hands-on experience in managing money has probably just made it easier for me to make stock selection decisions more quickly, not necessarily better.

As I said before, I have relied primarily on two investment services: Value Line and Securities Research Company. Value Line provides a 16-year statistical record of the numbers that are critical to an investor's insight into what a company has accomplished. There are other services like Standard & Poor's, but they are not as valuable to me. Value Line also provides recommendations that have stood the test of time. The quarterly charts prepared by Securities Research on stocks traded on the New York Stock Exchange and in the Over-The-Counter market provide the pictures that guide me in most of my investment decisions. These charts provide a 12-year record of each stock's monthly price range, earnings and dividends per share, volume of trading activity, relative price strength of each stock and a few other factors related to the price action of each stock. Some business magazines are sources of ideas, as is the *Investors Business Daily* newspaper, which, on a daily basis, sets forth the relative strength of both the price and earnings of the company. These services are important to me now, but in the future there will probably be similar publications that improve on these.

Not to be ignored is a good broker. A broker is important for several reasons, but an important one is access to the output of the investment research department of the firm. I do not use discount brokers because good ideas from a broker who is with a firm that has a large, capable organization are worth far more than a few commission dollars that may be saved by trading with a discount broker.

Let's assume with all of this in place that an individual's broker contact calls with a suggestion. If the idea has come from some other source, still obtain the broker's recommendation. Listen carefully. Then begin to look for some answers. Question the broker initially on thoughts that come to mind, but before taking any action, look at the charts and numbers to see what they say. From that study and analysis, call the broker and enter the order if that is the decision. If unable to decide, an investor should review his or her thinking with the broker in the hope that the answer will become clear. Never forget the broker's motivation in calling in the first place was to make money and make the investor happy. To make the decision, the following is a summary of what an investor probably will want to explore:

The Business

Is this a company that is growing steadily, or is it vulnerable to the cyclical nature of our economy? Is the company a significant factor in the industry? Can it influence or affect price changes in its product line or lines? How fast are they growing? Can a fast growth rate be maintained? What is the risk of someone undermining their sales efforts? Do they have a new product or special expertise that sets them apart? To whom do they sell? If they are dependent on one or even just a few buyers (airlines, automobile companies and the government), it may be a red warning flag, or depending on the relationship with the buyer (Wal-Mart), it may be a haven of safety. Have they been growing by acquisitions, or have they done it internally? Do they depend on just a few products (like a drug company), or is it just the opposite?

Answers to questions such as these will give important insights into what the company does. Remember the purpose behind this group of questions is to determine the speed and volatility of their growth. Value Line shows the annual rate of growth in revenues during both the last five and last 10 years and the estimate for the next five years.

I have touched upon sales and revenues, but some comments and illustrations to supplement the above questions may be of help. At one time, McDonald's looked as if they might stop growing as they saturated the United States with their restaurants. Then they proved to themselves and investors generally that they could invade the rest of the world. The same thing is happening to Johnson & Johnson, Coca-Cola, Pepsi Cola, Anheuser Busch, Whirlpool and many other companies. The chemical and drug companies have always known this. With younger companies like Casey's General Stores, Sonic Corporation, Applebee's and other franchisers, the question becomes one of when they will exhaust their growth opportunities in the United States. Other questions revolve around the need for new products. Minnesota Mining & Manufacturing, Rubbermaid and companies in the toy business are examples that come to mind. The drug industry is an example of great reliance on having products in the pipeline. That problem is compounded by the length of time it takes for the Food and Drug

Administration to approve a new drug. The whole process frequently takes around 10 years. Fortunately for investors, they can solve this great uncertainty by owning more than one drug company. In my personal investments, I have always followed this policy when I invested in the industry.

Earnings

A historical record of the earnings on each share will tell whether a company is growing steadily or with significant down years. Steady growth at a high rate is normally what one hopes to find. But very rapid growth may be a cause of concern because, if anything interrupts or slows that growth, trouble may be ahead. Annual earnings should be the focal point of the analysis, but changes in quarterly earnings are the clue to whether the rate of growth is changing. This means it is logical to compare the most recent quarter with the one a year earlier as well as the previous quarter. Value Line provides quarterly earnings during the past five years. They also show quarterly sales for the same period. Value Line also makes an estimate of the rate of growth in earnings for the next five years. Understanding these numbers and trends is a step towards getting to the heart of the decision-making process.

The Balance Sheet

At the outset, this may seem to be a formidable obstacle or challenge. But it is not, for all the investor is attempting to obtain is a general feeling about the financial strength of a company. Foremost is the question as to whether the company is highly leveraged. Have they borrowed so much money that, in a prolonged period of adversity (meaning a slow down in sales and earnings), they might run out of cash and additional borrowing power?

An investor does not have to analyze this for at least two reasons. One is that an individual investor should be staying away from selecting high-risk companies such as those who are small or in the technological and international areas that are difficult to analyze. The second is that a service like Value Line provides their assessment of financial risk. So, do not spend much time on this because balance sheet problems seldom affect the kinds of stocks the investor should follow.

In a general way, just know that a company does borrow a small or large proportion of the money they need to operate their business. Again, in the capital structure section of the Value Line data, they show the percentage of the company's capital coming from debt or preferred stocks and common stocks. A glance at their numbers is all that is necessary. The amount of capital coming from debt varies from company to company and industry to industry. Some industries, like banking, borrow almost all their capital and usually have only about five percent of equity in their capital structure. Because of this risk, they are highly regulated, and that is the way the investor is protected. It is the type of business that makes the amount of leverage an important decision for the management of a company. If one combines lots of borrowed money with vulnerability to the business cycle, the inability to control costs (union power has been important in the past), and a highly competitive market place for the companies' products, there are some ingredients for trouble. Most of the time companies such as these are not attractive investments and are easy to pass over. My answer is to not spend much time searching for stocks that are potentially vulnerable to the fluctuations in the business cycle. Leave that to the managers of mutual funds and employee benefit funds, who have large amounts of money to invest, a great need for diversification and a big, highly professional research staff.

Price Earnings Ratios

This is probably the most important factor to understand because it is crucial to the success of most investment decisions. The ratio of the price of a share of stock to the earnings of a share of stock tells what the marketplace (investors all around the world) thinks about the company. To evaluate the importance of the price to earnings ratio (p/e) it must be compared with what it has been in the past, how it compares with the p/e of other companies in its industry and the p/e of the stock market as measured by an index such as the S&P 500 or DJIA. A starting point is to look at the history of the p/e ratio on a relative basis.

Let us say a stock is selling at 10 times its earnings and the DJIA is at 20 times earnings. Therefore, on a relative basis, the p/e ratio is at 50 percent. That in itself might indicate that the stock is cheap and attractive. But if the stock has seldom, if ever, sold at a ratio higher than 50 percent of the DJIA, it means nothing and an investor might just as well look elsewhere. But what if this stock is selling at 20 times earnings, the DJIA is at 10 times earnings, and in the past the stock has never sold at a p/e that is twice that of the market? A warning flag is very obvious, for the stock may be overvalued. But perhaps something new has developed, such as a new product or a merger with another company. Changes in p/e ratios develop because a company is a living organism that adapts to its environment in order to survive and grow.

Most of the time the growth rate in sales and earnings will control the level of the p/e ratio. As a generality, a stock selling at 15 times earnings with sales and earnings growing at 15 percent each year will represent sound value. The same is true of a company selling at 10 times earnings and growing at 10 percent each year. This is a simplistic illustration, for many factors have a bearing on the p/e ratio. It is obvious, but an investor should always be looking for companies selling at low p/e ratios and a high growth rate in sales and earnings. Early in 1995, Intel was selling around 10 times consensus earnings estimates for 1995 with an estimated increase in sales and earnings well above 50 percent for the year. Furthermore, there were strong indications that the momentum of sales and earnings would continue. Those who bought the stock liked the valuation, whereas those who sold were worried about sales in 1996 and beyond. Since the stock doubled in price, the optimists about the future were the initial victors. Under most market conditions, striking illustrations like this are few and far between.

This leads me to mention that most of the time the stock market is an efficient mechanism for determining a reasonably accurate price for a stock. Another way to look at this is that millions of investors on a world-wide basis are attempting to look into the future and hopefully outsmart the buyer or seller on the other side of the market. Accordingly it is logical to make decisions on the assumption one is not over-paying or under-paying, and in time, the investment will accomplish the desired objectives. This means that the time horizon for holding a new purchase should be several years. If one makes purchases in order to obtain instant gratification, the investor will probably be frustrated and disappointed. It is important to be patient. When successful with an investment, it is probably because the company consistently does the right things at the right time. In summary, it is advisable to keep in touch with investments by reading the quarterly reports, glancing through the annual reports, and supplementing them with relevant newspaper and magazine articles. This information plus contact with a broker should reassure an investor as to the soundness of decisions. At the same time, data as provided by Value Line will be important.

The Price Action Of A Stock

For some money managers, this is the only thing that is important. They track the price action of stocks in a variety of ways and can be quite successful. I observe some of the criteria that influences them but do not make investment decisions solely on the basis of technical (price) considerations. Technicians are not new to the investment business. One of my good friends and associates at The Northern, who was trained in fundamental analysis, became a technician because of his frustration with picking stocks in the way I have been discussing. There is no question about the price action of a stock being a forecaster for the future. There are many ways that the market begins to move a stock without any new fundamental developments being obvious. Some examples are: insider trading by the management, employee insights into new products, firsthand observations by the competitors of a company and last, but not least, the perceptiveness of fundamental analysts who are in frequent contact with the company. There is nothing unethical about this. It is simply the marketplace at work. In time, whether it takes days or months, the fundamental factors come to the surface.

Technicians have a variety of statistical approaches toward

attempting to predict price action. One of these is a moving average of the price as determined by perhaps 30 or even 200 days of duration (shorter and longer periods are also used). When the price moves above or below this average, it is considered a buy or sell signal depending on the direction. The volume of trading when a stock moves up or down may be indicative of the attitude of investors toward moving in or out of a stock. Another tool (and there are many) is to look for periods when the price of a stock seems to resist either going above or below a certain level. Studies such as these are of some value, but my experience over the years is that they are of more value to a trader than they are to long-term investors. I have much more confidence in interpreting the meaning of price action as shown in the charts provided by Securities Research Company.

The Securities Research Company charts show the monthly price range of a stock along with annual earnings (during the last 12 months) on a scale where prices are 15 times earnings. If the price of a stock is selling at 15 times earnings, the two plots are at the same point on the chart. Accordingly, whenever the price is more or less than 15 times earnings, the relationship is highly visible. These charts make it very easy to observe when the price action of a stock is changing its relationship to its earnings. This enables an investor to ascertain when a stock is beginning to look either over-valued or under-valued as the stock trades at p/e ratios away from its normal pattern. It is the change from the historical pattern that is meaningful, not as a trading vehicle, but as an indication of whether this is a logical time to either accumulate the shares or consider a reduction in the size of the investment.

But even more important than this is the visual picture of 12 years of price changes and earning trends. One glance at such a chart immediately brings out the stability, volatility or growth of earnings. The rate of growth of those earnings is also visible and can then be related to the p/e ratio. An example of a stock becoming over-priced is Wal-Mart. Historically, for many years, Wal-Mart consistently traded above 20 times earnings, with sales and earnings growing more than 20 percent annually. However, early in 1993, it appreciated to where it was selling around $34 per share when earnings were around 70 cents per share. This p/e ratio of about 50 times earnings was substantially higher than in the past, with the exception of 1987 when it sold at 40 times earnings. The price began to decline as investors gradually adjusted expectations toward slower growth in sales and earnings. After three years of performance below the market averages, at the beginning of 1996, the shares traded around $20, which is about 15 times earnings estimates for 1996. In the first nine months of 1996 the stock appreciated about 35 percent, even though earnings are now only growing between 10 percent and 15 percent annually.

For 10 years, International Business Machines Corporation's (IBM) price and earnings moved together in what turned out to be a serious downtrend. The shares reached a peak of around $170 in 1987 and a low of under $42 in the fall of 1993. At the low point, IBM was losing money. Earnings have been improving, and the shares traded above $110 in 1995 with a p/e ratio of less than 10 times earnings. In a situation like this, the chart had somewhat limited value for "timing" purposes because earnings were nonexistent. However, now that the trend of earnings is becoming more visible and predictable, the chart becomes a natural decision-making tool. I have used the IBM record simply to emphasize that charts are helpful most of the time, but not when earnings are volatile and unpredictable. Under those conditions, I believe most individual investors should look elsewhere until information is available to provide insights into the future trend of earnings.

Building a Portfolio

Studies have shown that most individual investors own less than 10 companies. Much, of course, depends on how much money is available, whether the individual is just getting started and whether savings from a paycheck are being used. Starting from nothing means that initially only one or just a few stocks will be held. Unfortunately many investors believe that it is necessary for them to speculate and attempt to hit a home run the first time up. It is much more logical to make the initial investment in a rather conservative situation that will not produce unpleasant surprises. An investor's employer is an ideal candidate, because one can think through the factors I have been discussing and be comfortable with the decision. A second alternative is a local company that receives a great deal of attention from the local newspaper. It might be the largest company in that part of the country. The telephone company might be a candidate. A third alternative might be the employer's most successful competitor. Again, the investor knows the business and the questions to ask himself or herself and the broker. It is also logical to think of local companies: Target (owned by Dayton Hudson), Taco Bell (owned by PepsiCo Inc.), J. C. Penney, Sears Roebuck, Exxon and many other companies that operate across the country. It was firsthand experience that led me to investigate McDonald's and Wal-Mart and profit as a result.

Once started, progress will depend upon having a disciplined savings program. It will also depend to some extent on not having a bad experience. Bad results often come from acting on a "hot tip." Perhaps a respected colleague at work says that the wife of his boss is on the board of XYZ Company and they just landed a very large account. Or a golfing buddy tells how much money he has made on ABC company and has only owned it for one month. They may be good ideas, but do not hurry to a telephone and call a broker. Do some homework.

After an individual has accumulated enough money to conclude that enough stocks are owned to achieve adequate diversification, what should the number be? Much depends on how deeply involved the investor believes he or she can be in knowing the companies and making good decisions. It also depends on the broker or some other source of information (such as your investment club). Many investment advisors of personal portfolios like to have between 25 and 35 companies in an account. Any number is arbitrary because there is nothing that dictates a specific number provides something magic. An investor must use good judgment and common sense. If the investor follows my advice and uses mutual funds as the way to own stocks in the technology, international and small company mutual funds, it then becomes logical to own fewer stocks. Any involvement in owning specific stocks in these three difficult-to-manage areas means the investor should make a significant increase in the number of stocks owned. This is because the investor must have good diversification in these three areas. At the end of 1995, I owned about 50 stocks, with all the extra holdings in technology and small companies. Normally, I would be very happy with 15 to 20 companies.

Also remember not to be afraid of concentrations in familiar and attractive companies. But, let a concentration evolve gradually as a common stock appreciates and still seems to be a good value. It is risky and dangerous to jump in and immediately take a big position in a company as a first time investment. With the benefit of hindsight, the investor may wish he or she had been more aggressive, but moving ahead more slowly may protect the investor from the agony and discouragement that follows a big, unexpected decline in the market value of an investment.

When to Sell

I continue to hold stocks I bought 40 years ago, but I also frequently sell stocks I have owned for less than a year. Never set a price at which to sell or a specific development that will happen. A company has a life of its own, and only time will tell what should be done. Decisions to sell should be based on considerations that, to some extent, will be the reverse of what made an investor like the company in the first place. Something has changed. The price of the shares has escalated and cannot be explained, or the price has weakened for reasons that lessen confidence in the future of the company. Perhaps the earning power of the company has become questionable because of the loss of senior people in the management or a new product that the market does not like. Most of the time when an investor's confidence has been shaken, it is best to move slowly and only sell part of the holding initially. For me, nothing is more frustrating than to liquidate a holding for reasons that later proved to be false. Most of the time, it means the investor has been emotional and is guilty of either poor research or none at all. In such a situation, I do not hesitate to reestablish my position. The inability to buy a stock because of inadequate funds can also be frustrating when an investor knows his or her assessment of the situation had been accurate. Just shrug it off and look forward to the next opportunity to invest.

Capital Gains and Losses

An important portfolio problem is how to handle capital gains and losses. Too many people become emotional and refuse to either take a loss or take a profit. My advice is never to hesitate to take a loss. Many times I have heard people say they will not sell until they get their money back. Nothing is more ridiculous. I grab a loss, no matter how big it may be, because I know that sometime in the future I will use that loss to offset a capital gains tax. There are things to do to keep from making a bad mistake when a stock is sold to take the loss for tax purposes. One is to double up the number of shares owned, wait for 31 days (the period our tax laws require when you buy back a stock you sell at a loss), and then take the loss on the original holding. This is what to do if the outlook for the company is favorable. An alternative is to take the loss and reinvest the proceeds in a similar company whose market action may be similar to the stock sold. There is also some logic to taking the loss, sitting on the sidelines for the 31 days, hoping it does not go up, and then buying the stock back. If the question is whether to take a profit, the answer depends first on the reasons for selling and second on the net price at which the sale would be made, taking into consideration the capital gains tax. If the reasons for giving up on the company are convincing, the only answer is to bite the bullet and pay Uncle Sam. When a profit is taken, there are no time constraints (from a tax viewpoint) on when to buy back the stock.

A Final Summary

By ending this book by writing about "picking stocks," I do not want to leave the wrong impression. Most of the investment segments of this book have been devoted to the mutual fund industry, not because I ended my career managing mutual fund money, but because I sincerely believe that an overwhelming proportion of individual investors will be more successful if they use mutual funds. Where can individual investors obtain full-time money management by money managers who are the best in the country? The answer is no place. However, I hasten to say that the trust departments of banks have similar expertise in the management of their common and collective trust funds. These funds are quite similar to mutual funds, but one must have personal trust accounts or employee benefit money that is managed by the bank in order to benefit from their ability to manage money in the same way that mutual funds are managed. Insurance companies that manage annuities are also characterized by very good management. The institutions that manage money dominate everything that transpires in both the equity and bond markets. This does not mean they always obtain superior results. It does mean that the individual investor who owns his own stocks should understand the institutional world. The big advantage of the individual is the ability to concentrate on a relatively few number of stocks. The institutions have so much money to handle that they are handicapped by the need to own a large number of stocks. Examine any of their portfolios; frequently, they have their largest positions in as few names as they can justify ... meaning their favorite, most comfortable and most attractive positions. The institutions are also handicapped by the challenge of how to accumulate or reduce their positions in hundreds of thousands, if not millions, of shares without affecting the prices of the stocks.

Recently, I read where a large institution had liquidated its entire holding of a stock when the market believed they still liked the stock. That stock lost half its value while this was being done. My advice is to recognize that institutional investors try to avoid disclosing their intentions in regard to the sale or purchase of a stock. Always beware of recommendations to buy or sell when money managers are being interviewed on television. Assume that, when they say they like a stock, they have already accumulated the position they want. A recommendation to sell is not likely if they still hold a large position This is just plain common sense, so do not be naive. Recognize that an individual investor will not know when institutional investors change their mind and start to liquidate investments. Today, more than any time in the past, large amounts of money are being placed in common stocks where the money managers make their decisions on the price momentum of a stock. Most of the time they ignore, or at least de-emphasize, the fundamentals, such as p/e ratios. As a result, the bottom of a decline is an elusive target. This does not mean an individual should never own individual stocks. It does mean that the longer-term outlook should be the dominant objective of the investor.

Even though I encourage individuals to participate in the stock market by having their own portfolio, I will emphasize again that I believe managing fixed-income investments, small company stocks, science and technology stocks and international stocks should usually be with mutual funds.

My comments have always been directed toward more conservative investors. I have not covered options, puts, calls, hedging and arbitraging. I have attempted to discourage the use of mutual funds that take above-average risks and mutual funds that specialize either domestically or internationally. This does not mean they are not important. It only means that the vast majority of individual investors should leave those things to professionals and organizations who have large research staffs and large amounts of money to manage.

If an individual or family wants to accumulate enough wealth to have a satisfactory and comfortable standard of living when the retirement years come, equity type investments, i.e. common stocks, should be thoughtfully considered. This is because they enable an individual or a family to benefit from the natural growth of our country. For most investors, the answer is common stock mutual funds.

APPENDIX A – AUTHORED ARTICLES

◆

Publications:

1966 – St. Louis Union Trust Co. Booklet:
"European Economic Report" 140

February, 1967 – Missouri Business: "The Outlook
for Common Stocks".. 140

1968 – St. Louis Union Trust Co. Booklet: "Performance
Achievement for Pension and Profit Sharing Funds" 140

April, 1968 – St. Louis Union Trust Co. Booklet Co-Author with
Ed Anderson of "European Economic Report" 140

January, 1969 – Trusts and Estates: "Common Stocks in
Tax-Free Funds".. 140

March, 1972 – Trusts and Estates: "Investment Strategy" 140

August, 1975 – Mutual Fund Forum: "ERISA: A Blueprint
for Mutual Funds" Assisted by John Watts 223

July-August, 1977 – Financial Analysts Journal: "Prudent
Investing—Before and After ERISA" 223

October, 1977 – Mutual Fund Forum: "Capitalism and the
Stock Market".. 223

August, 1978 – Financial Analysts Journal: "Quantitative
Evaluation of Investment Research Analysts".................... 224

January/February, 1979 – Financial Analysts Journal:
"Long-Range Planning in the Financial Analysts Federation"....... 225

January, 1981 – Mutual Fund Forum: "Why Mutual Funds
Outperform Banks" 225

March 6, 1981 – American Banker—The Same Article 225

May, 1981 – Sky: "The Maturation of Mutual Funds" 226

September, 1981 – Kansas City Times: "More Investors Cash
in on Chance to Use Fund Exchange Privileges".................. 226

November, 1981 – Mutual Fund Forum: "The Exchange Privilege
is for All Investors"....................................... 226

July, 1982 – Mutual Fund Forum: "The State of the Fund Industry 227

May, 1984 – Kansas City Business Journal: "Mutual Funds
Come in Many Shapes and Sizes"............................ 227

APPENDIX B – FAMILY TREES

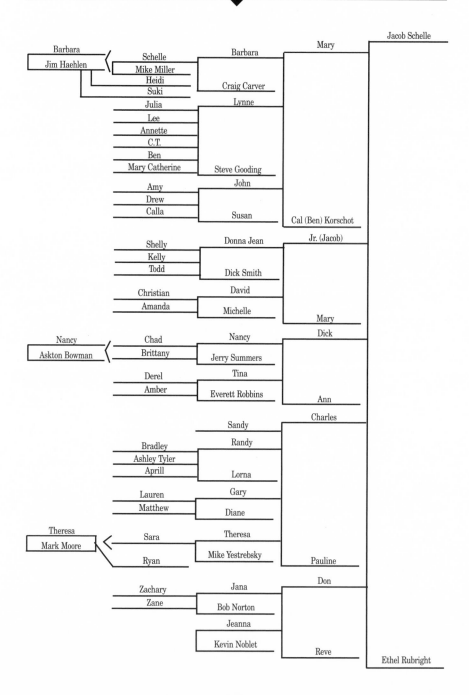

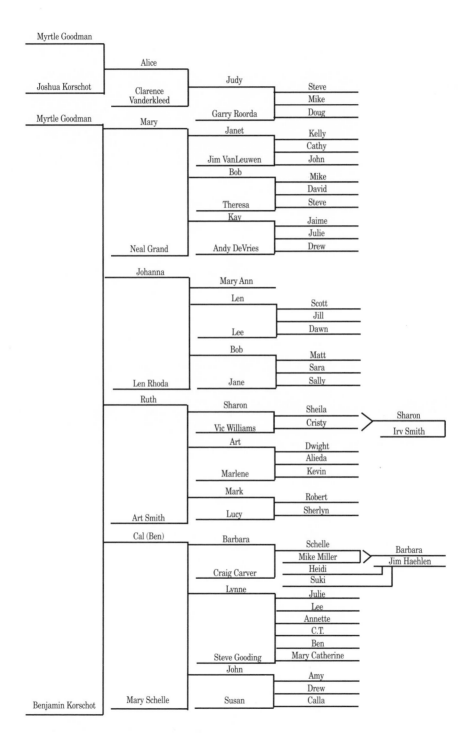

INDEX

◆

Abdou, Dr. Nancy, 258-262, 267-268, 271, 274, 276

"Abreast of the Market", 215, 217

AIDS, 255, 257, 259-263, 265, 267, 269, 271, 276, 278

Albala, Dr., 256

Alley, Robert, 177

Amare, Dr., 257

American Banker, 225

American Banker's Association, 74, 104

American Cancer Society, 114

American Depository Receipts (ADR), 322

American Express Financial Advisors, 311-312

American Marketing Association, 222

American Medical Association, 114

American Red Cross, 203, 262, 295

Amsterdam, University of, 89

Anderson, Ed, 140, 144

Andrews, George, 130, 134

Andrews, Marybill, 130, 134

Angell, Wayne, 239

Arkansas Bankers Association, 141

Arthur Anderson & Company, 250

Ask IMD (Investment Management Division), 181, 183

Association for Investment Management & Research (AIMR), 203

AZT, 269-271, 276

Badger & Guthman, 72

Bailey, Herbert, 114

Baker, Alex, 67-68

Baker, J.H., 35

Barron's, 199, 314

Beaver Lake, 249, 284

Becker, A.G., 97

Beckers, Carl, 127-128

Beckman, Steve, 157, 159, 164, 169-170, 194-195, 234

Behrens, Roland, 105-106, 126-127, 140

Behrens, Ruth, 126

Bellerive Country Club, 129, 150, 246

Benson, Lowell, 174

Bergers, 111

Bergstroms, 111

Black, Dr. Donald, 268

Bodwell, Henry, vi, 75, 78, 90, 93-94, 96, 103, 106, 109, 124

Bodwell, Marian, 109

Boehm, Barry, 130, 134

Boehm, Elmer, 130

Boehm, Jan, 130

Boettcher, Jerry, 173, 175

Bol, Bennie, 2, 18

Bol, Ed, 9

Bol, Frances (aunt), 2, 6

Bol, Johannes, 2, 6

Bol, John, 2, 41

Bol, Otto, 1, 2, 4

Bolliger, Walter, 147, 235-236, 240

Boswell, Ted, 128

Bouwer, Dennis, 225

Bradshaw, Stanley, vii, 239-241

Breeden, Doug, 239

Brown, Captain W.B., 59, 61, 64-65

Buchanan, Dodds, 165

Buck, Robert, 67-68

Bulldozer, 248-249

Burridge, Richard (Dick), 203

Burroughs-Welcome Drug Company, 269

Business Week, 218

Butin, Dr. Richard, 267

Butterfield Savings and Loan Association, 282

Butterfield Securities Corporation, 282

Buzzy, 120-121

Calhoun, Dave, 106, 126, 128, 145, 147

California Bankers Association, 142

Calvin College, 133

Campbell University, 211

Carlson, Arthur, 198

Caroll, Dr. D.C., 201

Carver, Craig, iii, 134-135, 284

Carver, Mischelle (see Mischelle Miller)

Centers for Disease Control, 262

Central Value Index, 151-152, 216

"Certified Financial Planner" (CFP), 234

Certified Public Accountant (CPA), 283

Chartered Financial Analyst (CFA), 127, 202, 283-284

Chase, Lloyd (Bill), vi, 34-35, 279

Chase, Louise, 279

Chicago, University of, 69-77, 110, 124, 151, 200, 203, 323

Chicago Board of Trade, 16, 37

Chicago Club, 105

Christian Reformed Church, 4, 20, 26-27, 36, 43, 278, 288, 294

Clayton, Alden, 67-68

"Closed-End Funds", 316-317

CNBC, 215, 297

Coleman, Dean, 100, 203

College for Financial Planning, 234, 313

Colony Woods, 125, 130, 138-139

Columbia University, 50-51

Combined Insurance Company of America, 123

Commerce Bank, 138, 164, 187-188, 283

Commonwealth Edison Pension Fund, 323

Continental Illinois Bank & Trust Co., 73, 129

Continental Investment Corporation (CIC), vi, 146, 155-157, 160-169, 179, 187-191, 212-213

Coopers, 111

Corcoran, Joseph, 68

Cotsonas, Betty (Westbrook), 66, 68

Country Club United Methodist Church, 221

Creesman, Ralph, 139

Croscutt, William, 20

Dale Carnegie, 78, 140

Davis, John, 114

Davis, Rolly, vi, 110, 112, 114, 250, 256

Davis, Sam, 127

Davis, Virginia, vi, 110, 249-250

De Paul University, 77-78, 151, 323

Deaconess Hospital Foundation, 132

DeAngelis, Peter J., 198

DeKinder, Sam, 179

Del Mar College, 282

Delaney, Ed, 158-159

Delnor Hospital, 255-256

Demarche Associates, 179

DePauw University, 130, 134, 136

DesPeres Presbyterian Church, 130

DeVries, Andrew, 286

DeVries, Andy, 286, 299

DeVries, Jamie, 286

DeVries, Julie, 286

DeVries, Kay, 286, 298

Dillingham, Jay B., 165, 233

Doerr, Julie, 210

Doerring, Dr., 263

Dordt College, 135, 289

Drake Hotel, 66

Duff & Phelps, 114

Dunnewold, Garrett, 1, 4

Dunnewold, Lawrence, 5, 36

Dunnewold, Mary (aunt), 1, 4

Eagan, John (Jack), 66-67

Eggers, Ken, 127, 132

Ellis, Jack, 144, 147, 200

Enright, Jack, 158

Erdman, Paul, 201

Erickson, William (Bill), 99

"ERISA: A Blueprint for Mutual Funds", 223

"ERISA, The Employee Retirement Income Security Act", 221, 223

Eubank, Dr. William, 258, 267-268, 277

European Society of Financial Analysts, 200

Evans, Mary, 130

Evans, Tom, 130

Evert, Charlene, 192

Evert, Herb, vii, 192, 196, 203, 229-231

Farm and Home Financial Corporation, 242, 244

Federal Reserve Board, 100, 215, 319

Fehring, Dutch, 41

Fields, Louis, 67-68

Financial Accounting Standards Board (FASB), 206-207

Financial Analysts Federation (FAF), 99, 127-128, 139-140, 142, 175, 190, 195, 197-205, 207, 209, 212, 221, 225, 234

Financial Analysts Journal, "Prudent Investing—Before and After ERISA, July-August 1977, 223

Financial Analysts Journal, "FAF's Current Planning Activities", Jan.-Feb. 1978, 225

Financial Analysts Journal, "Quantitative Evaluation of Investment Research Analysts", July-August, 1978, 153, 224

Financial Analysts Journal, 153, 202, 223-225

Financial Analysts Society of Chicago, Illinois, 197

Financial Analysts Society of Detroit, 99

Financial Analysts Society of Japan, 200

Financial Executives Institute, 143, 220-222, 296

Financial Institution Reform, Recovery and Enforcement Act (FIRREA), 237-238

Financial World, 201

Fink, Mathew, 207-209

First Methodist Church, Glen Ellyn, Illinois, 109-111, 122, 292

First National Bank in St. Louis, 106, 126, 140-141, 143, 147

First National Bank of Chicago, 73

First Presbyterian Church-Chicago, 110

First Reformed Church of Lafayette, Indiana, 287

First Union Inc., 143

Fleischer, Ernest, 239

Forbes, 189, 314

Forbes, "Survival Game", February 1, 1977, 218

Ford Motor Company, 48-49

"Formula Timing Plans", 151

Fortune, 314

Forum, 142, 223, 225-227

Foster, Bernice, 35

Franklin Savings Association, 239

"Freedoms Foundation of Valley Forge", 132

Frisby, Mrs., 10

Frohboese, Ernie, 200

Galema, Charlie, 15-16

Galema, Hattie (aunt), 15-16

Galema, Martin, 36

Garcia, Abel, 178

Garrison, Loyd, 241

German, Bill, 34

Ginsberg, Dr. William, 271, 275

Glen Ellyn, Illinois, 92, 107, 109-124, 132

Glen Oaks Country Club, 115-116

Glenbard High School, 113, 118

Gooding, Annette Marie, 282

Gooding, Benjamin Calvin, 282

Gooding, Charles Thomas (CT), 266, 274, 282

Gooding, Julia Marie, 282

Gooding, Lynne Denise (nee: Korschot, daughter), v, vii, 77-78, 80-81, 85, 110, 113, 116, 118, 120-122, 125-126, 129-132, 135-137, 248, 257, 261, 266, 268-269, 274-276, 278, 282-283, 285, 293

Gooding, Mary Catherine, 282

Gooding, Scott, 137

Gooding, Stephen, 137, 266, 268, 282-283

Gooding, Stephen Lee, 282

Gooding Partners, 283

Goodman, Amanda Tillotson (grandmother), 28-29

Goodman, Calvin, 28

Goodman, Charles, 30

Goodman, Clarence, 30

Goodman, John, 30

Goodman, Lester, 30

Goodman, Mary, 30

Goodman, Raymond, 30

Gray, Gloria, 203

Gray, William (Bill) S. III, 203

Great Falls Tribune, 215

Green, Reg, 210, 213

Grond, David, 286

Grond, Mary (nee: Korschot, sister), vi-vii, 3, 18-19, 26, 121, 136, 266, 281, 285-286, 288, 290, 298-299

Grond, Michael, 286

Grond, Neal, vi, 19, 89, 285-286, 299

Grond, Robert (Bob), 286, 290

Grond, Stephen, 286

Grond, Theresa, 286

Gusnard, Raymond T., 235-237, 239-240, 242

Gysels, James, 27

Habib, Dr., 264

Haehlen, Barbara Elaine (nee: Korschot), iii, v, vii, 53-54, 59-60, 64, 70-71, 76-77, 80-81, 90-92, 110, 113, 116, 118, 121-122, 132, 134-135, 137, 251, 255-257, 268-269, 274-278, 284-285, 290

Haehlen, Jim, 268-269, 274, 278, 284-285

Haehlen, Suki, 285

Halsey, (Admiral), 54, 56-58

Halverson, Richard, 183

Hammel, Ethel, 29

Hammel, Lloyd, 29

Hammel, Lloyd Jr., 29

Hammel, Mary Ann Click, 29

Hammel, Ruth Amanda, 30

Hannibal, Missouri Rotary Club, 142

Hansen, Howard, 110, 114-115

Hansen, Maxine, 110

Hardin, Hord, 127

Harlan, Dr. Woody, 273

Harriman, Mrs., 10

Harris Trust and Savings Bank, 73, 203

Hausmann, Frank Jr., 99, 203

Hechler, Robert (Bob), vii, 159-160, 167-168, 172, 187

Hein, Margie, vii, 178

Held, Chris, 9

Helping Hand of Goodwill Industries, 295

Henson, Tom, 128, 147

Hermes, Dorothy, 30

Heron, Catherine, 210

Herrmann, Hank, vii, 174-175, 192, 194, 229, 231, 233

Hertz, Dr. David B., 201

Hill, Bill, 76

Hill, Clara Jane, 76

Hillary, Fran, 130

Hillary, Harry, 130

Hillcrest Country Club, 268

HIV Virus, 260-263, 268-269, 276

Hoag, Robert (Bob), 67-68

Holekamps, 130, 133

Holliday, John, 176-177

Holt, Charles, 278

Hood, Robert, 168

Huey, Richard, 131

Huff, Emory, 67-68

IBM, 229, 321, 333

Image, 181

Indian Hills Country Club, 150, 245, 248, 269, 271, 284, 293

Indiana State University, 142

Individual Retirement Accounts, (IRA) 205-206, 212-214, 298

Institute of Chartered Financial Analysts (ICFA), 202-203

Institutional Investor, 142-143

Intagliata, Antonio, 176

International Association of Financial Planners, 222

International Telephone and Telegraph Company (ITT), 145, 156

Investment Analysis Standards Board, 198

Investment Company Institute (ICI), 192, 195, 197, 199, 201-210, 212-213, 218, 220, 222-223, 226-227, 230, 232-234, 267

Investment Dealers Digest, 227

Investors Business Daily, 215, 326

Investors Diversified Services, 312

Ivy, Andrew C., M.D., 114

Ivy Cancer Research Foundation, 114

Jensen, Julius "Reb" III, 157-158, 160-161, 188, 193, 196, 227

Jensen, Richard, 297

Johnson, Al, 210

Johnson, Glendon E., 166

Johnson, Leslie (Les), 67-68

Johnston, Harry, 128, 147

Jones, Sherman, 159

Judd, Jim, 222

Junior Achievement, 132

Kansas, University of, 221, 257

Kansas City Business Journal, 227

Kansas City Chamber of Commerce, 221

Kansas City South Chamber of Commerce, 222

Kansas City Kings, 247, 293

Kansas City Securities Corporation, 156, 159, 161, 165

Kansas City Society of Financial Analysts, 201, 221

Kansas City Star, 164, 188, 213, 218, 224

Kansas City Star, "Korschot's Dream Shifts from Coaching to Mutual Funds", October 7, 1980, 218

Kansas City Star, "Korschot Nursed Funds to Growth", December 7, 1986, 218

Kansas City Times, 164, 188-189, 213, 226

Kanter, Erick, 210

Keigher, Donald (Jamie), 66-68, 79

Keigher, Mary Lou, 66-67

Kemper, James, 187-188

Kester, William, 141

Ketchum, Marshall, vi, 72, 200

Keystone Group of Mutual Funds, 323

Kidder Peabody, 297

Kiwanis Club of Downtown Kansas City, Missouri, 295-296

Kiwanis Club of Downtown St. Louis, Missouri, 132, 141, 147, 220

Kiwanis Club of Glen Ellyn, Illinois, 112-115, 132, 201, 256

Klondike School, 10, 17, 19, 33-37, 41, 287

Kneebone, Robert, 74

Koning, Cecilia, 35-36

Kornhauser, Al, 115

Korschot, Alice (see Alice Vanderkleed)

Korschot, Amy Elizabeth, 283

Korschot, Barbara Elaine (see Barbara Haehlen)

Korschot, Benjamin Calvin (Cal, a.k.a. Ben), 74

Korschot, Benjamin Garrett (father), v, 1, 3, 4, 6-9, 11-12, 23-28, 34, 39, 43, 116-117

Korschot, Charley, 2, 41

Korschot, Edna, 14

Korschot Family Reunion, 16, 200, 286, 291-292

Korschot, Gertrude Einink (grandmother), 4, 19, 21

Korschot, Henry (uncle), 1, 2

Korschot, Jacqueline Calla, 283

Korschot, Jess (uncle), 4, 8

Korschot, Johanna (see Johanna Rhoda)

Korschot, John (cousin), 8

Korschot, John Andrew, 283

Korschot, John Bernard (grandfather), 4, 19-21

Korschot, John Calvin, v, vii, 81, 85, 91, 110-111, 113, 115-116, 118-122, 125-126, 129, 130-133, 136-137, 246-248, 255-258, 268-269, 274-275, 278, 283, 285

Korschot, Joshua, 29

Korschot, Lynne Denise (see Lynne Gooding)

Korschot, Maggie (aunt), 4

Korschot, Mary (see Mary Grond)

Korschot, Mary (Marian Marie) (nee: Schelle, wife), iii-vi, 41-55, 59-60, 64, 66-71, 76-81, 85-86, 91-92, 104, 106, 109-117, 119-123, 125-126, 129-132, 139, 144, 146, 150, 200-202, 211, 220, 232, 243-250, 253, 255-297

Korschot, Mary Susan Skipton, 138, 247, 283

Korschot, Myrtle Goodman (mother), v, 1, 3-5, 10-11, 18-19, 23-24, 26, 28-31, 34, 42, 85, 91, 105, 287-288, 290

Korschot, Ruth (see Ruth Smith)

Kortschot, Gertrude (great grandmother), 20

Kortschot, Henry John (great grandfather), 20

Kortschot-Rensink Farm, 90

Kostmayer, John, 156-160, 204

Kozminski, 77

Krebiozen, 114

Krebiozen: The Great Cancer Mystery, 114

Kroh, John A., Sr., 166

Kushner, Harold, 294

Lady, Larry, 172

Lafayette Journal & Courier, 41, 200, 213

Lafayette Leader, The 213

Lake Metonga, 120

Lakewood Oaks Golf Club, 245, 293

Lambert, "Piggy", 37-40, 42-43

Lambert Field House, 44

Lambrecht, Carl, 99

Lazzaro, Paul, 190

Lemenager, Jackie, 42, 44

Letendre, Dr., 259

Levine, Alexandra, 260-261, 276

Liberty National Insurance
    Company, 190-191

Lilley, Theodore, 202, 225

Lindquist, John, 65-66, 68

Lindquist, Lois, 66

Linwood Grade School, 5, 10

Lionel D. Edie & Company, 139

Little League, 118-119

Logan, Hugh, 127, 147

Logansport, Indiana State Hospital,
    288-290

Luton, Julie, 285

MacArthur, General, 56

Mackey, Guy, 44

Maddox, Frank, 130

Maddox, Sue, 130

Marchesi, Robert (Bob), 179

Margolies (Doc), 67-68

Marinella, Sam, 157-158, 160-161,
    167-168, 171-172, 187, 189, 191,
    193, 196

Maui El Dorado, 267

Mayo Clinic, 259

McCarthy, John Peters, 145, 147

McConnell, Walter S., 203

McDonald's Corporation, 116, 137-138,
    252, 270, 320-321, 327, 334

McKelvey, Jim, 111-112, 132, 134-135

McKenzie, Dr., 271-272

McLaughlin, David (Dave), 173

McWhinney, Rod, vii, 160, 172

Mendelson, Sid, 160

Mensink, Bryce, 278

Metcalfe, George, 147

Metcalfe, James, 147

Meyer, Janet, 213

Miami Herald, 199

Michigan, University of, 29

Midland Loan Services, 283

Miller, Mischelle "Schelle" Marie
    (nee: Carver), iii, vii, 135, 137,
    274, 284

Miller, Harry, 127

Miller, Michael Glenn, vii, 284

Miller, Oren, 127

Miller, Wayne, 159, 167-168, 187

Minnesota Mining and Manufacturing
    Company, 102-103

Minnick, Gwyn, 150

Minnick, Ockie, 150

Missouri Business, 140

Missouri United Methodist
    Foundation, Inc., 295

Mitchell, Fred, 174, 179, 194, 229,
    231-232

Mitchell, Richard, 158-160, 167-168, 187

Money, September, 1974, 214

Money Managers Memo, 181, 183, 188

Morgan, William "Bill", 171-172,
    194-195, 227, 232-233

Morningstar Mutual Funds, 313-314

Morton, John, 67-68

Mount Moriah Funeral Home, 278

National Association of Investment
    Clubs, 141, 215, 220-221

Nave, Tom, 167

Navy, 49-51, 61, 63-64, 67, 79, 81,
    83-87, 89-92, 288

Neal, Larry, 174, 176

Nelson, Jim, 100

New York Society of Financial
    Analysts, 198-199

New York Times, "Talking Business
    with Korschot of Investment
    Company Institute", October 7,
    1980, 218

New York Times, "A Big Bear Joins the
    Bulls", February 17, 1985, 216

Noblet, Jeanna (nee: Schelle), 271-272, 274, 291

Noblet, Kevin, 291

Northern Illinois Gas Company, 97

"Northern Trust Alumni Association", 143

Northern Trust Company, 73-81, 90, 93-107, 112, 115-116, 123-125, 127, 139, 143-144, 151, 192, 202-203, 256

Northwestern University, 50, 67

Norton, Jana (nee: Schelle), 271-272, 275, 291

Norton, Robert, 291

"New York Society of Security Analysts vs. Financial Analyst Federation" (NYSSA vs. FAF), 199

O'Conner, Don, 210

O'Hara, Art, vi, 74-75, 78, 93-94, 99, 101-105, 124, 143, 203, 211

O'Neil, C. Roderick (Rory), 203

Ochsner, Dorothy, 178

Olsen, Jack, 178

Olson, Don, 74

Optimists Club of St. Louis, 141

Oregonian, The, Portland, Oregon, October 25, 1974, 215

Overton, Jim, 250

Ozment, Roy, 127

Pacemakers, 299

Packard Motor Car Company, 71

Paine Webber & Co., 297

Panday, Shreekant, 175

Parkway High School, 129-130, 133, 135

Partee, Charles (Chuck), 100

Patterson, Doyle, 166, 233

Patterson, Solon, 199, 225

Pearl Harbor, 47, 54, 59

Pet, Inc., 141

Pine Rest, 288

"Plankowners Celebration", 68

Poettgen, Dick, 178

Pogue, Richard, 209-210

Presbyterian-St. Luke's Hospital, 256

Pridemore, Menlo, 36

Public Works Administration (PWA), 8

Purdue University, 8-10, 13, 18, 25-27, 29, 33, 35-45, 51, 67, 69, 72, 134, 290

Quer, Eric, 258, 263

Reasoner, William, 159

Regional vice presidents (RVP), 163-164, 168-171, 176-177, 183, 212, 218, 248, 264-265

Register-Guard, Eugene, Oregon, October 24, 1974, 214

Research Management Associates (RMA), 173, 175, 178-179, 185, 222

Research Medical Center, 248, 257-258, 263

Retirement System of the Federal Reserve Banks (RSFRB), 75, 93-96, 101, 151

Reusche, Robert (Bob), 107

Rhoda, Dawn, 289

Rhoda, Helen Korschot, 287

Rhoda, Hilda Korschot, 287

Rhoda, Jake, 287

Rhoda, Jane, 289-290

Rhoda, Jill, 289

Rhoda, Johanna (nee: Korschot, sister), 3, 12, 18-19, 286-288, 290

Rhoda, Lee, 133, 135, 289-290

Rhoda, Leonard (Len, nephew), 133, 135, 289-290

Rhoda, Leonard (Len, brother-in-law), 19, 287-289

Rhoda, Mary Ann, 289

Rhoda, Matt, 289-290

Rhoda, Robert, 287, 290

Rhoda, Sally, 289-290

Rhoda, Sara, 289-290

Rhoda, Scott, 289

Rhoda, Stuart, 287

Richey, Ronald, 191-195, 232-233

Rieke, Louise, 178

Ringenberg, Wade, 75

Rist, Doris, 268

Rist, Les, 268

Robbins, Belle Bogardus, 10

Robbins, Bill, 10

Robbins, Gordon, vi, 10, 12, 14-16, 18, 27, 34-37, 41-42, 53

Robbins, Professor Fred, 36-38

Roberts, Dick, 146, 157-160, 162, 193

Rodgers, Dr., 263

Roorda, Carolyn, 290

Roorda, Doug, 290

Roorda, Garry, 290

Roorda, Judy, 290

Roorda, Mike, 290

Roorda, Steve, 290

Roosevelt Federal Savings & Loan Association, 147, 230, 246

Roosevelt Financial Group, Inc., vii, 235-242, 295, 297

Rosen, Steve, 218

Rosenthals, 111

Rotary Club, Liberty, Missouri, 220

Rotenstreich, Jon W., 229-233

Rouse, Bob, 94

Rubinstein, Harvey, 30

Rubinstein, Sharon Hammel, 29

Rubright, Elizabeth, 17

Rukeyser, Louis, 216

Samford Frank P. Jr., 191-192

Sand, Dr. John, 273

Sauer, Dr. Gordon, 266-267

Scates, 111

Schafers, Ted, 141, 143

Schelle, Ann, 291

Schelle, Arevia (Reve), 271-272, 275, 291-292

Schelle, Charles, 291-292

Schelle, David, 292

Schelle, Don, 120, 271-272, 275, 291-292

Schelle, Donna, 292

Schelle, Ethel (Rubright), 43, 80

Schelle, Gary, 292

Schelle, Jacob Jr., 80, 291-292

Schelle, Jacob Sr., 80

Schelle, Jana (see Jana Norton)

Schelle, Jeanne (see Jeanna Noblet)

Schelle, Mary (sister-in-law), 291-292

Schelle, Mary (see Mary Korschot)

Schelle, Mary Elizabeth (see Mary Elizabeth Todd)

Schelle, Nancy, 291

Schelle, Pauline, 291-292

Schelle, Randy, 292

Schelle, Richard, 291

Schelle, Sandy, 292

Schelle, Teresa, 292

Schelle, Tina, 291

Schifman, Ben G., 213

Schwab Corporation, 314

Scottish Rite Club of St. Louis, 142

Securities & Exchange Commission (SEC), 156, 160-162, 189, 204, 207-209, 227, 237, 311, 315

Securities Research Company, 297, 326, 332

Security Pacific Bank, 145, 147

Shepherd, Fred, 127

Silver, David, 204, 206, 209

Simmons, Tom, 210

Simpson College, 118, 134

"Sinawiks", 132

Sirridge, Dr. Marjorie, 257, 261

"60-60" Club, 109-110, 292

6259 Investment Club, 114-115

Sky Magazine, 226

Slopsema, Fred, 5

Smith, Aleida, 286

Smith, Arthur (Art), 19, 34-35, 47, 286

Smith, Arthur Calvin, 286

Smith, Brice R. Jr., 147

Smith, Cristy, 286

Smith, Dr. David, 268-269, 271-272

Smith, Dwight, 286

Smith, Edward Byron, 96, 105

Smith, Greg, 239

Smith, Kevin, 286

Smith, Lucille, 286

Smith, Mark, 286, 290

Smith, Merlene, 286

Smith, Robert, 286

Smith, Ruth (nee: Korschot, sister), vi, 3, 13, 18-19, 26, 34-35, 47, 121, 286, 290

Smith, Sharon, 286, 290

Smith, Sheila, 286

Smith, Sherlyn, 286

Smith, Solomon A., 96

Smith, Solomon B., 96

Smith Breeden Associates, 239-240

Southern California, University of, Kenneth Norris, Jr., Cancer Hospital & Research Institute, 259-260

Southern Methodist University, 104, 135, 137, 211

Southwestern Graduate School of Banking, 104, 211

Spot, 6, 12-13, 19, 249

Springer, Lester, 109, 111

Springer, Ruth, 111

St. John's United Methodist Church, 221-222, 245, 284, 292

St. Lawrence Catholic Church, 3

St. Louis Association of Financial Planners, 201, 221

St. Louis Globe Democrat, 132, 141, 201, 213

St. Louis Post-Dispatch, 141, 213, 236

St. Louis Society of Financial Analysts, 139-140

St. Louis Union Trust Company, 105-106, 125-149, 151-153, 176, 202, 251-252

St. Louis University, 138, 141, 283

Stern Brothers, 283-284

Stoddard, George D., 114

Stone, Fred, 74

Stout, Charles, 240-241

Strader, Robert (Bob), 158-159, 164, 168-169, 171

Studebaker Corporation, 73

Sturgeon, Gene, 178

Sullivan, John (Sully), 67-68

Swanson, Ann, 210

Sweet, Murray, 152

Swift, Carolyn, 91

Symonds, Mike, 76, 78, 101

Tabscot, Robert, 131-132

Taube, Mel, 38

Te Kortschot, 89

Texas, University of, 136-137, 282

Thomas, Betty, 130

Thomas, Don, 130

Thomas, Dr. Rollin, 69

Thompkins, Lowell, 76

Thompkins, Ruth, 76

Thompson, Malcolm, 67-68

Thompson, Russell, 174

Tillotson, John, 30

TMK United, Inc., 194, 229, 233, 265

Todd, Al, 42, 51

Todd, Mary Elizabeth (nee: Schelle), 42, 51

Torchmark Corporation, 187, 189, 191-195, 229-233, 265, 321

Trudell, Robert, 67-68

Trust & Estate, 140

Turley, Clarence M. Jr., vii, 147, 241

Turley, Ethan, 35, 37

Turner, William, 100

U.S. Army Ordnance Department, 47, 50

U.S. News & World Report, 199, 217

U.S.S. Harold J. Ellison DD864, 81, 83-89, 91

U.S.S. Knapp DD653, 51-68, 79

U.S.S. Missouri, 63

"Unit Investment Trust" (UIT), 316-317

United Accumulative Fund, 174, 176

United Bond Fund, 174, 177

United Cash Management, 176-178

United Continental Growth Fund, 175

United Continental Income Fund, 174, 176

United Daily Dividend Fund, 176

United Group of Mutual Funds, 146, 158-159, 161, 164-166, 172, 192-193, 204, 232-233

United High Income Fund, 174, 176, 205

United Income Fund, 174, 184

United International Growth Fund, 175

United Investors Life Insurance Company, 157-158, 164, 188, 190, 194, 265

United Investors Management Co., 233

United Municipal Bond Fund, 174, 177, 184

United New Concepts Fund, 175

United Retirement Shares, 174

United Science & Technology Fund, 174, 178

United Vanguard Fund, 175, 178, 183, 192, 229

Upshaw, David, 178

Valicenti, Mitchell, 160-161

Value Line Investment Survey, 297, 313-314

Value Line Mutual Fund Survey, 313

Van Dyke, Marion, 175

Van Leeuwen, Cathy, 285

Van Leeuwen, Janet, 286, 290

Van Leeuwen, Jim, 286

Van Leeuwen, John, 285, 298

Van Leeuwen, Kelly, 286

Vanderkleed, Alice (nee: Korschot, sister), 3, 29, 34, 47, 290

Vanderkleed, Clarence, 3, 34, 47, 290

Vanderweilen, Becky, 2, 5

Vanderweilen, Cecil, 2

Vanderweilen, Charles, 1, 2

Vanderweilen, Chuck, 2, 5, 18

Vanderweilen, John, 2

Vanderweilen, Ruth, 2

Vaughan, Eugene (Gene) Jr., 203

"Veiled Prophet" Organization, 135

Vickroy, John, 130

Vickroy, Mary Dean, 130

Vinnick, Barbara, 52

Vinnick, Eli, 52

Virden, Captain Frank, 54, 58-59, 67-68

Vogel, Frederick, iii, 166

Volcker, Paul, 215

W & R World, 181-182, 216

Wabash College, 37

Waddell & Reed, iii, vi-vii, 146, 148-149, 152-153, 155-182, 184, 188-191, 193-196, 201-202, 205, 212-213, 215-216, 218-219, 222, 224, 227, 229-235, 237, 243, 246, 251-252, 265, 283, 297, 312, 321, 331

Waddell & Reed Asset Management Company, 180, 194-195, 229, 231-232

Waddell & Reed Investment Management Company, 196, 231-232

Wall Street Journal, "Abreast of the Market", November 11, 1974, 215

Wall Street Week, 192, 216, 218, 257

Wallace, Monte, 189

Wallace, Neil, 189

Wallaces, 111

Washington University, 141, 176

Watts, John, 179, 222

Webster Hills United Methodist
Church, 132

Weil, John, 128, 147

Welch, William, 35

Westbrook, Vern, 66, 68

Wheaton Drama Club, 112

Wheaton, Illinois, 80, 92, 109, 112

Whitehouse, Horace (Hocky), 66-68

Who's Who in America, 234, 291

Who's Who in Finance and Industry,
234

Who's Who in the Middle West, 234

Who's Who in the World, 234

Wiggins, Millie, 211

Wiggins, Norman, 211

Williams, Art (A.L.), 169-171

Williams, E.P. (Ted), 166

Williams, Eugene, 105, 126, 128-129,
135, 143, 145, 147

Williams, Jim, 171

Wills, John, 94, 101

Wilson, T., 201

Wineland, Jim, 178

Wyngarden, Dr., 255